A FACE FOR PICASSO

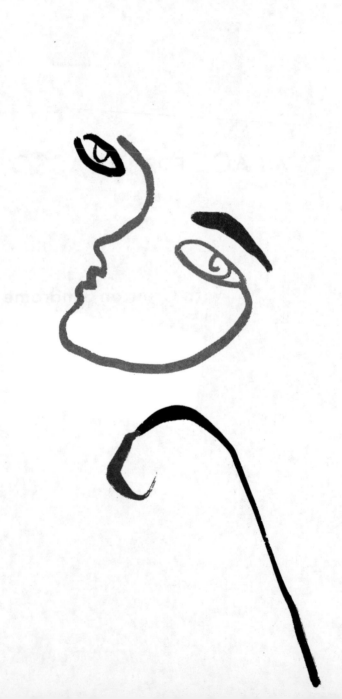

A Face for Picasso

Coming of Age with Crouzon Syndrome

ARIEL HENLEY

SQUARE
FISH

FARRAR STRAUS GIROUX
NEW YORK

SQUARE
FISH

An imprint of Macmillan Publishing Group, LLC
120 Broadway, New York, NY 10271 • fiercereads.com

Our books may be purchased in bulk for promotional, educational, or business use. Please contact your local bookseller or the Macmillan Corporate and Premium Sales Department at (800) 221-7945 ext. 5442 or by email at MacmillanSpecialMarkets@macmillan.com.

The Library of Congress has cataloged the hardcover edition as follows:
Names: Henley, Ariel, 1991– author. Title: A face for Picasso : coming of age with Crouzon syndrome / Ariel Henley. Description: First edition. | New York : Farrar Straus Giroux Books for Young Readers, 2021. | Includes bibliographical references. | Audience: Ages 12–18 | Audience: Grades 10–12 | Summary: "A YA nonfiction story about Ariel and her twin sister's experience living with Crouzon Syndrome"—Provided by publisher. Identifiers: LCCN 2020053393 | ISBN 978-0-374-31407-1 (hardcover) Subjects: LCSH: Henley, Ariel, 1992—Health—Juvenile literature. | Craniofacial dysostosis—Patitnes—Biography—Juvenile literature. Classification: LCC RD763 .H38 2021 | DDC 617.5/2—dc23 LC record available at https://lccn.loc.gov/2020053393

An earlier version of Chapter One appeared as a story in *Narratively* on July 18, 2016.

The names of certain organizations and all characters outside of the Henley family have been changed to respect their privacy.

Please note that this book contains mentions of disordered eating and vivid descriptions of surgery and post-surgical recovery, including vomiting, severe pain, and depression.

The information in this book is a first-person account and is not intended to be a substitute for professional medical or treatment advice. Always consult your doctor or qualified health professional with any questions regarding your health, medical condition, and/or treatment options.

Originally published in the United States by Farrar Straus Giroux
First Square Fish edition, 2023
Book designed by Aurora Parlagreco
Square Fish logo designed by Filomena Tuosto
Printed in the United States of America

ISBN 978-1-250-89557-8 (paperback)
10 9 8 7 6 5 4 3 2 1

LEXILE: 880L

To my incredible family:
Mom, Dad, Alexis, Marissa, Aaron, and Zan.
I could not have done this without you.
I love you endlessly.

—A.H.

I want my story heard. Because, ironically, I believe Picasso was right. I believe we could paint a better world if we learned how to see it from all perspectives, as many perspectives as we possibly could. Because diversity is strength. Difference is a teacher. Fear difference, you learn nothing.

—Hannah Gadsby

A FACE FOR PICASSO

FINDING MY VOICE

If you ask me about my childhood, I will tell you how magical it was.

My twin sister, Zan, and I were the youngest of five kids, and together we grew up in a big white house that our father built and our mom decorated. It was a home filled with life. My siblings and I always had friends over, and if Zan and I weren't inside, we could be found playing on the swing set with the neighbors in the field behind our house.

These were the stories I had planned to write about in my memoir, because at the end of the day, I want to normalize experiences like mine. But the more I wrote, the more I realized my childhood was anything but normal. I had a beautiful, privileged upbringing in so many ways, but my story is one rooted in the *idea* of beauty. So to write honestly about coming of age with Crouzon syndrome, I had to write about beauty through a lens of disfigurement. As a woman, I am defined by beauty; and as a woman with a facial difference, I am also defined by my very lack of the thing. This is a lesson I began learning in childhood. It's a lesson I want to destroy.

Zan and I were born with Crouzon syndrome, a craniofacial condition where the bones in the head don't grow. Throughout our childhood we had numerous operations that changed our appearance and saved our lives. Though we were born identical, with each surgery, we looked less like each other and less like ourselves. My changing appearance felt like being stripped of my identity. Who was I if I did not recognize my own reflection in the mirror? Who was my twin sister if she no longer looked like the person I knew—if she no longer looked like me?

Though the physical aspect of our condition was sometimes painful, it was nothing compared to the emotional toll of navigating life with a facial difference. The everyday stares, comments, and subhuman treatment were constant reminders of our painful medical history and perceived shortcomings. We were treated as less attractive, less intelligent, and less worthy of basic respect.

And yet, for the first eighteen years of my life, I rarely spoke of my appearance or acknowledged that I was different. I got angry anytime anyone asked me about my face—my differences. *How dare they*, I thought. I tried to deny that people made fun of me, even though it happened openly every time I was in public. If I could deny the way I was treated, I could pretend it wasn't happening. But ignoring my experiences meant denying an entire aspect of my identity.

So no, I didn't write about all the magical moments of my childhood and teenage years. There are definitely some joyful memories and plenty of funny stories. But this memoir is mostly me exploring my differences, as honestly as possible.

———

Throughout this book you will see that I use the terms "facial difference" and "facial disfigurement" interchangeably. Both describe an appearance that differs from the norm. Both describe individuals with craniofacial conditions and noticeable physical differences. Both describe me. And faces like mine are not as rare as you might think. This is a global issue, but popular media rarely explores what it's like to look different. And though Zan and I were just two of millions of people around the world living with facial differences, we grew up thinking we were outsiders. We grew up feeling alone.

Part of this isolation came from growing up without stories about disfigurement. Not stories we related to, anyway. Most of the stories I've seen—both as a child and as an adult—were written or told by people outside of the facial difference community, by people who didn't understand the complexity of our experiences. When disfigurement and other facial differences *are* discussed in mainstream media, they are typically used as tools to signify that a character in a story is evil (think Scar in *Lion King* and Dr. Poison in *Wonder Woman*), or as a token of inspiration for those without visible differences (think Auggie Pullman in *Wonder*).

The derogatory treatment of people with facial differences isn't new. It has roots in physiognomy—a pseudoscience claiming a person's physical appearance represents their moral character. This ableist belief that a facial difference can indicate a lack of morality is how moviegoers, for example, know that characters like Scar and Dr. Poison are evil simply by looking at them. Without positive, normal reflections of my experience to contradict these hateful depictions, I assumed it was true.

This is why visibility is crucial. Without it, people with faces like Zan's and mine are pushed further into the margins. Even now, I'm disturbed by how easy it is for others to ignore our humanity simply because we do not look like them. People assume that because I had an unconventional appearance growing up, I did not have friends. People assume that because my eyes are crooked and far apart, I am not intelligent. People assume that because I do not meet arbitrary standards of beauty, I am not a strong, beautiful woman.

This is why I wrote *A Face for Picasso*. I did not know of any children's or young adult novels about teenagers with Crouzon syndrome, and so I wrote the story I wished I'd had growing up.

———

I start my story with a memory from middle school, because in that moment in seventh grade, I began to view my life leading up to that point—and everything that came after it—in a new light.

When I think about my life, I think of it in terms of before and after. Before and after seventh grade. Before and after doctors expanded my skull and face for the third time. Before and after I was old enough to understand the emotional implications of my appearance changing overnight. Before and after

I had to discover who I was outside of my face; outside of my perceived ugliness. This is why you will find my story divided into three parts: before, after, and healing. I start my story in seventh grade, then rewind and walk you through the things that led up to that point and everything that came afterward. Because for me, this was where it all began—my turning point.

Seventh grade was when the pressure to fit in with my peers became inescapable and my inability to do so became undeniable. It was when I realized that the way I was treated by my peers was far worse than any surgery I'd had. Seventh grade was where I discovered that putting pen to paper and speaking my truth on my own terms would one day make me feel less alone. In middle school, I began to dream that one day I, and others with Crouzon syndrome, would finally be seen for who we are: normal.

I used to understand beauty as little more than symmetrical features. My early definition of beauty was shaped by the white, Western beauty standards I grew up with. And as I write about beauty, you will see I use words like "corrected" and "fixed" when describing my appearance. This is the language that was used to describe my surgeries. This is the language I knew—the language I internalized. If my face had to change, I wanted it to be made into one that was acceptable to society. This is partially why I went to such great lengths to reach an unattainable standard of beauty. But my changing appearance and my desire to have a symmetrical face resulted in body dysmorphia and an eating disorder.

Though my struggle with both disordered eating and a full-blown eating disorder plays a large role in my journey to healing, I've tried to be careful in how I write about it. So while disordered eating is woven throughout the narrative, I made the decision to not include the specifics of my experience with bulimia. I could not write about this aspect of my life in a way that was healthy for myself or for readers. It's an illness that never completely goes away, but something you learn to live with. And so I do not want to glamorize it for those who are struggling. I only want to show how toxic beauty ideals impacted every aspect of my life. Our surgeries, like the golden ratio that you'll read about in Chapter 1, reached toward a very specific, white-centric standard of beauty. I did not understand this at the time, but the operations we had, as well as my obsession with achieving symmetry, reinforced impossible beauty standards, misogynistic ideals, and racism.

Picasso, who plays a big role in this memoir, was a racist and misogynist. While I talk about his legacy at length, I don't focus specifically on his racism. It is an extremely important topic, but I don't have nearly enough knowledge to do it justice. I do want to acknowledge the basics of what I know to give you further context for his artwork: Picasso was an avid collector of African masks and textiles. Not because he cared about the culture or the function of the masks, but because he viewed African people the same way he viewed women: as objects he could use to further his own work. He appropriated African art and used African masks as a symbol of savagery, showing that physiognomy is rooted in both ableism *and* racism. He studied African art, copying the abstract nature of the works. This, along with his desire to depict more than one side of something simultaneously, was what inspired cubism.

For a deeper perspective on this topic, I encourage you to celebrate Black artists like Chéri Samba and Black art historians like Roslyn A. Walker, the senior curator of African art at the Dallas Museum of Art, and Denise Murrell, the associate curator for nineteenth- and twentieth-century art at the Metropolitan Museum of Art in New York City, who are working to decolonize modern art by highlighting the role of racism in Picasso's legacy and bringing attention to the erasure of Black culture and African influence in art history.

———

Writing *A Face for Picasso* helped me find my voice. In the same way I've separated my story into before and after, I've also separated myself. It is only by accepting and piecing together the many fragmented pieces of my identity that I found a path toward healing. I had to find the beauty in myself and in my story at every stage.

So, yes, this is a book about beauty. But more than that, it's a story of strength, survival, and sisterhood. It's a story—my story—about what it means to grow up with a disfigured face in a beauty-obsessed world.

ONE

I am ugly. There's a mathematical equation to prove it. Or so I was told by the boy who sat behind me the first day of seventh-grade art class.

"I'm going to stick my pencil through the back of your eye," he told me, laughing. "It's not like you could get much uglier. Even the teacher thinks so."

He continued poking me in the shoulder with his pencil, but I said nothing.

At twelve years old, I was already used to people identifying my flaws and commenting on my ugliness. It comes with the territory of being born with a facial difference as a result of Crouzon syndrome—a rare craniofacial disorder where the bones in the head fuse prematurely. My eyes were too far apart and too crooked, my nose too big. My jaw was too far back, my ears too low. There were regular appointments with doctors and surgeons trying to fix me and my twin sister, Zan, who was also born with the condition. Some of it was for medical purposes, other times for aesthetics. We would sit in a room while doctors took pictures of our faces from every angle. They would pinch and poke, circling our flaws. We would sit and let them pick apart our every imperfection, and we wanted it, we did.

"Fix me," I would beg.

They would do their best. We'd have surgery, recover, and return for more pictures, more circling, and more detailing of every flaw. By the time Zan and I were eighteen, we'd each undergone over sixty surgical procedures to alter what we looked like.

My art teacher that year was a woman named Ms. J. She had a laugh so loud it echoed down the corridor. She wore beautiful, bright colors and taught us about artists and movements I had never heard of and encouraged us to explore what art meant to us both collectively and as individuals.

On the first day of class, Ms. J introduced herself, then asked us to state our names and what we were most looking forward to learning. There were students in the class who were naturally gifted, who wouldn't need a reference photo or outline to guide their creations. I was not one of them. I couldn't even draw a straight line without a ruler, and even then, it took me two or three times to get it right. So when it was my turn to answer, I told the class I wanted to improve my skills. After every student answered, Ms. J passed out a syllabus and told us that every week, we would be required to research an artist, a movement, or a piece of artwork we were drawn to. We would write a one-page report explaining our topic and what it meant for our art.

"By the end of the year, I want everyone in this room to understand art as more than a pretty picture," she told us. "Art isn't about what you see. It's about what you feel. I want you to show me what you feel." But if having a disfigured face had taught me anything, it was that without beauty, nothing else mattered. My physical appearance was often mistaken for my character, and to those who did not know Zan and me, our disfigured faces were imperfection personified. When strangers looked at us, they did not see normal children. They saw crooked, asymmetrical eyes. To them, the crookedness was who we were—it was *all* we were. So I spent my childhood obsessed with symmetry, obsessed with bridging the gap between the person I was and the person I felt I should be.

That afternoon, after I told Mom about the boy in my art class who said I was ugly, I told her I wanted to die. She brought me to my therapist the following day.

━━

My therapist's name was Beth. She was a middle-aged woman with red, curly hair that fell just past her shoulders. She had a round stomach and round glasses and almost always wore green. Every week, I would sit in Beth's office, play mancala, and tell her of my dreams to travel and write. By the start of seventh grade, I had only been seeing her for a few weeks, and the topic of my appearance had not yet come up.

When I entered Beth's office the next day, she sat facing the burnt-orange plaid couch that looked straight out of a 1975 home furnishings catalog. We did not play mancala. Instead, Beth looked directly at me and asked me if I was happy.

I did not know how to answer, so I cried. Beth took a tissue from the small table next to her and gave it to me, still listening as I sobbed. When the tears stopped, we sat in silence for several minutes.

"It's like when you reread the same sentence over and over again without understanding what it means," I said, finally. "That's how I feel about my life, about what I look like."

She nodded as I spoke, looking at the tablet and pen sitting next to the tissues on the small table. She began to reach for them but stopped. Instead, she folded her hands and put them in her lap.

"I don't understand it," I continued. "These things, they just keep happening, and I know it has to mean something. It has to. I want my suffering to mean something."

She responded by giving me an assignment. She told me that she wanted me to take a picture of my face every day for the next few weeks. She said I had no connection with my physical self, because my appearance had undergone drastic changes so many times. This made sense to me, and I was surprised I had never made the connection.

"You don't have to show these to anyone," she told me. "Just take them for you."

For weeks afterward, I cried at the sight of a picture of myself. The tears consumed me, and I spent the following days refusing to leave the house. Seeing images of the person I was made me angry.

I was ugly.

—————

Later that week, Ms. J spent the first half of class discussing the role of beauty in art. Though the very idea of beauty is subjective and dependent upon the interpretation of the audience, she said in order to develop our understanding of art, we had to first understand the role of aesthetics in determining what makes art *art*. She taught us about the "golden ratio," the mathematical equation that, in many ways, explained beauty.

During the Renaissance period, artists would use an equation to create balance, symmetry, and ultimately beauty in their work. It was first explained over two thousand years ago in Euclid's *Elements*, which describes a sequence frequently found in nature. The ratio was later supported by the Fibonacci sequence—a series of numbers where each number is the sum of the two numbers before it. Using the same math found in the Fibonacci sequence, the golden ratio combines symmetry and asymmetry in a way that is alluring and attractive to the eye. The closer an object's measurements were to that ratio, the more beautiful it was considered to be. I didn't fully grasp what the equation meant for physical beauty until days later, when during a discussion on facial structure and drawing portraits, Ms. J mentioned the golden ratio again. She told us that scientists had studied this equation, using the formula to try to quantify beauty.

"They analyze and they measure," she told us. "They measure the hairline to the root of the nose, right between the eyelids. And from right between the eyelids to the base of the nose. And from the base of the nose to the bottom of the chin. If these numbers are equal, the individual is said to be more attractive." She gestured as she spoke. According to the ratio, she said disapprovingly, the ear should be the same length as the nose, and the width of an eye should equal the space between the eyes. In order to be considered beautiful, the length of a woman's face divided by the width should have a ratio of 1:1.618. She showed us work by Renaissance artists like Raphael and Botticelli. Her tone made it clear she did not subscribe to such a narrow definition of beauty, but I found the existence of these algebraic and geometric formulas oddly comforting. At least there was an ideal—something to work toward. I did not understand mathematical equations or ratios at the time, and so the only thing I learned from her lesson was that these were the standards a woman must meet if she wanted to be deemed worthy. Beautiful.

Ms. J went further, telling us that the golden ratio had been used to create an attractiveness ranking system for women. I do not remember the studies she referenced, only that individuals, mostly women, were rated on a scale of one to ten, based on the symmetry of their facial structure, with most people scoring between a four and a six. Never had an individual been ranked a perfect ten, but still, she said, we lived in a society that found the need to measure and rate and rank and score.

"These ideas are everywhere," Ms. J told us. "Look around you." She said that once we looked for it, we'd start to notice the ways beauty standards shaped our society. "How many times do you see a magazine article about the most attractive celebrities?" she asked the class. "We celebrate their beauty—their facial proportions, as if that is all they are. As if achieving a specific aesthetic is all any of us should ever hope for."

This expectation, though daunting and unrealistic, felt familiar to me because I was raised in a family that understood the privilege of beauty. My sisters Marissa and Alexis were ten and twelve years older than Zan and me, but even as a child I understood the rare, natural beauty they possessed. With dark eyes and long, dark hair, their looks were classic and timeless. Even my sixteen-year-old brother Aaron knew what it meant to be admired for his appearance. In my fantasies, I imagined myself having symmetrical bright blue eyes like my brother and thick, sleek hair like my sisters. But alas, my eyes were brown and crooked, and my curly hair left a row of frizz across my head that was neither sleek nor stunning.

My siblings inherited their beauty from my parents. My dad had perfectly coiffed dark hair and a beard that highlighted the green in his eyes. He was exactly eight inches taller than my mom, who stood two inches over five feet. Until her late thirties, my mom had always been tiny, weighing barely ninety pounds. For years I watched her cling to this fact, because in her thinness and beauty she found her worth.

I grew up in Alamo, California, surrounded by beauty and wealth. Dad owned a construction company and Mom issued building permits in the next town over. Though my family was well off, I felt out of place among my peers. I wanted to look like my siblings and resemble my parents—to experience the world as they did. I wanted to blend in, to be normal. When strangers stared at me in public, I desperately wanted to believe it was because they were in awe of me. I told myself their stares of disdain were actually ones of admiration. But the more Ms. J taught us about art, the more I couldn't help but think that if my appearance had been measured against the golden ratio, my formal rating wouldn't have been higher than a two.

———

I was reminded of my ugliness again a few weeks later, when I found a *Marie Claire* article about Zan and me buried beneath memories and a thick layer of dust in the attic. We were nine years old when we were interviewed by journalists from the French edition of the magazine. Two women came to our home. My mom put us in dresses and curled our hair and we sat at the dining room table, which we were only allowed to do on special occasions. The women took pictures of us and asked us questions about our life. All I can remember of them is their accents and the way I felt confused when they kept implying that I was different.

In the center of the table sat a framed picture of my sister and me from when we were five. We were in coordinating blue-and-white sweaters and holding strands of pearls. It was one of those forced mall photos that families like to hang in their homes to convince everyone else they are happy. I hated the picture. My eyes were bloodshot and I looked weak. It was taken only months after Zan and I had surgery to expand our skulls and advance the middles of our faces. They broke our bones and shifted everything forward. The procedure was necessary to rectify the premature fusion of our skulls. They took bones from my hips and put them in my face. I had to learn how to walk again.

After I found the article, I sat on the plywood floorboards in the attic and began translating it with the basic French I had learned in school. What I couldn't decipher, I plugged into an online translator. The words spoke of the way the bones in my head had fused and described the devices that were invented in the garage of our surgeon's home as a last resort. I cried as I read the words, because it all felt so simple. The way they described it, I mean. They didn't mention the weeks spent in the ICU or the fact that my mom spent her nights hunched over the edge of my hospital bed, too afraid to leave. The article didn't mention that Zan and I were people and not a medical condition. Then, stretched across the page, in big bold letters, I saw it:

Their faces resembled the work of Picasso.

The words were stamped on the page right below a picture of my sister and me sitting at our kitchen table, laughing like *normal* children. But we weren't normal children, because normal children don't get written about in French magazines. Normal children don't get called ugly in French magazines.

I was embarrassed, or maybe I was more ashamed, and I found myself wondering how I could ever have thought someone could think I was special. It was like the whole world was laughing at a joke I wasn't in on. I slammed the magazine to the floor and spent the rest of the night in my room.

"They compared us to Picasso!" I yelled when Mom came to check on me.

"They did not compare you to Picasso, they compared you to his artwork," she clarified. "Picasso was an artist. You are God's artwork."

"God should take up a new occupation," I said back. I shredded the magazine that night.

Separating the art from the artist did not make sense to me. Zan and I never had the luxury of separating ourselves and our appearance from anything we did. We *were* our faces. To compare us to Picasso's artwork was to compare us to the man himself.

—

Before Picasso, art had been primarily focused on portraying classical beauty. In a 1945 interview with André Flores, Picasso said, "Art is not the application of a canon of beauty but what the instinct and the brain can conceive beyond any canon. When we love a woman we don't start measuring her limbs. We love with our desires—although everything has been done to try and apply a canon even to love. . . . It's not what the artist does that counts, but what he is."

But Pablo Picasso *was* a terrible person. He was abusive and cruel. Of his eight long-term relationships, two of his partners had mental breakdowns from his abuse and had to be institutionalized. Two of them committed suicide. He was a volatile hypocrite with a God complex. He painted disfigured faces and distorted bodies as a way of dismantling realistic depictions of objects and people in order to remake them in his image. He painted the women in his life—the women he "loved"—this way. It wasn't enough to physically and verbally abuse them. He had to take his misogyny to the canvas, because he found pleasure in stripping them of their humanity both in art and in person.

Picasso often started his paintings by creating a representational portrait of one of his wives or his mistresses. Then, one by one, he took their features and disfigured them, placing them on the canvas wherever he saw fit. It didn't matter who they were as women—as people. It only mattered how he saw them. Disfigurement was how he symbolized what he believed to be their character. It was a way to control them by controlling how others saw them—another way of forcing women to exist within society's patriarchal image. It was also how he kept some of his affairs a secret, how he concealed the women's identities so they would not find out about each other.

It wasn't just the fact that Zan and I were compared to paintings of women with asymmetrical and sometimes bizarre faces that upset me. It was being associated with Picasso himself—an old man—that was so humiliating and offensive. The way I saw the world, and the way people saw me, was always an extension of my face. I understood Picasso's artwork to be an extension of him.

The *Marie Claire* article shaped the way I understood every memory that came before it. It forced me to internalize the conventional standards of beauty I did not live up to. For that, and for so much more, I hated Picasso.

After I found the article in my attic, I told Ms. J about it. About how my face had been compared to a Picasso painting. I told her of the assignment Beth had given me and asked her if I could incorporate my own personal project into my class assignments. Ms. J liked my idea. She told me that appearance, much like design aesthetics, is arbitrary and exists only to assign meaning and purpose for those seeking it, but that ultimately our unique attributes are our signatures. They're the stamps on the world that only we can leave. They're the things that set us apart and make us beautiful.

Ms. J walked over to her desk and began punching the keys on her computer. I stood there, unsure whether I was to follow.

"Leonardo da Vinci explored beauty and symmetry through what he called the 'divine proportion.' He was a math guy," she told me, "so he frequently incorporated mathematics into his works to ensure that they were visually appealing."

She turned her computer screen toward me, scrolling through an article with images of da Vinci's *Profile of an Old Man*, *The Vitruvian Man*, and *Mona Lisa*, all famously beautiful pieces. Ms. J stood behind her desk, one hand on the computer mouse, looking up at me.

"Do you know what da Vinci looked like?" She enlarged an image of an old man with long white hair. "I don't know about you," she said, "but he doesn't look too pretty to me." I laughed.

What I didn't understand then was that art was not about beauty. As Ms. J told our class, art was supposed to make us feel something. Though I didn't know it yet, my appearance was my art. My body, my face, my scars told a story.

My story.

PART I

Before

TWO

A few days after my mom brought my sister and me home from the hospital, in late January 1991, I had a seizure and stopped breathing in the back seat of her car—a brown Ford Aerostar she and my dad had bought the year before. Without stopping to call the paramedics, Mom rushed back to the hospital, removed me from my car seat, and ran through the emergency room doors with me in her arms—my entire body blue and purple from lack of oxygen.

"Help my baby!" she cried.

When Mom details the story, she tells of how swiftly the nurses moved from behind the counter and, with me in their arms, ran into one of the vacant exam rooms. "It was pure instinct," she tells me as she snaps her fingers. When the doctors finally got me breathing again, they kept me in the NICU for observation before sending me home.

"You were so tiny," Mom says. She holds her hands out in front of her as she speaks, as if to imagine my four-pound body resting in her palms.

After my seizure, Mom began taking Zan and me to the

hospital so frequently, the hospital staff thought she was paranoid and suffering from postpartum depression.

"There's something wrong," she'd tell them. "I can feel it." Still, they'd assure her that her babies were fine, that things would get better. But Mom refused to listen—always taking us to different hospitals, doctors, and specialists, desperately seeking confirmation for what she had known all along: We were sick, and it wasn't just in her mind.

Zan didn't have seizures like I did, but our symptoms aligned weeks later when we both began vomiting daily. Zan and I were still breastfeeding. Doctors assumed it was an allergy to Mom's milk, so she eliminated foods from her diet every other day. But even after trying every formula available, the vomiting persisted. "There's something really *wrong*," my mom kept saying, but nobody listened.

It didn't help that Zan and I *looked* like healthy children for our first few months, until our eyes began to bulge so much they looked like golf balls in the center of our faces. By then, it was clear our faces were different, but nobody could figure out why. As the intracranial pressure caused increased swelling from our brains trying to grow beyond the confines of our fused skulls, large bumps formed on the tops of our heads. The bumps were so prominent they became part of us—like an extra finger or toe. When Zan and I were learning to talk, Mom began teaching us to identify the parts of our body. She would point to her eyes, and my sister and I would mimic her, pointing to our own faces, saying *eyes*. We would do this for every feature: eyes, nose, mouth, ears, *bump*. It was just another part of our appearance. Sometimes I imagine myself as a child, walking around with my sister and our bumps, like characters in *Coneheads*, and the experience feels easier, lighter even.

As the bumps on our heads grew larger and the vomiting became more frequent, doctors were even more confused by what was happening inside our bodies. First they thought we were epileptic. Then they thought we had Down syndrome. Then they suggested a host of other conditions, but none of them explained our symptoms. And so my mom spent her days alternating between cleaning up vomit and waiting to clean up vomit. As time passed, the physical act of our getting sick became increasingly violent. We'd fling our bodies forward, spewing all that was inside us outward. When there was nothing left, we'd scream in agony.

That August, when our pediatrician realized we needed more care than he could offer, he suggested that Mom take us back to the hospital once more. "Don't leave without answers," he told her. Because Mom was unwilling to return to the same hospital she'd already been to so many times before, the man suggested that she take us somewhere that specialized in pediatric care.

The Children's Hospital on 52nd Street in downtown Oakland, California, had towering beige walls that were visible from the freeway. At the time of our appointment, Zan and I were just under a year old. Mom says this was the hospital that saved our lives, because it was here that my parents met Dr. Vaughan. It was here that they finally found answers to questions they didn't even know they had.

Once inside the hospital, my parents found Dr. Vaughan to be efficient—in and out of each exam room quickly and with a purpose. Thick gray hair covered the space above his ears but was sparse across the top of his head. He had a large chin and an even larger mouth that pinched his eyes closed when he smiled. He specialized in pediatric epilepsy and neurodegenerative diseases. Though Zan and I had neither of those things, it was within moments of meeting us that Dr. Vaughan offered up a diagnosis: Crouzon syndrome. The condition was rare and only occurred in one of every sixty thousand births, but Zan and I got lucky. We were the first known set of twins to survive it. This was a syndrome that had been thought to be only genetic, but our family had no history of the condition. With us, it was a fluke, a mutation of the genes. Nothing but pure bad luck. And even though my parents didn't know what the diagnosis meant for us, they were relieved and optimistic.

"Great," my dad said. "Give us medicine and we'll be on our way."

Dr. Vaughan smiled sympathetically.

My parents spent the rest of that afternoon at the hospital, seated in an exam room as specialists from various departments came in and out so quickly, they struggled to keep track of whom they spoke with.

"We understand you've gotten some bad news tonight," one of the specialists—a woman with long brown hair—told my parents. From Mom's descriptions, I imagine she wore a high-waisted light blue pantsuit with her hospital identification badge clipped to her left breast pocket. The title on her badge said she was a social worker.

"We're here to help you however you need," she continued. My mom says she spoke with an ease that made it clear she was either well rehearsed in her message or well practiced in delivering bad news. Neither was ideal. My parents appreciated her kindness but were confused as to why they'd need her help.

After the woman left the room, my dad turned to my mom. "What was she talking about?" Mom was just as confused as he was.

So when Dr. Vaughan returned, she asked him to explain what was going on.

"Who are these people?" She was standing now, bouncing Zan against her hip to keep her calm. We'd been at the hospital for three hours, and my parents weren't the only ones growing restless.

"Did the others not come talk to you?" the doctor asked.

"Yes, they did. We just don't know why."

Leaning against the dark blue exam table, Dr. Vaughan

told my parents about the surgeries Zan and I were going to need, surgeries that would break our bones and restructure our faces.

"When babies are born, their skulls are soft," Dr. Vaughan said, tucking his clipboard under his arm. "As babies grow, their skulls grow with them. What's happened here is . . . well, their bones have fused." He touched his fingers together, as if to demonstrate what was happening inside us. "If the skulls don't grow, there's nowhere for their brains to go."

"So, what does that mean?" Mom asked.

"That means surgery."

"And what will these surgeries do exactly?" My dad was still seated in the wooden chair.

"Well, if all goes according to plan, they'll make the girls' skulls a normal size and allow them to live a normal life."

Mom sighed with relief.

"But the surgeries are risky. Due to the Crouzon syndrome, the girls have abnormally small airways." My parents nodded along. "The procedures they're going to need will decrease some of the pressure they're feeling." Dr. Vaughan tapped his index finger against his temple. "But I want you to know that there *are* risks."

My parents listened as he spoke about the possibility of brain damage. He told them that our eyes and our ears and our bodies might not work the same way other children's did, but that it was going to be a waiting game. For Zan and me, having

Crouzon syndrome meant we had bilateral coronal synostosis, which basically meant that the coronal sutures—the seams connecting the bones that go from the ear to the top of the scalp—had closed too early. Our metopic sutures—the seam connecting the bones from the nose to the top of the head—were also closed. This was why our heads were long and pointy in length, but short and flat in width.

"It's hard to say what the outcome will look like until we see how the surgeries go," he said. But even after Dr. Vaughan attempted to explain the severity of the condition to my parents, there was still a disconnect.

"You were such happy babies," Mom told me years later. "It was so hard to understand how something so horrible could be going on inside you when you were just *so* happy."

Weeks later, Zan and I had our first surgeries to release the sutures and expand the bones in our heads—a procedure that helped make room for our brains to grow. We were eight months old.

———

The first surgery Zan and I had involved removing the top part of our skulls, reshaping the bone, and reattaching our craniums with plates and screws. Then our eyes were repositioned and remodeled. It was an operation that prepared us for the surgeries to come—surgeries to further advance our skulls and the middle of our faces. These operations were known as the Le Fort procedures—Le Fort I, Le Fort II, and Le Fort III, with each surgery focusing on a different area of the head and face. The procedures were performed periodically as we grew, because our bones did not grow on their own. Surgeons would cut our scalps from ear to ear, peel the skin covering our foreheads down, and break the bones in our heads and in our faces, shifting them closer to where they were supposed to be. They used titanium plates and screws to keep everything in place. Each procedure had to be done separately, because individually they were dangerous, but together they were deadly. Zan and I were too young to remember the first surgeries that expanded the bones in our heads, but it didn't matter, because we were sedated for most of it anyway. Mom has told me of the surgeries so many times, I feel as though her memories are mine. Like an out-of-body experience, it feels like I witnessed the world happening around me.

Our first surgery, which Zan and I had one day apart, lasted eleven hours. Afterward, Zan and I were only supposed to be in the ICU for a few days, before being transferred to the fifth floor, where patients were moved once their recovery no longer required specialized care.

Mom still has photographs from that time. In one of them, my sister and I are next to each other in hospital cribs. At the foot of each crib is a picture of Zan and me hugging each other. The photo had been taken just before our surgery.

The reality of our recovery was a stark contrast to the photos my mom displayed. Zan and I had IVs in each of our arms, heart monitors on our chests, and breathing tubes covering our mouths. Our bodies appeared the same as the bodies of other babies—soft and small and helpless. But our faces were like something from the scene of a car wreck—too horrific to imagine. Our eyes were bruised and so swollen they could no longer close. The skin around them was a deep purple, but with the blood and drainage that seeped from each eyelid, it became hard to tell. As nurses worked on decreasing the swelling, they protected our eyes by adding eye drops and lubricating ointments to the open slits between the top and bottom eyelids. Then they covered them with a thin Saran Wrap–like plastic. The clear plastic strips clung to our faces, stretching from the middle of our foreheads down to the tips of our noses, just above our nostrils. The material trapped the blood, if only temporarily. When the plastic was removed to add more drops and ointments, blood from our eyes dripped down our cheeks like runoff to a river.

The skin around our eyes continued to bubble, until our eyes looked like giant blood-filled blisters sitting atop our faces. And though surgery eased the pressure in our skulls—the pressure that had caused the bumps and the vomiting—the shape of our heads remained slightly too oblong to be normal.

Years later, I asked Mom why she'd attached photos of us to our hospital beds.

"Because you were my babies," she said sheepishly. I had half expected her to say she did it for identification purposes, and so I was surprised by the sweetness in her tone. I was even more surprised by the underlying sadness in her eyes as she spoke. For a brief moment, it was as if I was peering into the eyes of the same tired, terrified Mom she had been all those years before.

"I wanted the nurses who helped us to know what you looked like before. Because you weren't just a baby," she added. "You were *my* baby."

Though Mom said the photos were for the nurses to remember who we were beneath the blood, bruising, and bandages, there was a part of me that wondered if she'd done it more for her memory than for theirs. Because there are certain things in life that change you. Certain events that, even as they're happening, create an awareness in the very core of your being that nothing will ever be the same again—that *you* will never be the same again. And so I couldn't help but question if there was a part of my mom that knew our surgeries were propelling Zan, me, and our entire family into a life none of us could have prepared for. If she wanted to remember who we were, because she somehow knew there would be no going back. Still, Mom never revealed the parts of her that perhaps still wanted to cling to the life she knew before our diagnosis. Instead, she fought for us as we spent that month in the ICU lying flat as boards in our cribs. And next to our photo at the end of each of our cribs, she tied a red, heart-shaped balloon with the words *I love you* scrawled across it.

Three years after my family first met Dr. Vaughan, after we had surgery to expand our skulls, Zan and I underwent the Le Fort III procedure to move the centers of our faces forward and open our airways. At the time of our scheduled procedure, the blood banks had such a low supply, my dad called every family member and friend he could think of, begging them to donate. One of our nurses, Ruby Clem, helped too. She got members of her church's congregation to donate the rest of what we needed for a blood transfusion. Zan and I were four years old and preparing to enter kindergarten. After the operation, our faces changed so much, we looked like different children.

The Le Fort III, or the midface surgery, as we called it, involved a method that was invented by our maxillofacial surgeon, Dr. Long: gradual distraction using internal devices. Before he developed this new way of moving the bones in the center of the face forward, it was standard for patients to undergo a procedure invented decades ago by a surgeon named Dr. Paul Tessier. Dr. Tessier's procedure required the patient's scalp to be cut open and the forehead peeled down. Since people with Crouzon syndrome have abnormally shaped skulls and the forehead had to be removed from the rest of the skull and shifted, large areas of the brain were exposed. With a survival rate of only 50 percent, Tessier's procedure was dangerous. And while surgical methods improved over the years, they were still dangerous and sometimes even ineffective. Once, while performing a Le Fort III operation on another child, Dr. Long realized the method being used was not actually expanding the length of the skull as intended. And so he created his own.

Dr. Long's idea to design a new device and surgical method came from his desire to improve the surgery results and decrease the mortality rate associated with such a dangerous procedure. He based his invention on the Ilizarov apparatus—a device attached to two sections of bone. For the new procedure, Dr. Long created titanium plates in the garage of his home and, during surgery, inserted them into our skulls. Afterward, screws protruded from right below each of our eyes. In the days following, he'd turn the screws to shift our bones. Days later, after our faces had been shifted, the screws were removed.

Dr. Long's inspiration for the new surgery came not only from the research that had been done on Dr. Tessier's procedure or the realization that the Le Fort III needed improvement, but also from the fact that he'd worked with the surgeon before. During Dr. Long's residency, Dr. Tessier visited the hospital where he worked and spent hours performing what was, at the time, the standard midface procedure for children with craniofacial disorders. Of the four children Dr. Long watched undergo the procedure that day, only two survived. When I learned this, I thought of Zan—of the fear I had every time we had surgery that we wouldn't wake up. Or worse, that only one of us would. Because statistically speaking, if Zan and I had undergone Dr. Tessier's procedure, only one of us would have made it out alive.

At the time of our midface surgery, I went first. We were

both four years old, but I was still older than Zan by thirteen minutes. I took my role as the older sister seriously. As children, Zan and I were strong in different ways. Physically, she was stronger and healthier. Her body responded to surgeries better than mine did. Though I was the weaker twin, medically speaking, I was stronger in spirit. I wanted to protect Zan, so I often insisted on having my surgeries first. I told myself that surgeons could better prepare for Zan's procedure after seeing how my body responded. But there was a part of me that only did it to avoid confronting the reality of what recovery would look like. Going into the operating room was easier when I was unaware of how mangled I would look when I woke up. It was easier to accept the idea of pain when I didn't have to see it in action first.

———

The morning of the second Le Fort procedure, Zan and I sat on gurneys in the middle of the hospital room floor. The railings of our beds were pushed against each other and other children— other patients—were in beds all around us. We were waiting for surgery. We'd had the operation before, and we'd have it again, but still it did not get easier. I cannot remember how long we had been waiting, only that I passed the time by playing with the strings on my hospital gown and picking at the grip on the bottom of the hospital socks, as they scratched at the skin on my feet.

Sweat and saline permeated the sterile air of the room. My arm was draped over the side of the railing, and I held my sister's hand in mine. There were patches on our hands to numb the skin where the IVs would go. Mom stood on the other side of Zan, dressed in a white medical gown that zipped over her clothes. She had blue booties over her shoes, and a matching blue bouffant cap covering her hair. A white mask covered her nose and mouth, muffling her voice as she spoke with the nurses like they were old friends. She wore this uniform whenever Zan or I had surgery, so she could be in the operating room with us—to hold us and talk to us as we fell asleep. Then she had to leave.

While I sat on the gurney in the preoperative wing, a nurse drew a line ear to ear across my scalp with a plastic comb and parted my hair as she continued making conversation with my mom. Knowing her hairstyling tricks were to make room for the surgeon's scalpel, I tried to distract myself. I tried to dig deep and find courage. But as I sat there holding on to my sister, I could only focus on the glare of the fluorescent lights as they bounced off the speckled tiles covering the floor. It was almost time to go.

As a child, I often tried to hide my fear. Our surgeries were hard on everyone in my family, and I didn't want to make things more difficult than they needed to be. Especially for Zan. I wanted to be strong for her, to carry the burden and the weight of the emotional trauma. I wanted to protect her. I thought that maybe if I pretended to be brave, acting as though there were nothing to be frightened of, she'd believe it. I wanted to take her pain for her. It allowed me to focus on something more than myself. It gave me courage I would not have had for myself.

"You have to let go now, honey," one of the nurses told me, as she tried to gently pry my sister and me apart. Another nurse clicked to release the brake on my bed with her foot, but I tightened my grip, looked at my sister, and quietly whispered, "Don't let go." Finally, one nurse wrapped her arms around me and another around my sister and together they separated our beds and our hands. When I could no longer hold on, I began screaming. I screamed so loud, my voice cracked and trembled. *Please, no.*

"We have to go into the other room." The nurse's voice was soft, but her tone was firm. "You will see your sister again after surgery."

"Please, I'm not ready. I'm not ready," I shouted. "I want my sister. Please don't take me from her." I screamed over and over again through tears, my whole body shaking. My face throbbed and my head ached, but I sat with my knees at the end of my bed, slamming my fists against the pillow in front of me. I screamed as though my life depended on it. Until the sight of Zan got so small with distance, she was no longer visible through the doors of the operating unit. Until I had to be sedated, because the stress of knowing what was coming became too much. My screams were not for myself, though. They were for Zan, because I knew she was next and there was nothing I could do to stop it.

For many years following the operation, I'd wake in the morning, my cheeks red and swollen from tears and my pajamas soaking wet, drenched in my own urine. Sometimes, in my dreams, I was able to make a sacrifice. I was able to take my sister's pain and do it for her. But reality was always far crueler.

For months after the surgery, Zan and I struggled to accept our new appearance. We'd walk around with our heads lowered to the floor and cry anytime we caught a glimpse of our new reflections. The surgery had shifted our bones, as the surgeries before it had done, and the surgeries after it would do again. And each time, we came out looking and feeling less and less like ourselves.

Despite our facial differences, Zan was an adorable child. After the swelling from the first midface surgery went down, her features developed in a way that resembled more traditional standards of beauty. Her light brown eyes, which once bulged from her face, were straighter and more doe-like. Her jaw had been pushed forward, eliminating the underbite that had accentuated her once-odd facial proportions. Her cheeks were now round and full, and she had a button nose just like Mom's. She had shoulder-length brown hair and bangs that weren't quite long enough to hide her eyes.

My new face didn't suit me the way Zan's suited her. My differences were more noticeable. I was smaller than Zan—awkwardly so. My eyes were farther apart and more crooked.

My upper jaw had been moved forward, but my front teeth were missing, so I wore fake ones on a brightly colored plastic retainer that clung to the roof of my mouth. I had a slight lisp when I spoke. My cheeks were hollow, and when I smiled, one side of my face rose higher than the other. Though not quite as prominent as they'd been before the surgery, my eyes were still large and misshapen.

"I want my old face back," I would tell my mom, violently tugging at my cheeks.

"But Belle, you're so beautiful," she would say as she cupped my face with her hands. Belle[1] was a nickname my family had given me after they found out we were sick.

"It means beautiful," Mom told me. She'd whisper it every morning and every night as she kissed my cheeks and my forehead and told me that she loved me. Still, Zan and I cried for months, always begging to go back to the way we'd been before.

While adjusting to the appearance of my new face, I avoided mirrors and I avoided my sister. I couldn't bring myself to look directly at Zan, because she was a reminder of what we'd been through. But at night, as we lay in the bed that we shared, my sister would gently place her hands on my face, just above the bruises, and I would place my hands on hers, and together we would cry about the way we could no longer recognize each other by anything but the sound of our voices.

---

1   My family called me Belle and Bella. Both mean *beautiful*.

"I don't like my face," Zan would say.

"I don't like mine, either."

Zan and I weren't the only ones who felt this way. To our family, our faces were those of strangers. They'd watch us as we slowly recovered, as our bruises faded and swelling decreased, revealing the final product. But our slow healing didn't make the drastic difference any easier to adjust to. My parents struggled to understand our change in appearance and asked the doctors to put us back the way we were.

"These aren't my kids," Dad told Dr. Long. "I want my girls back." But it was too late. There was no going back.

And so our faces were like masks we couldn't remove. Because even if we could have gone back to the way we were before, it would have meant more surgery. And so the fear of surgery was always there, taunting us. A reminder of what was, what had been, and what could be. A reminder of who we were and who we would never be again.

THREE

A week after we entered kindergarten, my parents were called in for a parent-teacher conference because Zan kept apologizing to people at school for her appearance.

"I'm sorry I'm so ugly," Zan told her teacher, Mrs. Martin, one morning. "I'm sorry you have to look at me." Then she placed her square plastic lunch box in a cubby in the corner and shuffled to her seat—her eyes never leaving the tops of her shoes or the gray carpet beneath them.

Mrs. Martin had short brown hair that curled just above her ears. She was round and soft, with kind eyes and a gentle smile. She had skin like porcelain and wore floral-print dresses that went down to her ankles. Every morning she stood by the classroom door and hugged each student as they entered.

"How are you, Miss Alixandria?" the woman always asked. That was my sister's full name. My mom chose it for its versatility. Because it gave my sister freedom to decide what she wanted to be called. *Alix. Andrea. Ali. Alexa.* We called her Zan. And every day at school, she would cry because she didn't want the other students to see her.

Stunned by my sister's comments, Mrs. Martin tried to let it go. But after listening to Zan apologize every day for a week, she approached her.

"Why do you say you're ugly, sweetheart?" Mrs. Martin asked once, as she crouched beside Zan's desk.

With unabashed honesty, my sister quietly whispered, "Because I am."

———

After the first Le Fort procedures, there were periods of time where I separated my experiences from my sister's. The surgeries had forced me to go inside myself—to retreat deep within my own mind. It's how I survived. The only way recovery was bearable was if I let my mind go dark to numb my feelings. But to retreat inside myself also meant to withdraw from my sister. It meant blocking out the memories I had of her suffering and healing and suffering again.

I told myself that if I pretended none of our surgeries had happened, the memories couldn't hurt me. That was why Zan and I were in separate classes that year. When Mom asked us earlier that fall if we wanted to be in the same class, we chose separation. Rather, I demanded it.

"Sissy, can I please be in your class with you?" Zan would plead. I always told her no.

But my attempt to disassociate myself from my experiences in the hospital impacted not only the way I viewed the world, it also impacted my relationship with Zan. She was the source of my strength. I remember always wanting to make sure she was never far from me, never without a reminder of how much I loved her. But as we recovered from surgery and adjusted to our new faces, I couldn't think of my sister beyond the idea of her, because that made all that we went through real. That made her pain and my pain *real*. And I was excited about the freedom that came from not having Zan around as a constant reminder of my differences.

Though Zan's new face brought her appearance closer to the norm—closer to what the golden ratio deemed beautiful— she was more bothered by it. She'd yet to learn how to get comfortable, how to make a home in her new body. Whereas I could compartmentalize and temporarily forget about my differences—my pain—she could not. Pain was all she could think about—hers and everyone else's. In class, she would cry if another student was upset or got hurt playing at recess. When her teacher tried to comfort her, my sister would ask for me. Other days, she would remove her hearing aids and tell her teacher that I was the only one who knew how to put them back in. An office aide would come to my classroom and escort me down the hall to Zan's classroom. Zan lit up when she saw me, and we would laugh discreetly as I placed her hearing aids back in her ears. We would hug each other tightly before I returned to class.

In hindsight, my choosing to be in separate classes despite Zan's wishes to stay together was probably a mistake. Though there was pain in always reminding each other of what we'd gone through, there was a certain isolation in never seeing others who looked like us. That isolation made our truth undeniable and strengthened our bond. We were different, but together we could get through it.

Mrs. Martin already knew of the surgery Zan and I had undergone just months earlier. That summer, when Mom had submitted the paperwork to enroll us in school, she spoke with Mrs. Martin about our adjustment and how she and my dad were trying to help us move past the experience by keeping things as normal as possible.

"It's like when a child falls down on a playground," Mom told me years later. "When a child falls and they look at you stunned, unsure whether they want to laugh or cry. It's how you react in that moment that sets the tone for their response," she said. "If you smile and help them up and distract them, sometimes they can forget why they were scared in the first place. Sometimes they can forget they hurt at all."

I appreciated the analogy, but our experiences were impossible to forget. They were too big. There are some things in life that never stop hurting.

My parents arrived for Zan's parent-teacher conference just before five p.m. Zan and I accompanied them as they met Mrs. Martin in the classroom at the back of the school. While the adults discussed Zan's behavior, we played on the playground.

Mrs. Martin thought Zan was depressed. And though the teacher didn't say it, Mom knew she was worried Zan would try to hurt herself.

"Alixandria seems very distant in class and is struggling socially." The woman paused for a moment. "She's started apologizing to me for being . . . *ugly*." She put her hands to her chest, as if to cover her heart.

"I was worried that might happen," Mom said. "Ever since the operation, she's been so focused on wanting her face to go back to the way it was." I watched from the swings as Dad put his arm around Mom and pulled her in. "I don't know how to help her through this."

"The doctors said it's going to take time for the girls to adjust," Dad said, still looking at Mom. "We just have to give them time."

"I know it's a process," Mrs. Martin interjected. "And one that is not easy for you or the girls." She smiled sympathetically. "I wish there was a guidebook or a manual on how to help Alixandria get through this, but unfortunately, all we can do is offer support."

Mrs. Martin went on to suggest weekly check-ins with Zan. So once a week for the rest of the year, Zan would get to have lunch in the classroom with her teacher. This allowed Mrs. Martin to keep an eye on my sister. Zan loved it.

I read once that when a child experiences trauma, the best way to help them is to talk about it, to hold a light up to their experience, acknowledge it, and say, "This was not your fault." And with that permission to talk about it should come a space that is safe and supportive, and most importantly, free of whatever the trauma was. But for Zan and me, this was impossible. We carried our traumas with us in our bones and in our faces. We saw our experiences reflected in the shocked and horrified reactions of strangers when they looked at us. We saw our pain in our very reflections. And worst of all, we saw every awful memory reflected in the face of each other. Everything we were at that time, every aspect of our identity, was a result of our suffering.

After my parents' meeting with Mrs. Martin, my family did their best to help me and Zan fit in with the other students. They signed us up for dance classes, so we could meet other kids. They took us to weekly social outings at the park and coordinated playdates with other students in our grade. They even dressed us in clothes that they hoped would distract from our appearance. Because if people were focused on our outfits, maybe they wouldn't see our faces. Despite my family's best efforts, it didn't matter what clothes we wore or how we did our hair—we stood out.

And though we did make friends at school, the truth was inescapable: We were alone in our differences.

Even on days like Halloween, when everyone appeared differently in costume, Zan and I could not escape the fact that we would never be like our classmates.

Every year, the elementary school celebrated Halloween by inviting all the students to participate in a school-wide parade. Groups of kids in costumes marched around the blacktop while parents cheered and took photographs. Zan and I dressed up as princesses that year. Her costume was pink, with satin and tulle. Mine was white. We wore plastic tiaras and carried wands that were decorated with feathers and beads.

Since we were both in kindergarten, we were able to march together. As we stood with our classmates, waiting to show off our costumes, a group of boys walked by. They were older and took classes in a different part of the school.

"Your face looks like a mask," one of them yelled to me.

"Is every day Halloween?" another boy added. They laughed together, turning around to stare at me even after they passed.

"I look so ugly in my costume," Zan whispered, pulling at the sleeves on her dress.

"No you don't, sis," I assured her.

Though the insult wasn't directed at her, Zan took it personally. We were twins. And so Zan continued calling herself ugly. Because if she identified and verbalized her own perceived flaws first, maybe others wouldn't feel the need to do it, too.

The following year, Zan and I were still struggling to adapt to our new appearance, so my mom visited every classroom in our elementary school to teach the other kids about our condition. One day, while I was home recovering from a minor outpatient surgery to put tubes in my ears—tubes that helped ventilate the middle ear and prevent infections—she went from one class to another, stood in front of the students, and told them about Crouzon syndrome. She even brought our pictures and explained our surgeries. At the end, she offered to answer any questions the students had.

"Does it hurt them?" one boy asked.

To answer his question, Mom asked each student in the room to hold out their arm and pinch their skin.

"Did that hurt you?" she asked them. The children all nodded.

"It hurts them, too," Mom told them. "They are no different from you. They feel the same things, like the same things, think the same things. They just look a little bit different from you on the outside."

As I got older, I often found myself wishing I could bring Mom with me to explain my appearance to everyone I was forced to encounter. "Hold your arm out and pinch your skin," I imagine her saying. Because pain is universal. Maybe then people would get it.

Unlike Zan, I don't remember openly hating my face during those early years. I hated the pain of the surgeries. I hated seeing my sister suffer. I hated seeing the way she despised her very existence. I even hated the change that came with adjusting to my new face, my new identity. I hated all that my new face stood for, but I did not hate my face itself. Not at first, anyway. I'd like to say that unlike Zan, my change in appearance didn't affect me, but it did. I just didn't process the pain in the same way as my sister—she released it and let it out into the world. I held it in.

Even then, it wasn't so much the appearance of my face that impacted me. It was my inability to process pain. Exposure to trauma made me feel things so deeply, there were times I thought I was drowning. It was a sensitivity to the people and the world around me so extreme, so troubling, I wanted to save everyone. Sometimes the magnitude of my feelings would overwhelm me, and unsure how to process what was happening, I'd shut down.

In second grade, my teacher, Mrs. Fargo—a short, older woman with laugh lines that wrinkled the skin around her mouth—gathered the class in a circle on the carpet in the front of the room to watch a cartoon. In *Why, Charlie Brown, Why?* Charlie Brown's friend Janice Emmons gets diagnosed with leukemia. As the cartoon played, I focused on the chairs and the row of computers next to me to distract myself from what was on the screen. I was only eight years old. I was too young to understand the severity of cancer, and yet I ached for the character on the screen. It was like I felt her pain and her fear in my bones. So I curled myself up into a ball on the floor, making myself as small as I was physically able to.

There was a scene in the show where the child was teased as though her cancer was contagious, and it resonated with me in a way that was almost spiritual. But in the cartoon, the child had friends who stuck up for her and defended her—something I'd never experienced. Because when your condition is physically apparent—when your condition *is* the appearance of your face, it becomes who you are. And there was no defending that. Still, I tried to watch the program, but my skin tingled and tears formed in my eyes and ran down my cheeks. I began to panic. All of a sudden, I felt trapped in a body, in a life that did not feel like my own. I wondered how my teacher could ask us to watch such a show. But as I looked around the classroom, nobody else seemed fazed. To cope, I put my thumbs in my ears to block out the noise from the television and my pinkies over my eyes to hide the images of the little girl with bruises on her legs. It didn't matter to me that it was fictional. I understood it wasn't real. But I also understood that, in many ways, it was. I'd seen children just like Janice in the hospital. I wanted Janice to be okay. I *needed* Janice to be okay. Because if a fictional character on the screen couldn't fight her illness, what hope was there for Zan and me?

It often happened like this. I was okay until I wasn't. I didn't think about everything Zan and I had been through until I did. I didn't hate my face until I remembered what it symbolized. And then I did.

The next day, after seeing my reaction to the film, my

teacher held my hand as she walked me to the office of our school's psychologist. The psychologist was young, with brown hair like my mom's. She had soft eyes, and her words felt sincere when she spoke. She didn't mention the movie my teacher had shown us in class the day before, but I knew that was why I was there.

After my teacher left the room, the psychologist handed me plain white paper from the printer on her desk and a plastic cup filled with colorful crayons and pencils. She asked me to draw how I was feeling. On the paper, I drew a picture of the field behind my house. I drew the play structure my parents had installed earlier that summer, with Zan and me swinging on the swings. I drew the sun shining and birds singing, and I told her I was happy. She smiled before sending me back to class. She saw nothing of concern.

It was hard to explain my feelings to the psychologist. It was hard to explain my feelings to anyone, really. Except Zan, because with her I never had to explain. I didn't lie to the therapist. I *was* happy. I was happy, but with an underlying sadness. Because my life was a constant reminder of my own mortality and the mortality of those I loved.

I wish I could say I was grateful to have someone to go through it all with. I wish I could say it made it easier to have someone know what it was like, someone to relate to, but it didn't. They say when you become a parent, having a child is like having a part of you live outside of yourself. Being a twin is a similar feeling. It's this other part of you that you wouldn't want to exist without. Zan felt like half of me, and the only thing worse than having the surgeries was watching her have them, too.

FOUR

The idea that Zan and I resembled Picasso's artwork is rooted in cubism, an early twentieth-century modern art movement created by Picasso and Georges Braque. Cubism stemmed from the artists' desire to present multiple perspectives of something all at the same time. They did so by painting from more than one angle. This is why many faces in Picasso's artwork were disfigured.

Before modernism, most painters focused on creating realistic, three-dimensional portrayals on two-dimensional canvases. Artists used depth and space so viewers felt they were looking at something real. But for cubist artists, it did not make sense to paint three-dimensional portrayals of their subjects, because they were not using a three-dimensional medium. Three-dimensional objects could not exist on a two-dimensional surface. Instead of trying to reflect physical reality or nature, they focused on capturing the true essence of their subject.

Like a cubist painting, my features appeared to be out of place—a puzzle whose pieces had been scattered. The older I got, the more unrealistic my features became.

———

I was eight when I discovered that one of my missing front teeth had grown into the right nostril of my nose.

It was early June and the first weekend with hot enough temperatures to go swimming. My family had a pool in the backyard, so I spent the entire day in and out of the water. Hours later, when I was called inside for dinner, I stripped my wet swimsuit and hung it to dry over the side of the claw-foot tub in the Jack and Jill bathroom Zan and I shared. I showered and rinsed the chlorine from my tangled hair. After drying off, I grabbed a tissue from the counter to blow my nose. As I pressed down on the outside of my nostril, I felt something hard against my finger.

I was only in second grade and had little understanding of my anatomy, but a feeling in the pit of my stomach told me that something was not right. I tossed my towel to the floor and with both hands, grabbed the light-up magnifying mirror from the drawer. I tilted my head back as far as possible, trying to see as far up my nose as I could. When this didn't work, I tried blowing my nose again. I even grabbed a Q-tip and, with one eye on the mirror, tried to remove whatever was up there. All I could see was something with a rounded edge. It looked like bone.

———

I did have front teeth once. Baby teeth, anyway. I had only had them for a year before I was rushed to the hospital after a seizure. I was two. Doctors in the emergency room could not get me breathing, so they had to remove my teeth to make room for a breathing tube. With a small mouth and an even smaller airway, they said it was a matter of either saving my teeth or saving my life.

"Her teeth will grow back," they told my mom, but they never did.

At five, I began hiding the blank space in the front of my mouth by wearing a retainer with fake front teeth attached to it. Mom called it my flipper. Aaron called them my dentures. I fiddled with it constantly, always using my tongue to click it in and out of my mouth. For Mom, the sound of my retainer slapping against my teeth was maddening. One week, it irritated her so much she called the orthodontist for prescription-strength dental paste so she could glue my retainer to the roof of my mouth. She'd smear a thin layer of the salmon-colored paste onto the plastic arch of my retainer and then press it up into my gums, holding it in place until it dried against the roof of my mouth. Within months, I decided against wearing the retainer altogether.

—

After dinner the night I found something stuck in my nose, I returned to the bathroom to try to figure out what it was. I was used to things going wrong inside my body, but the fear that a bone had somehow grown through my face was overwhelming.

Eventually, I wandered down the hall to my parents' bedroom, where Mom sat beneath blankets with a book. "Momma, there's something wrong with my nose."

"What do you mean?" Mom put down her book and looked at me nervously. "Are you okay?"

"There's something there," I said, as I lifted her finger and placed it on the outside of my nostril. "Feel it." When Mom jumped, I knew my instincts had been correct. Something *was* off.

Mom sat up, opened the nightstand drawer next to her, and removed a flashlight.

"Tip your head back," she said, positioning the light up my nose. Before I could say anything, she lowered the flashlight and called for Dad.

"Joe, can you come take a look at something?" When he didn't answer, she hollered again.

"Call your dad, please," she said, pointing to the intercom on the wall next to the door.

"Dad," I said into the white square, "Mom needs you in your room right now, please. There's something wrong with my nose." I released the button and pressed Listen, waiting for my dad's response, but his words were unidentifiable over my brother's.

"Belle, stop picking your nose," Aaron yelled from his room, as if he had solved a medical mystery. Mom rolled her eyes. "Oh, just ignore him," she said, swatting her hand.

As my dad made his way up the stairs, Mom continued digging around my nostril with a Q-tip and a flashlight.

"Does that hurt?" she asked, swabbing the tooth.

"No." I could feel pressure when she pressed on it, but not pain.

"Tilt your head back more," Mom ordered. "What about now? No pain?"

"My nose doesn't hurt, but my neck does."

Mom removed the swab and placed the flashlight back in her lap. I slowly lowered my neck forward, reaching up to massage it.

"Hang on, Belle," she said. "One more so Daddy can see."

"Joe, come take a look," she said as soon as Dad reached the doorway. "There's something in her nose."

My dad bent down, placing his hands on his knees for stability. Mom held the light as he looked. "Oh yeah," he mumbled, still squinting. "What is that?"

Mom chortled. "I don't know what it is. That's why I'm asking you."

"Well, I don't know," Dad said. "Did you put something in it?"

"Why would I put something up my nose?" My neck was cramping and I was annoyed.

"I don't know." He shrugged. He took the flashlight from Mom to try to get a better look. "It looks like a bone."

Mom sensed my panic and shot my dad a look that said, *Why would you say that?* She promised to schedule an appointment to see a doctor first thing in the morning and sent me to bed. But who could sleep after something like that?

———

There was a bridged, enclosed walkway above 52nd Street in Oakland. It connected the Children's Hospital to the medical offices across the street. The morning after finding something in my nose, Mom and I drove underneath it for an appointment with a doctor in one of the offices.

We parked in the adjacent parking structure, and I held Mom's hand as we scurried down the concrete steps, onto the sidewalk, and through the automatic doors of the medical offices.

"I know you!" the woman at the welcome desk said, smiling, as she stood from her chair. She'd been a security guard at the hospital for years. We often saw her during our visits, but her name always escaped me. As Mom and I neared the desk, the woman swung open the waist-high door and left her security post to give us each a proper hug.

"Long time no see!" the woman laughed. "What's it been? A week?" Her voice was deep and warm.

"A week? I wish!" Mom said, and they laughed again.

The center of the medical office building was open from the ground floor all the way up to the fourth-story skylight. From the entry hall you could see each floor's caged railings, allowing visitors to look down into the lobby. Mom and I rode the elevator up to the third floor.

From high up, the gray tile we'd walked across just moments before looked like concrete. While Mom checked in with the receptionist, I stayed by the window, looking down at the entrance below me. Toward the back of the main floor, past the security guard and welcome desk, there was a curved wooden platform with what looked like giant papier-mâché trees. As I stood there, my fingers gripping the tiny squares in the metal window guards,

I admired the different shades of green that made up each of the leaves. Above the trees, large birds and butterflies with colorful wings hung suspended from the ceiling. The creatures' inner wings were the same yellow as a school bus. The yellow changed to a bold, crimson red, and at the outermost tips of the feathers, faded into purple. I liked waiting here for appointments because looking through the black caged windows made me feel like I was in a zoo. But for once, I wasn't the one on display.

I only had to wait a few minutes before a nurse opened a door and called for me to meet with the doctor. "All right, Ariel, come on back." She led us down the hall to an exam room. In it was a chair like the one at the dentist's office—the kind that with a press of a button could lie flat—and a cushioned bench with a stack of family-friendly magazines at the end of it. I decided to sit on the bench next to Mom.

Making a last-minute appointment meant seeing whichever doctor had availability, even if I was not familiar with them. So when the doctor entered, he quickly introduced himself to Mom, before turning to wash his hands in the sink. "Go ahead and hop on up here," he said, pointing to the seat with his elbow. Still, he did not look at me.

"I'll hold your stuff, baby." Mom pointed at the book in my hand. I gave it to her before climbing up into the chair.

The man removed his otoscope from his pocket and placed it at the edge of my nostril. He scrunched one eye closed as he looked through the device. Then, to get a better view, he placed his thumb on the tip of my nose and pointed it upward like a pig. The entire exam took less than one minute. When he'd seen enough, he sat back on his stool and lowered his hands to his lap.

"And when did she first notice the object?" He pointed to his nose and swiveled his stool around to face Mom, who shrugged and looked at me.

"I don't know." Mom seemed confused as to why he was asking her and not me. "Belle, how long? Just one day?"

I began to recount the story, but the man cut me off before I could finish.

"It's a bead," he said confidently.

"Like when you put the pieces from the Life game into your ears," Mom said, looking at me, relieved and almost amused.

"No, it's not." I was equally confident.

"It's an easy fix. We can knock her out and remove it, no problem." The way he said it sent a shiver down my spine. I imagined a scene from the old cartoons where a character got hit on the head with a frying pan, sending a dizzying *boing-oing-oing* reverberating across the screen. The character would see stars before falling face-first into the dirt. But this was real life. And if the doctor didn't listen, it was only a matter of time before instead of stars, I'd see the surgical light above me as they administered anesthesia.

"No!" I shouted. I had never been so vocal or defiant with a new doctor before. I had never felt so belittled by a doctor before. It wasn't the idea of surgery that upset me, it was how dismissive the man was. When I made a joke about my appearance or what I was going through, people listened. But when it came to my actual medical care, I was no longer seen as an expert on my own body. "I did *not* shove a bead up my nose."

Mom's eyes were wide and she wasn't sure who to apologize to—me or the doctor. I could feel my neck growing warmer by the second and quickly threw my hands in front of my face, turning my body into the back of the chair to hide my tears.

"Could you give us a moment?" Mom's voice was soft, barely above a whisper. I heard the man's footsteps as he walked to the door and closed it behind him. Then I felt her gently place her hand on my back. I turned to face her. She was sitting on the stool where the doctor had been. Her elbows on her knees, she leaned forward and took my hands in hers.

"He wouldn't listen to me," I said as my eyes blurred from tears. "He's wrong. It's not a bead."

"Hey." Mom cupped my cheeks. "Look at me, please." I shifted my eyes from the floor to meet her gaze. "You know I would never agree to anything you weren't okay with, right?"

I nodded.

"I believe you. I always believe you."

We left the doctor's office immediately.

On our way out of the hospital, Mom suggested we stop to see if Dr. York was in.

Dr. York was middle-aged, and only slightly older than my parents. An esteemed plastic surgeon in San Francisco, he always wore pin-striped shirts and slacks or blue surgical scrubs. His upper lip was speckled gray with stubble from the mustache he kept clean-shaven. He had a large forehead, with skin so tight it never wrinkled. Sometimes during appointments, I found myself wondering if the skin beneath his hair was as smooth as the skin on his face.

Dr. York had a reputation: He was known around the world for his extreme skill and precision in cosmetic surgery. He could perform face-lifts so easily, it was like patients shed ten years from their appearance overnight. His true passion, however, was working on children with intracranial deformities: children living with rare diseases and disfigured heads and faces. While Picasso took the faces of beautiful women and mangled them on his canvas, Dr. York took abstract faces like Zan's and mine and sculpted them to make them beautiful.

Dr. York was one of my main surgeons. I trusted him. He not only heard me when I made jokes about myself, but he listened when I spoke about my fears. He didn't treat me like a child. Before surgery—any surgery, no matter how minor or complex—he would go through every step of the procedure with me so that I would understand what was being done.

"And I won't die?" I'd always ask him.

"And you won't die," he'd promise.

Dr. York had a private practice in San Francisco but saw patients at the hospital on certain days. "To what do I owe this surprise?" he asked when he saw me.

We told him about the object in my nose, and he asked if he could take a look. "I won't do anything. Just looking." He held his hands up to show he had nothing in them.

"It's a tooth," he said a few seconds later. His tone was casual, as if this was common sense. He told us it wasn't dangerous, that the tooth got confused and instead of growing downward through my gums, it went up into my nose. Before we left the hospital, he told us to start scheduling follow-up appointments with Dr. Long to see what the next steps would be.

"Good news!" I told my dad when I got home that evening. "My front tooth came in." I paused dramatically. "Bad news: It's in my nose."

It was easier to laugh about the situation than confront my new reality: that my body was once again wrong and would need to be corrected. It was easier for everyone this way—for me, for my family—if I hid my fear and instead acted amused by the strangeness of it all. I wanted to be normal. I wanted my body to be the same as everyone else's.

———

Mom had kept the remnants of my front baby teeth in a purple plastic retainer case. When I was eight, sometime after finding the tooth in my nose, I asked if I could have them. I started keeping my real teeth in my nightstand drawer next to my retainer with the fake ones. I liked being able to hold on to them, my own reminder that I'd once had a smile that looked like everyone else's.

Having no front teeth was socially acceptable as a toddler, but the older I got, the stranger it became. It seemed like every time I'd invite a girl from school over to my house for a playdate that year, they'd work up the courage to ask me about my mouth.

"What happened to your front teeth?" They would hesitate for a moment, unsure whether it was okay to ask.

I always responded in the same way. I would look off into the distance, as if contemplating a dark event from my past. Then I'd examine the room suspiciously, making sure nobody was around to hear me.

"Want to know a secret?" The answer was always yes. So I'd lead my guest up the stairs to my bedroom, where what was left of my teeth sat in their plastic case.

"Stand here," I'd say. Then I'd remove both retainer cases from my nightstand, positioning my body to hide what I was doing. I'd quickly shove the too-small retainer into my mouth. The retainer was tight from disuse and the wire hugged my gums uncomfortably, so I maneuvered my tongue underneath the back of it to ease the pressure. After the retainer was in, I'd slowly turn around and smile. Whenever someone got close enough to examine the teeth, I'd use my tongue to flick the retainer. This would send my teeth flying and my friends screaming.

"I'm just kidding," I'd tell them. "My teeth are right here."

Then I would open the second plastic container and show them the tiny pieces of shattered teeth. "This is what they used to look like," I'd say seriously. "This is what they look like now." I'd grab a flashlight from my dresser, and just as I'd watched my mom do the night I first realized something was in my nose, I'd tilt my head back and shine the light up my nostril for people to see where the tooth had positioned itself. After this, they usually stopped asking me to explain my appearance.

I didn't do this often, but I had fun with it when I did. Though I only ever told a few girls from school about the tooth in my nose, somehow everyone in my grade found out. I was embarrassed at first, until the other kids were fascinated and asked if they could see it, too. I spent recess tilting my head up to the sunlight as my classmates did their best to get a peek up my nostril. One boy even brought a flashlight of his own so that he could get a better look. I felt like a science project. I never liked discussing my medical experiences at school, because it shattered the illusion that I was just like everyone else. But I told myself that being around the same students in class every day forced them to adjust, to get used to a face so different from their own. Besides, having the attention of the other students felt nice. Like for once I was one of them. That is, until I found out the reason for their fascination.

The kids I'd shown my tooth to started a rumor about me: that when my tooth traveled upward, it had not stopped in my nose.

"It went up, up, up until it lodged in her *brain!*" one boy said at recess. He pointed his index finger up to the sky as he spoke. "That's why she looks so weird." By this time, it had been years since the midface advancement surgery Zan and I had when we were four, and I was slowly outgrowing my face. The more time that passed, the more out of place my features looked.

While the rumors were just rumors, the tooth in my nose *did* cause more surgeries. I'd gotten braces put on in second grade, so instead of removing the tooth altogether, doctors attached a small silver chain to my nose-tooth through the roof of my mouth. One end of the chain was attached to the tooth and the other to the front wire of my braces. Every couple of weeks, Mom would take me to the orthodontist, where they would thread more wire through the chain and make a knot. Every knot pulled the chain downward. They hoped that with time, the chain would bring the tooth back down through my gums.

Tightening the chain was simple but painful. It didn't help that my orthodontist was a large man with hands the size of my face. His fingers were thick and bulky and did not fit easily in my mouth. I dreaded the appointments so much, I'd often cancel them without Mom knowing. I'd simply erase the voice-mail reminders from the answering machine or write the same appointment down multiple times on the family calendar so Mom would get confused.

"Oh shoot," she would mutter to herself. Then, like clockwork, she would ask me if I remembered which day my appointment was. I always told her the wrong information. With a full-time job and five kids to keep track of, she relied on that calendar to tell her where we needed to be and when. Eventually the doctor sat Mom down in an exam room and threatened to stop seeing us if we missed any more appointments. She didn't tell him it was me. She just nodded and said okay.

The more things that went wrong inside my body, the harder it was to laugh off my tooth growing into my nose. Instead, it became easier to think my face really was like one of Picasso's cubist paintings. Even if my facial features appeared scattered, like puzzle pieces, my pain was linear. One problem always led to another.

FIVE

I grew up in a house in Alamo, California—a small suburb to the east of San Francisco. The house, which was over one hundred years old when my parents bought it, sat on a private, three-acre plot of land, tucked away from the main boulevard, partially hidden behind overgrown trees and tangled bushes. It had a wishing well in the front yard, and a small white cottage in the back. There were two other houses and a barn at the end of the property. An elderly woman lived in one of the houses for a while. When she passed away, my parents bought the rest of her land.

I don't remember much about that first house on Vine Lane, only the yard. The house was small for seven people, so my parents converted the garage into a bedroom for my older sisters to share. But in May 1994, after Mom made tacos for Marissa's thirteenth birthday, the house burned down. Zan and I were only three. Mom forgot to turn off the stove, and a newspaper on the counter caught fire. Nobody was hurt. The house wasn't totally destroyed, but the damage, along with Zan's and my health issues, made it uninhabitable, so it was torn down. There were no rental homes or apartments in the area that could fit our family of seven, so the insurance company gave us four rooms at a nearby hotel: one for my parents; one for my older sisters; one for my brother; and one for Zan and me. My family lived at the hotel for the next three years, while my dad got to work on rebuilding our house on the same plot of land where the first one had burned.

After the fire, my parents found healing by pouring themselves into anything that got them closer to the life they intended to rebuild. And though I know they must have been stressed by the challenges they faced, they never showed it. There was no time to be sad when my dad had a business to run. There was no time to be angry or have regrets when there was work to be done. This was how they dealt with our surgeries, too: There was no time for fear or worry when, with each surgery, we were closer to health and closer to reaching an aesthetic ideal.

My dad finished rebuilding our home in 1997. It was a large white house with eight bedrooms, three floors, and a brick wraparound porch. I loved the house my dad built because it was a reminder of what beauty could come from chaos and tragedy. In some ways, I saw it as a symbol for Zan and me, and what we went through. Our bodies, like the walls of our house, had to be taken apart and reassembled. With every operation, we learned how to put ourselves back together. We had no choice but to learn how to rebuild. But in this divide, I left parts of myself. I knew how to be in one place or the other. My life was constantly oscillating between the two—heaven and hell, surgery and recovery. I did not understand how to be both versions of myself at the same time. I did not know how to be both normal and different; sick and healthy.

After years in a hotel room, Zan and I dreamt of living in a neighborhood with other children our age. Hotel living was fun, but moving home was magic. Especially in 1998, when the Gallaghers, a family of twelve, moved in next door.

With ten children in their family and five in ours, we had an entire neighborhood between us. We learned this the very after-noon they moved in, after Mom invited one of the children—Nina, a girl the same age as Zan and me—to come swimming in our pool.

"Can my sister come?" Nina asked politely. Mom told her yes.

That afternoon, dressed in a one-piece bathing suit and a beach towel draped over her shoulder, Nina followed the short dirt path to the fence that divided our yards. Her younger sister Victoria trailed closely behind. Victoria was four years old and the youngest in the family. Her hair was cut into a bob, with soft brown strands that fell to the center of her ears. She wore her bangs pinned back with a bendable barrette.

As the children started over, Mom saw another child from the kitchen window—a boy named James, who was just one year younger than Zan and me—hoisting the girls up and over the wire fence that divided our yards. Mom tossed the dishrag she'd been holding onto the counter and rushed to the fence to help. When my dad saw this from the window of his office, he joined her. After they helped lift Victoria over the sharp edges of the fence and placed her safely onto the grass below, Mom invited James to join his sisters by the pool. "Anyone who wants to can come," she told him. James smiled and took off running back into the house, where he'd spent the day with his family unloading boxes. Within minutes, the rest of the Gallagher kids—five girls and four boys—flung themselves over the fence.

The Gallaghers understood what it meant to be suspended between two realities: the desire to go back and the desire to move on. Months before they moved in next door, their mom had died of a brain aneurysm in her sleep. Victoria was asleep next to her when it happened. After their mom's death, the family couldn't bring themselves to stay in the home, so they moved in with their grandma until the house next door to mine was listed for rent. Their dad remarried within a year. The single-floor home had four bedrooms and a large backyard that was overgrown with ivy, but it was small for twelve people. Every room besides the master, which Mr. Gallagher shared with his new wife, had black metal bunk beds. The boys' room had two sets of bunk beds, but the oldest brothers often slept sprawled out on the living room couches instead.

Living next door to the Gallagher family was the highlight of my childhood. After school, we'd meet at the fence and spend the evenings playing games of kickball and capture the flag until the sky was too dark to see. During our summers, our parents all had to work, and so we were often left unsupervised. We'd rummage through our cabinets and hold bake sales on the walking trails across the street, using whatever ingredients we could find. One summer, we even went door to door down the street next to ours, selling expired orange juice that we found in the back of the pantry. In a rusted Radio Flyer wagon, we loaded up red Solo cups and a lukewarm pitcher of the bright orange drink.

"Lemon-*lade*!" Victoria would shout enthusiastically. Most of our neighbors bought a glass just to be nice, and when they thought we weren't looking, used the neon liquid to water their lawn. We didn't mind, though. We used the money we earned to treat ourselves to ice cream cones from the local Baskin-Robbins.

As we got older, Zan and I grew closer to Nina and Victoria, because they were closest to us in age and in spirit. They'd sleep over most weekends—arriving after school on Fridays and returning home after dinner on Sundays. They became family.

Zan and I rarely spoke about our medical condition in the first few months we knew Nina and Victoria, and they never asked. It was like they did not see anything different about us. Being with them allowed me to forget about all the things that set me apart from other children my age.

Our friendship gave us the sense of normalcy we'd been craving. It showed us that we could exist, that we could have friends, without the appearance of our faces impacting how we were treated. That not everyone would treat us poorly because of the way we looked. More than that, it taught us that we did not have to be defined by our faces. That we could separate ourselves from all we had been through.

Their friendship also showed me the kind of life I wanted to have and the kind of person I wanted to be. When I was unsure of myself or nervous about meeting new people, I channeled who I was with them. I did not owe anyone an explanation for my face. At school, Zan and I did not talk about our surgeries or our appearance. We pretended we were just like the other children in our classes. The less emphasis I placed on my appearance, the less the kids in my class did, too. And we only ever let our friends see the parts of us we wanted them to see. When we had surgery, we never had visitors from school. We would only see our friends after we healed. There was never any crossover. Because outside of school and outside of my home life, where people didn't know Zan and me or our story, our appearance was what defined us. Returning to school after a procedure was exhausting, because it meant switching personas. Zan and I were used to having to maintain a facade, to assimilate, to pretend we were just like the other students. But we weren't. Surgery forced me to confront what I spent my life denying: I was different. And I was not ready to let Nina, Victoria, or anyone else see that.

——

Months after the chain was attached to the tooth in my nose, it came off. It detached itself and worked its way down through my gums. I only knew it happened when I felt the soft, dainty metal hanging from my braces. It was smooth against my tongue.

I was mostly relieved when it happened. Trying to move

the tooth was painful and yielded no results. I finally asked the doctors to just remove it altogether.

"This is your permanent tooth," one of the dental assistants explained to me as if I didn't understand. "If this one is removed, there's no tooth to take its place."

"I don't care." I sat in the dental chair with my arms folded across my chest.

"You might not care now, but what about in a few years, when you're the only one without teeth?"

"Well, I guess I'll deal with it then." I wanted her to stop explaining things I already knew. Did she honestly think I did not know what it was like to be ridiculed for not having teeth? During lunch at school, I could not even take a bite of my sandwich without at least one comment about how gross my mouth was—how gross *I* was.

I'm already in pain, I wanted to tell her. *Why does my suffering have to be physical, too?*

Weeks later, the team of specialists agreed to do the surgery.

The operation to remove the tooth from my nose meant once again cutting through the roof of my mouth and into my nose. It was a simple outpatient procedure and required minimal recovery time. A couple of hours after the operation, I got sent home with gauze and a swollen lip.

When we got home from the hospital, Nina and Victoria were sitting on the couch with Zan. Since we never talked about our medical problems with our friends, Nina and Victoria found out about my surgery that afternoon when they stopped by the house after school to see if Zan and I could play.

It wasn't that my surgery was a secret; I just worried that if Nina and Victoria knew about our surgeries, they would stop seeing us the same way. I had not learned how to explain that there were two versions of me—my hospital self and my healthy self—and I did not want them to treat us any differently.

Victoria stood from her place on the couch when she saw me. "I made you this." She handed me a piece of light pink construction paper that she'd folded in half to make a card. She had drawn a red heart on the front in crayon and had written *FEEL BETTER ARIEL* in squiggly letters on the inside.

"Thank you." I tried to smile, but my lips and mouth were still numb.

When I sat down on the couch, Zan and Nina covered me with the blanket that had been draped over the back of the couch.

"I'm sorry I didn't tell you guys." My words were slurred from the medication, so I leaned my head back and closed my eyes.

"It's okay," Nina assured me. "We're glad you're home." Victoria nodded in agreement and squeezed her way back onto the couch with us.

"Want to put a movie on?" I asked Zan. "We can watch whatever you want." I liked the company but did not feel like talking. I was asleep by the time they found something to watch.

The movie was only halfway over when I jolted awake again.

My mouth was beginning to throb as the anesthesia wore off. It was like my jaw had a heartbeat. My head was spinning and my ears rang and I felt like I could sleep for a thousand years.

"Are you okay?" Zan asked, sensing my discomfort.

I placed my hand to my lips and nodded.

Nina and Victoria got up from the couch and returned moments later with a glass of water and an ice pack from the freezer. I thanked them and took a sip, before falling back to sleep with the ice pressed to my face.

I couldn't show this side of my life to the kids at school. I couldn't tell them about what my experiences were really like. That was how I knew Nina and Victoria weren't like our other friends. They never made Zan and me feel like we were different.

—————

Though I compartmentalized my experiences, each procedure changed me. My personality had been fractured like my skull, resulting in two halves making up the whole. I was divided into two people: one who identified as being disfigured and one who did not. Each time, I would return to school determined to get back to normal, only to find myself once again retreating inside myself.

Being taken apart physically meant being forced to re-assemble all the parts of me. This work of rebuilding my internal world left me with little energy for existing in real time. I spent so much time inside my own head, trying to process my experiences and what I'd been through, I rejected the people around me. After surgery, I did not want friends, I wanted myself. For weeks, I avoided other kids at recess and did not talk as much in class. I was lost inside my own mind—my own pain—leaving my classmates to wonder why I was no longer interested in them. I was selfish in my suffering, desperately trying to work through my thoughts and feelings so I could move on.

Zan was the same way. Since we never gave our school friends the opportunity to understand the emotional impact of what we were going through, the number of friends we had at school fluctuated. When we were healing, we lost friends because we stopped wanting them. Once we recovered, we went back to being social and craving the community of friends we'd rejected before.

By the time I had the tooth removed from my nose, Zan and I had each already had dozens of operations. But from then on, Nina and Victoria were at our house after each one. Even on days when our eyes were too swollen to open and our bodies too sore to move, they sat in the darkness with us and kept us company as we healed. We didn't have to talk. We could just be. Their presence offered up a silent *I love you*. Sometimes I think our friendship came so easily because in our own ways, we all understood grief and loss. Theirs was much more concrete and substantiated: the loss of their mom. Zan's and mine: the loss of ourselves.

SIX

When Picasso was young and could not afford new canvases, he painted over his own paintings. Beneath *The Blue Room*, a 1901 painting of a naked woman bathing in the middle of Picasso's Boulevard de Clichy studio in Paris, is a portrait of a bearded man in a bow tie, resting his head on his hand.

Art experts had long suspected something underneath *The Blue Room*. In the 1950s, they noticed areas where brush-strokes were inconsistent and pigments differed. By 1997, X-rays confirmed there *was* something there, but it wasn't until infrared technology was used in 2008 that the man's face was revealed.

Sometimes it felt like Zan and I were one of Picasso's layered paintings, always being painted over. The truth of who we were was erased to make room for who we were becoming.

In October 2001, the year before I entered middle school—two years before I enrolled in Ms. J's art class and four years after we moved into the house my dad rebuilt—my mom mentioned an appointment with Dr. York to discuss our next midface advancement. Zan and I were ten years old and returning home from a weeklong camping trip in the Santa Cruz Mountains with our class. It was a week of hiking and sleeping in a cabin with our friends, a week of feeling normal.

We lived off the main boulevard, just a couple of miles from the elementary school. After a week of sleeping in a bed that was not my own, I was even more excited to be home. Until my dad drove past our driveway without slowing down.

"Where are we going?" I asked.

"To see Dr. York."

Zan and I exchanged confused glances.

"We're going all the way to San Francisco *now*?" I asked again. We had already been stuck on a bus for two hours that morning, and the city was another hour away.

"This was the only time he could see us." Mom shrugged. Zan and I were not buying it. It was like this sometimes, though. My parents were good at involving us in our own care until they weren't. They were trying to protect us. It was bad enough to have the stress of impending surgery hanging over us.

Months before our field trip to Santa Cruz, Zan and I had gone to see Dr. York for a checkup when talk of another midface surgery came up. At the time, he said he didn't foresee us needing to do it again. That once was probably enough. Once was enough for most children, but we had a more severe case, so I always tried to prepare myself for the worst. It was easier to be pleasantly surprised. I'd been so happy to hear Dr. York say he thought our major surgeries were out of the way,

I'd leapt from the exam chair and wrapped my arms tightly around him.

"Thank you," I whispered. "Thank you."

———

I sat on a medical stool in the exam room, still in my camp clothes, as Dr. York pushed the round wire frames of his glasses closer to the top of his nose. His glance remained fixed on the computer next to him, where pictures of my face from every angle covered the screen. The photos had been taken three months earlier, at the previous appointment.

Dr. York had asked me to stand against the back wall of the exam room.

"Smile," he'd said, as he held the camera just inches from my face. "Okay, now let's do one *without* you smiling." I let my face fall, and my mouth shifted into a frown.

He had me turn my body to one side, then to the other. "Look up. Now look down."

He'd been taking these photos periodically since I was a child. "It'll help us track the progress of your appearance," he always told me.

I'd never minded the photos being taken, but that afternoon was the first time I saw all of them displayed. I was fascinated by Dr. York scrolling through the photos on his screen. First he considered those from my previous appointment. Then he viewed before-and-after shots from each of my operations. Amid images of me with crooked eyes, then *less* crooked eyes;

missing front teeth, then a retainer with fake teeth; a flat nose, then a straight nose—I did not see progress. Only more flaws I wanted corrected.

There'd been a time when Zan and I were so identical, I could hardly tell where I ended and she began. In photos from childhood, I cannot tell you who is who. After our diagnosis, my parents had a portrait taken of Zan and me. For years afterward, it hung in the hallway of the craniofacial unit at the Children's Hospital in Oakland. It was part of the hospital's campaign celebrating patients' unique, diverse faces.

In the photo, Zan and I are three years old, dressed in matching cream-and-green dresses that frilled outward at our waists. We have soft brown hair that sits just above our shoulders. Our eyes poke out of our faces so far that just from looking at the photo, I fear they'll fall out. The children in the image seem unbothered and unaware of their differences. They are smiling and happy.

Zan and I would walk past the portrait on our way in for surgery. The nurses would often smile and point. "Look, it's you," they'd say, before asking who was who.

"That's me and that's Zan," I'd sometimes tell them, but if it weren't for the names on the plaque next to the photo, I never would've known. Because it wasn't our portrait that had been painted over, it was our physical bodies, our faces. And the older we got, the more our appearance reminded us of the change and pain we were forced to endure. Eventually, the nurses stopped pointing to the portrait every time we passed it.

Like the childhood image of Zan and me that had long been hanging on the wall of the hospital, the photos Dr. York took in his office emphasized my facial differences. It wasn't just the fact that my eyes were too far apart on my face. They were also crooked, with the outsides of my eyelids slanting downward, like scribbles running off a page.

Their crookedness was further enhanced by the differences between my eyes: Whereas my left eyelid cupped my eye as if to hold it and protect it, the lower eyelid on the right was flat and offered minimal support. This meant that more of my right eye was exposed, making it more sensitive to touch and wind and temperature. If the air outside was cold, or if so much as a fan swept air through my room, my eye would water uncontrollably. This caused half my face to almost always appear red and splotchy, as if I'd been crying from only one half of me. When this happened in public, strangers would stop me on the street to ask if I was okay.

"Oh yes," I would tell them. "My eyes are just watery." I would smile, but they'd look at me skeptically, convinced I needed help.

From the side, my small cheeks and shallow eye sockets made my large brown eyes protrude from my head like those of a fly. My profile revealed an underdeveloped upper jaw and a flat face to match my long, flat head. My ears sat too low. Zan's appearance was similar. She had large eyes that, like mine, slanted downward. Strangers often asked why our eyes were shaped the way they were, so crooked and far apart.

"I don't know," I would lie. "We just came that way." Sometimes I wanted to tell people the truth about our faces, but mostly I hated the way they felt entitled to our story.

At school, children compared our appearance to that of a pug or to Sloth from *The Goonies*. And seeing some of the images of my face on the screen, images from before my face changed, I finally understood why they'd done it. I'd seen the images before but never all at once. It was like I was seeing myself for the first time. Sure, we needed the surgery to stay alive. But more so, I grew horrified by the fact that I'd been walking around with features so unconventional, they were frightening. I wondered if that was how the children at school felt, if that was how strangers on the street felt when they passed us: frightened.

When I could no longer bear to look at the images on the screen, I focused on the varying shades of white paint covering the exam room wall in front of me. The colors overlapped, but the longer I stared, the more they blurred together. After a moment, I turned my head to look at Zan, seated next to my mom in the corner of the room. My dad stood with his back against the doorframe, hands resting casually in his pockets.

"This is the area I'm worried about." Dr. York was looking at an X-ray now. He dragged his mouse across the top of the image near the forehead.

"What are you worried about?" Zan asked, as she rubbed the sweat from her hands onto her jeans.

Dr. York opened a photo of Zan and me next to our X-rays, so he could view them side by side.

"When we did this surgery last time, the girls were, what, four . . . five?"

Mom nodded.

"It was great progress and served the girls well, but they were not fully developed. We knew there would be a chance we'd have to expand it again." He turned from the computer and placed his hands on my face. "We can see their faces changing." He massaged my cheekbones and stared intently at the outer areas next to each of my eyes. "See how hollow this is?"

I gently shook my head free from his grasp and watched as he walked over to Zan.

"Do you see the indents here?" he asked, pointing again at the outer edges of her eyes. "This is just one example that I want you to see, because if you look at the photos from a few years ago, you can see we are regressing."

My parents nodded along, looking from Dr. York to the computer, to Zan and me.

"The girls have outgrown their faces."

When had we grown *into* our faces? I wondered. The first time he did the surgery, there was so much talk of progress and how much better we looked. But there were always things that needed correcting. Zan and I could never just be content with the way we were.

"So they *will* need the surgery then?" Mom asked.

Dr. York nodded.

Zan and my parents remained calm, but I did not.

"I thought you said we didn't have to!" I was standing now.

Dr. York apologized, but it didn't matter. Nothing mattered.

"How could you lie about something like that!" Dr. York didn't answer.

"And you." I pointed at my parents accusingly. "You knew! You knew why we were coming here this whole time."

My dad said my name and touched my hand, trying to console me.

"Don't touch me!" I was yelling now. Under any other circumstances I probably would have been spanked for using such a tone. "I hate you! I hate all of you!" I told myself to swallow my sadness, but it showed up as rage.

My body curled into itself as I backed into the chair I'd been sitting in moments before. The pain too great, I could feel myself holding the air inside me for too long. I wanted to breathe, but I had forgotten how. I no longer had control over myself. I was light-headed and dizzy, drifting further and further away. I had not had a seizure in years, but I could feel one coming.

"Ariel." Dr. York placed one hand on my shoulder, trying to bring me back to them, to stop my seizure before it happened. I finally inhaled a breath so deep, it grounded me, forced me back into reality. I was crying too hard to speak, so I stared at my shoes, shaking my head back and forth. "Your parents love you so much. They really do."

After moments of silence, I spit out the only sentence I could muster: "No, they don't."

Dad's face softened. I knew he was hurt. Mom, too. They looked like they were going to start crying with me, but I didn't care. They had lied.

"They do love you, Ariel."

"It doesn't feel like it."

Zan slouched in her chair, her arms folded across her chest. When our eyes met, she quickly looked away. When I saw her lips quivering, I could tell that like me, she wanted to cry. But one of us had to hold it together, and this time, it was clearly not going to be me.

—

Zan and I stayed silent the entire drive home. Back at the house, we removed our camp duffel bags from the car and carried them inside. We had only been home for a few hours and already I wished to be back in the mountains with our friends. Away from doctor's appointments and surgeries and the feeling that no matter what I did, the appearance of my face would never be good enough. Zan and I climbed the stairs to the second floor and went our separate ways, straight to our own rooms. I'd barely put my bag down when Mom knocked on the door.

"Leave me alone!" I'd hardly stopped crying since we'd left San Francisco.

Mom opened the door anyway.

"I got you something last week." She met the anger in my voice with kindness. She placed a folded quilt on the bench at the foot of my bed.

I ran my fingers over it as Mom turned to leave. The back of the quilt had squares of pink and plaid and soft green florals. There was a garden embroidered on the top with hand-stitched bumblebees and ladybugs. It was beautiful. Underneath the quilt were matching pillows and sheets and curtains. I touched them gently, stroking the flowers. I was pleased that such a thing of beauty made Mom think of me. I did not let her see this, though.

Mom stopped to look back at me in the doorway and smiled. I looked her in the eyes and threw the quilt onto the floor.

"I hate it! It's ugly! Just like you." I stomped on the quilt as hard as I could. "I hate you," I screamed. "I hate you! I hope you die!"

Shock and pain flashed across Mom's face. "I can take it back."

I hated myself for being so cruel. I didn't mean it. I wanted to stop being angry. To sob into Mom's lap and beg her to hold me. To tell her I was scared. So scared. That I wasn't prepared for this. That I just wanted to be ten and do ten-year-old things. To tell her that I loved her. That I loved the quilt. That she was everything in the world to me. That she was the most beautiful woman in the world. That a life without her was not worth living. But I couldn't. Instead, I said, "Don't bother" and slammed the door behind her. It was easier to be angry than ask her for help.

Alone in my room, I fell to the floor. Looking back, I felt like the bearded man in the portrait beneath *The Blue Room*. How easily one person could be erased. Was the man in the painting proud of what he had been made into? Or was he like Zan and me, always living in fear of being painted over again? With my face buried into the quilt, I cried myself to sleep.

———

Zan and I were just four years old the first time our faces changed. The first time we looked in the mirror and didn't recognize ourselves. The first time we looked at each other and saw a stranger. The first time we understood what it meant not to belong in our own bodies. The first time we had to confront who we were if not our faces.

Now it was happening all over again.

SEVEN

In the spring of fifth grade, I found a flyer for cheerleading tryouts pinned to the wall near the front of our elementary school. A local team was holding a weeklong clinic at the end of May for elementary and middle school students in the district. I was drawn to the ad's image of girls with high ponytails dancing with glittery pom-poms. I nudged Zan and pointed to the poster. "That looks fun!" She read the flyer and agreed. When four other girls in our class expressed interest, we decided we would all try out together.

For weeks, cheerleading was all Zan and I talked about. We didn't know the first thing about it, but we dedicated ourselves to learning. Every day after school, we'd go out on the lawn in front of our house and stretch and run and jump, as if that would help.

We had been going to school with the same children since kindergarten. By now our classmates knew Zan and me. They were used to our faces. As we prepared to leave elementary school, we thought cheerleading would be a way to make friends at our new middle school. We were wrong.

The weeklong cheerleading clinic was open to girls ages five to fourteen and was held at an elementary school in the town next to ours. Participants would spend the week learning one cheer and one dance and perform them for a panel of judges on the last day of the clinic. The team had four divisions based on age and accepted twenty kids for each one.

Zan and I carpooled on the first day with Justine, who I'd befriended four years earlier in Mrs. Richards's first-grade class. Justine was tall—almost an entire foot taller than Zan and me, with a slim build and long red hair. She had what one coach called "excellent cheerleading potential."

After Mom dropped us off, we found the other girls from school standing in a circle on the grass. When they spotted us, they waved us over. Distracted by the easy conversation within our small, familiar group, I failed to notice that the other kids had already taken issue with Zan and me trying out. Their awkward stares quickly turned into comments.

"You don't look like a cheerleader," one girl told me during warm-up stretches. "Cheerleaders are supposed to be pretty."

I could feel my cheeks flush with embarrassment. I looked over at Zan and held her gaze. We didn't need words. Zan's nostrils flared and I could feel her frustration like she could feel mine. I whipped my head around to scowl at the girls talking the loudest. This only made them laugh harder.

"Just ignore it," Zan told me. When it came to instincts in difficult situations, Zan was flight and I was fight.

When Justine noticed what was going on, she let out a

dramatic groan. "It feels like I haven't stretched my hamstrings in a while," she said as she leaned her body forward, trying to touch her nose to her knee. "And by a while, I mean *ever*." The louder the girls around us laughed, the louder Justine spoke. She wasn't one to draw attention to herself, so I smiled when I realized she was trying to distract us from what the mean girls were saying.

As the warm-ups continued, Zan and I felt like we were only there for entertainment. Girls took momentary breaks from kicking and twisting to nudge their friends and point in our direction.

"Look at their eyes," they murmured. "Oh my God, do you *see* them?" They pulled the outer corners of their eyes down with their fingers.

Every time we heard a giggle, we knew it was another kid making fun of us. Zan and I didn't know what to say, and so we did what we always did: nothing. After all, they were right. We *didn't* look like cheerleaders. It wasn't just because of our faces, either. The other girls wore Spanx and spandex that hugged their slender prepubescent frames. Most of the other girls had no breasts and no hips and no fat that moved when they jumped or jiggled when they ran. But by fifth grade, my once petite frame had begun clinging to every ounce of fat on my body, refusing to let it go. I wore a baggy T-shirt to hide my figure and stole liquid foundation from my mom's bathroom drawer to color in the area from my armpit to my bicep, where the skin had stretched, leaving behind deep purple lines under my arms. Zan was not fat like I was, but she was the first of our friends to get boobs, and once they sprouted, it seemed like they'd never stop growing. Like me, she wore loose clothing to hide her body.

The other girls at the clinic had pulled their hair into tight, high ponytails with curls sprouting like perfectly arranged bouquets. But Zan and I had unruly hair. No matter what we did, a layer of frizz stood tall across our scalps. My ponytail, which always refused to stay in place, sagged lower and lower until it became a tangled mass at the base of my neck. In lulls between stretches, I nervously tugged at my clothes and my hair, dodging glances from the other girls and trying not to hear their insults.

After warm-up stretches, the coaches told us to take a water break while they prepped the music and discussed the plan for dividing into groups. Girls stood around chatting and practicing their kicks to see how high they could get their legs to go.

"Show me your kick," I told Justine, trying to distract myself. She smiled and shrugged, before putting her arms up in a high V, taking a step back, and swinging her leg forward and up. Her foot stopped next to my ear before she swung her leg back down.

Zan put her hand next to my head as if to measure how high Justine had kicked, then moved it upward toward my eyebrow. "Higher!" Zan said.

Justine kicked high enough to tap Zan's hand over and over. Finally, when she needed a break, she pointed to me. "You go."

I smiled and pretended to flip my hair. "If you insist."

Like Justine had done before, I put my arms up and got ready to kick. I could feel people staring at me, but I tried to ignore them. As I took a step backward, my foot landed on a wet patch of grass. As I went to kick, my legs slid from underneath me and I fell onto my back, my legs straight up in the air. Zan and Justine rushed to me, all three of us laughing so hard we couldn't speak.

"I'm broken," I joked, slowly rolling onto my side.

As I stood up, I could see other girls were laughing again. I was frustrated at having messed up in front of them, but at least this time, I was laughing, too.

After warm-ups, we were divided into groups by age. The woman in charge of the program called Zan and me over to her. "We are going to have you girls come over here."

We followed the woman to a section of grass where the five-through seven-year-olds were learning an easier routine. Even though we were eleven and preparing to enter middle school, the woman told us it would be more appropriate for us to learn with them. The gesture was cloaked in a fake kindness and felt like a mix of passive aggression and a full-blown slap to the face. I was embarrassed and angry, because though the other kids were the ones to *say* we didn't look like cheerleaders, the adults—the ones who were supposed to know better—believed it.

———

At school that week, I watched Justine and our other friends practice their routine together during recess. They all stood on the grass with their hands behind their backs in a diamond formation.

"Five, six, seven, eight," Justine yelled, and crossing one foot behind the other, the girls turned to face each other. Zan and I watched their arms make sharp movements through the air as they chanted about team spirit and Bulldog pride. When they finished, Zan and I clapped.

"Your turn," Justine told us.

"Oh no, that's okay," Zan said.

"Come on," Justine encouraged us. "You watched us, now we'll watch you."

"Ours is embarrassing," Zan said. "I don't want people to see it."

I laughed and nodded in agreement. Whereas their routine was complex and mesmerizing to watch, ours was juvenile. "We are the Bulldogs," we were supposed to yell. "Check. Us. Out." We were to tuck one arm against our rib cage and let our forearm stick out like we were holding a tray and extend our other arm into the air to make a check mark.

"Oh good," Zan had joked the day before. "Now we get to jump around and pretend we're doing the 'I'm a little teapot' dance."

It was one thing to have to perform it at the clinic, where everyone looked just as ridiculous as we did, but we didn't want anyone at school to see the routine.

"I'm sorry about everyone at clinic," our friend Nicole

added. Nicole was a returning cheerleader, so she already knew most of the coaches and the routines they taught.

"What do you mean?" Zan asked. It was easier to feign ignorance than acknowledge the fact that Zan and I had been unwelcome. An awkward silence lingered as Nicole looked at Justine, Kyla, and Taylor, each of them trying to decide which details to share.

"They were making fun of you guys the whole time."

Zan and I looked at each other. As her cheeks flushed, something in my sister snapped.

"Well, I actually wasn't aware they were doing that, but thank you so much for letting me know. I feel *so* great about myself now!" Zan's tone was sharp and sarcastic, surprising even herself when she spoke. "Do you want me to pat you on the back now for being such a *great* person?" Before anyone could respond, Zan threw in a "Yay you!" Then she rolled her eyes and pretended to clap her hands together.

I looked at my sister, equal parts shocked and proud. My sister was kind and soft-spoken, but she had her limits. We gathered our stuff and moved to a table where we could be alone.

"Why would she even tell us that?" Zan asked when we walked away. "Like what was the point?" I wasn't sure. All it did was make us even more embarrassed to return for day two of the clinic.

Justine called after school to apologize, and we agreed to put the issue behind us so we could focus on getting through the tryouts, but Zan and I still felt hopeless. We knew we wouldn't make the team. Even if we gave flawless auditions, team regulations prevented us from joining the division they were having us try out for. They wouldn't let middle schoolers cheer with kindergartners. Even if they did, why would we want to? It was all a ruse. A way for them to say they gave us a chance without ever having to actually follow through. Despite the fact that we had been set up for failure, we were determined to show the judges what they were missing.

After school that Friday, Mom curled our hair and pulled it up into ponytails on the tops of our heads. The team colors were purple and white, so she tied a plum-colored ribbon around each elastic. "I found them at the craft store." Mom smiled at me in the mirror.

When she finished our hair, she gave us each a white T-shirt and cotton practice shorts to put on. Then she dabbed blush on our cheeks and smeared red-tinted ChapStick on our lips.

"Do we look like cheerleaders now?" I flexed my hands outward and twirled.

"Like the cutest cheerleaders there ever were."

Our audition time slots were not until six forty-five and seven that evening. Of everyone at the clinic, we were last. Zan and I thought we would at least get to try out together, but when we checked in, they assigned us each a new partner—both were five years old.

Mom exchanged looks with us. "They're not all trying out for the same squad, are they?" she asked one of the coaches.

"Yes, this is for the Mascots and the Junior Pee-Wees," the woman said, before walking away. Even the names of the lower divisions were ridiculous, but not as ridiculous as the hope I clung to that we still might make the cut.

Mom was ready to put up a fight, but Zan and I begged her not to. We knew there was no point in causing a fuss. They'd already made up their minds.

Zan's audition was first. I watched her and her partner—a sweet girl who pronounced her *r*'s like *w*'s—run into the auditorium to perform in front of the judges, but the windows were taped off, so once the door shut behind them, I could no longer see inside. Ten minutes later, Zan exited through the same door with a smile and a thumbs-up.

"It went great!" She squealed and hugged me.

When my turn came, I plastered a smile on my face and rallied into the auditorium. I swung my arms and chanted the way I would when cheering on the sidelines of a football game. When I reached one of the two black X markers on the floor indicating where my partner and I were to stand, I put my arms in a high V and kicked my leg up by my ear, letting out one final "Go Bulldogs!" The judges smiled approvingly and made a note on their tablet.

My partner and I performed the cheer first. I proudly yelled and enunciated each word the way Mom and I had practiced. I hit every motion and nailed every jump. When it was time to perform the dance, everything I'd spent the week upset about melted away. I didn't care about the table of judges in front of me or the fact that I was too old to join the division I was auditioning for. In that moment, it was just me and the music. Once again, I did my routine perfectly, even remembering to smile the whole time. After both routines were finished, one of the judges pointed to the blue gymnastics mat and asked if I had any tumbling experience.

"A little bit," I lied. Zan and I had spent the days leading up to the clinic teaching ourselves as much as we could about tumbling. Did I have formal training? No. But I didn't want to give them any more reasons to doubt my potential.

As I stepped up to the mat, I smiled and took a deep breath. Before I could give myself a chance to overthink what I'd practiced, I went for it. I did a cartwheel, stretching my legs outward as I shifted the weight of my body sideways and over my hands. When I landed, I fell backward into a bridge, kicking my legs back up and over my head. When I stood up, I did a roundoff, landing with both my legs together, before sliding into a perfect split. The judges smiled and nodded again, and I felt an incredible rush—a *high*. It wasn't fancy, but it was something, and I was proud. So proud, I didn't even have to fake my enthusiasm when I rallied out of the auditorium at the end of the audition.

The coaches said they'd notify participants on Saturday, so Zan and I spent the entire next day waiting by the phone. The call never came.

"Maybe they're telling everyone who *didn't* make it first," Zan suggested, and we decided that made sense. We clung to this explanation until Justine called on Sunday morning to see if we'd made the team or not. She'd received a call Saturday morning telling her she was the first person on their waiting list. Nicole, Taylor, and Kyla each made the division for our age group.

When we still hadn't heard anything by Sunday night, Mom tracked down one of the coaches' personal phone numbers.

"Oh yes, the *twins*," the woman said, as if trying to remember who we were. "We appreciate the girls' time and spirit, but unfortunately, we just had too many talented athletes to choose from this year. Sadly, we cannot offer them a space on our team, but please encourage them to try out again—"

Mom hung up the phone before the woman could finish her sentence. I knew it had more to do with the appearance of our faces than our skill level, and so did she.

"You did the best you could, and that's all you can ever do," Mom said. "I'm so proud of you."

I rolled my eyes as I wiped a tear from my cheek.

"Try not to cry, baby. It won't do any good."

"It still sucks."

"There will always be ignorant people out there, but that is not about you."

It was always like this. My family believed Zan and I could do anything. They saw the surgeries we went through and the way we channeled our strength as our minds and bodies fought us. This was both helpful and harmful, because though they saw us this way, the rest of the world did not.

Despite our rejection, I was determined to be a cheerleader. I spent the rest of the weekend looking up all the other teams within a twenty-mile radius. I called coaches and inquired about tryouts. There was only one team that did not already have a full roster: the Bay Area Panthers. Since they needed more cheerleaders, we didn't even have to try out. They told us if we could make it to weekly practices and Saturday games—all held at a high school thirty minutes from our home—we were in. I didn't care where they were located so long as they would take us. After speaking with the coach, Zan and I called Justine. Within a week, all three of us were signed up.

EIGHT

"I want eyes like this," I told Dr. York at our next appointment. Over a year had passed since we'd last seen him, and our surgeries were scheduled for that spring. This time, I brought along our fifth-grade yearbook and circled the faces of the other girls in my class with features I admired. If my face was going to change, I should at least be allowed to give some input.

It was January 2003. Zan and I were twelve and in sixth grade now, and if we had learned anything from entering middle school, it was that to people who don't know you, you *are* what you look like. The pain of surgery had been looming over Zan and me all year, but we knew it was minor compared to what we would face if we did not conform. If we did not change. If our faces did not change. There was no way out and no way to avoid pain, but at least having the surgery meant things *could* change. Maybe it would even make us beautiful. Temporary physical pain for a decrease in emotional pain. This seemed like a reasonable trade-off.

It was during this appointment that we learned our next surgery would be divided into two parts: the forehead and the midface. To move our foreheads, Dr. York would go in through our scalps. To expand the middle of our faces, Dr. Long would break our upper jaws and move them forward. Due to Crouzon syndrome, Zan and I have always had tiny airways. Even at twelve years old, our airways were the size of an infant's. This made a dangerous operation, like the one Dr. York was planning to perform on our foreheads, even more high risk. In early May, Zan would have the operation on her jaw and I would have the forehead procedure. Six weeks later, we would swap.[2]

After going over the scheduling logistics, Dr. York asked if we had any questions.

"Can you, like, *actually* make my eyes straight this time?"

Dr. York seemed surprised by my blunt delivery and laughed.

"Yeah," Zan added. "Look at their eyes." She opened the yearbook and motioned to our classmates' headshots. "We want eyes like theirs."

---

2   While writing this book, my medical research indicates the surgeries happened in the opposite order: Zan had the jaw surgery, then I had the jaw surgery. Then, six weeks after the operation on our jaws, we had surgery on our foreheads. As I've combed through medical records, the documentation in my file and the way I remember it do not match up. But many records were written for insurance purposes or were overly vague because our medical team was already so familiar with our case. I also discovered information that was inaccurate and inconsistent. Though I remember having the surgery on my forehead first, it may have not been done that way.

To us, this seemed like a simple request. And it would have been, had our skulls and faces been made of Play-Doh. Instead, they were made of skin and bones, and scar tissue that had built up over time.

"I can't make your eyes look like someone else's, but there are tweaks we can try."

"Well, you can at least make them straight, right?" I asked. "I mean, you're a smart guy. Surely you can figure it out."

Dr. York looked over at Mom and smiled. "Are these your kids or what?" he teased. Mom had a reputation for being a fierce advocate for Zan and me.

"You have a voice, use it," she told me once. Watching Mom was how I learned to always fight back.

———

Zan and I had spent the summer before sixth grade excited to enter middle school, because it meant we would get our own lockers like the characters on *Lizzie McGuire*. I imagined Zan and me with a large group of friends, always at our lockers, talking and laughing and trading gossip. It never occurred to either of us that when we got to middle school, we would be surrounded by a hundred new kids. Classmates we hadn't grown up with, classmates Mom hadn't explained our condition to. It never occurred to us that the people we had been friends with would no longer want to be friends with us. This is not to say that Zan and I didn't have friends. We did. But the more time that passed, the more our circle dwindled.

Our new classmates didn't know what to make of our condition. In class, kids would either assume I was a genius (I was
ugly, I *had* to be a genius. Otherwise, what was the point of
me?) or that I had an intellectual disability. Though my ability
to consistently surprise people kept life exciting, there was nothing I hated more than being treated as if I were inferior. To make
matters worse, many of the students at my new school cheered
and played football for the Bulldogs—the team Zan and I had
tried out for but didn't make. They liked to remind us of this.

"Do you cheer for the Panthers?" a boy named Benjamin
asked the first week of school.

"Yeah!" I turned to face him. I thought he was being
friendly, so I matched his excitement.

"I thought so. People at practice were talking about the
weird-looking cheerleaders and I was like, 'I think I go to school
with them.'"

I turned back toward the front of the room, hoping he
wouldn't see the way his words embarrassed me. I don't know why
I was surprised. When the season began, Zan and I were mocked
relentlessly for our desire to dance and cheer, but we stuck with
it. I told myself that I needed to prove that "ugly" girls could be
cheerleaders, too. That we had as much a right as anyone else to
cheer on the sidelines, to take up space. I just wanted people to
believe we were normal. More than caring what others thought,
I needed to believe I was normal. By that point, it had been
eight years since our faces changed for the first time, and the

longer we waited to have the procedure again, the more notice-able our facial differences became.

As much as I was dreading the surgery, it also gave me hope. The first part of the surgery was scheduled for early May—the same week the entire sixth-grade class was set to take a trip to Chinatown in San Francisco.

"Will we make it back in time for the field trip?" Zan and I asked. It wasn't until this moment that my mom realized we didn't understand the severity of the procedures we were going to have. We'd been through it once before, but we were young then and had distanced ourselves from the memories enough to make them no longer feel real. I thought it would be difficult for a time, but that things would go back to normal. I didn't realize normal would have to be redefined.

"No, bug. You'll be out the rest of the school year."

It was 2003 and the SARS epidemic had spread panic across the country. A racist and incorrect theory began to circulate that the virus was carried by Asian people. It didn't matter that there had been almost no cases in the Bay Area. My classmates' parents didn't want their kids visiting Chinatown. So our field trip was canceled.

This mentality rubbed off on some of the students, too. Boys in class made jokes about how Chinese people were infected and diseased. During class one afternoon, they moved their desks away from Jeff, the only Asian American student in the class. Jeff sat on my left. But even after everyone around him moved, I stayed put. When I looked over and saw Jeff with his head bowed and looking at his lap, I glared at the boys laughing behind me and moved my desk closer to Jeff. It was weird being on the other side of bullying. Usually I was the one people moved away from. I was the one they called a freak.

"Ignore them," I told him. But Jeff did not want my help. When I scooted closer, he moved his desk farther away. The boys howled with laughter again. I knew something of what it meant to be feared, to be called disgusting, to be treated like nothing. So Jeff's rejection stung, but I was not angry. Sometimes when you're hurting, it feels better to deny others before they can deny you. Or so I told myself.

The natural order was restored a week later after I began coughing in class. The boys in the back of the room immediately started in with their comments. "It's SARS!" This time Jeff was laughing with them.

Later that day, when I told my friends about what had happened, they shrugged it off. *Boys will be boys.* This was the thing about being different. I was always on the outside. Even though Jeff and I were both teased, it was for different reasons. And just as I could never understand what it was like to be Asian American, he couldn't understand what it was like to live with Crouzon syndrome. There was nowhere for me to go to be with others who were like me. No clique I could join where I would be fully accepted. Nobody besides Zan who understood what it was like to go through each day knowing we would never truly belong. That there would always be an *us* and a *them*, and that was that.

The next morning, Zan and I were both coughing up thick green and yellow slime. The surgery was only a few days away, but we were already accumulating too many absences, so Mom said unless we were vomiting, we had to attend our classes. When she finally brought us to the pediatrician after school, he said we had bronchitis. This meant our surgeries would have to be rescheduled. I was too relieved to be disappointed. I'd spent my entire life being ugly. What was a few more weeks?

The night before Zan finally went in for surgery in mid-June 2003, before surgeons broke apart her jaw and, with metal plates and screws, once again expanded the center of her face, she asked me what the point of life was. Her head rested on the white pillowcase next to mine, and I lay there, just inches from her face.

"I have no clue," I told her, studying her expressions. I wanted to remember everything about her just as it was.

"Do you think it will be worth it?" Her voice was soft, barely above a whisper.

"It has to be," I assured her.

"If anything happens . . ." Her voice trailed off. "If anything happens, promise me you won't be sad." She was stern this time.

"That's a ridiculous promise to make," I told her, as if I *knew* everything was going to turn out okay. As if I *knew* she'd make it out of surgery, recover, and go back to the person she was before. But even at twelve years old, we both understood there are some things you never recover from.

"Seriously, though," she said. "If something happens to either of us, we need to promise we'll be okay. That's the only way I will go in tomorrow." She spoke as if she had a choice.

The room was silent.

"I promise if you promise," she continued.

I rolled onto my back and began counting shadows on the ceiling. I turned my head to look at her. "Okay. I promise."

We were both lying—to ourselves, to each other. We knew that if one of us went, it wouldn't be long before the other one followed. We were a team. A pair. And every night before surgery, we'd sleep huddled together, praying God would not take one of us *alone*.

Zan turned over, one hand resting under her chin. She closed her eyes and quickly drifted away. As I watched her sleeping that night, her knees pulled in close to her chest, I noticed how small she looked—so powerless and innocent, just a child. Tears rolled down my cheeks, and I repeated silent prayers.

"Please make this pain stop," I kept begging, over and over again. I was tired of living in a cycle of fear and pain. The tears were heavier now. I don't know who I was talking to. Maybe to God, maybe to myself. I just wanted it to end.

The next morning, I woke up to Zan nudging me. "Sis," she whispered. "You peed."

My pajamas were soaking wet, and I was lying in a puddle of my own urine.

"Bad dream?" she asked me.

I nodded and sat up. "I'm sorry, sis."

"It's okay." The side of Zan's pajamas was wet, too.

I knew getting peed on was gross, so I was grateful Zan never made me feel bad for my inability to control it. Instead of being upset, we got up and walked to the bathroom we shared. We peeled the soiled pajamas from our bodies and left them in a pile on the tile floor. She grabbed clean clothes from the closet while I started a bath.

"How are you feeling?" I asked her as she handed me a clean pajama shirt and sweatpants.

"Ready to get this surgery over with." Zan wrapped herself in a towel and walked down the hall to my parents' bathroom to use one of the other showers. I listened to the rush of the faucet for a moment before climbing into the tub.

Zan had stopped wetting the bed before we even entered kindergarten. My parents spent the following years trying to help me learn to regulate my bladder, too. When I was younger, they tried not giving me anything to drink after dinner. When that failed, they tried medications and waking me up throughout the night. Mom even tried having me wear a bed-wetting alarm—a device that clipped to my underwear and set off a piercing screech whenever it got wet. It was supposed to teach me how to recognize urges before accidents occurred but ended up just waking everyone throughout the night—everyone except for me. But knowing when I had to go was never the issue. I spent all day, every day, in a state of panic. I was stressed and on edge. When I finally went to sleep, it was a slumber so deep, nothing could disturb me. Nothing except the nightmares that left me so terrified, I peed.

It was my greatest source of shame. I'd often stay up until the early hours of the morning, determined to make it through the night, dry. Though part of me knew my peeing stemmed from the trauma of the surgeries I had and would continue having, I didn't know how to explain that my body remembered things my brain begged me to forget.

By the time I was showered and in fresh pajamas, it was time for Zan to leave.

"Well, I guess this is goodbye," she said. "Next time you see me, I'm going to be so beautiful, you won't even know who I am."

I laughed and told her she already was. Then I hugged her as tight as I could. "I love you."

"I love you, too," she said.

I kept my composure in front of her but cried as I watched her and Mom drive away. We were just kids.

NINE

When Picasso was thirteen, his younger sister Conchita died of diphtheria—a condition that caused her to slowly suffocate. She was only seven years old. Her death was slow and her suffering was profound. So profound that Picasso tried to make a deal with God to save her. If he spared Conchita, Picasso vowed never to paint again. He would give up his talent as an artist in exchange for his sister's life. In the weeks that followed, Picasso struggled to navigate his offer to sacrifice his art to save his sister and what it meant for himself. He alternated between wanting his sister to survive and wanting her to die. After mourning Conchita's passing on January 10, 1895, Picasso felt simultaneously angry toward God and relieved about what his sister's death meant for his future. He was still free to be a painter.

Like Picasso, Zan and I understood what it meant to grow up fearing the death of a sibling. We knew the helplessness of watching someone suffer and the guilt that often accompanies it. We, too, told ourselves we would do anything to save each other. We too felt guilty for hoping we would never have to.

———

Zan went in for surgery just before noon, but I didn't get to see her until a week later, when one of her eyes was still black and blue and too swollen to open. When I finally saw her, she sat slumped over the side of the chair next to her hospital bed—her pillows stained red and brown with blood from her mouth. She smelled like sweat and blood and could barely speak, but every now and then she'd let out a groan, as if to acknowledge my presence.

"It's good for circulation," the nurses assured her every time she made a noise.

I hated seeing her like this. Though she couldn't say it, I knew she was in pain. I could see it in her face—the way she struggled to hold her head up—and the way she tightened her fists around the edges of her hospital gown, as if the tighter she squeezed, the less she would feel. I found comfort in knowing that she was almost through the worst of it.

"Bella is here with Daddy and Aaron," Mom announced when we arrived.

Zan tried to smile, but the skin on her face was round and swollen and didn't want to move.

"Hi, sis!" My voice cracked when I spoke, and I laughed nervously. It was all I could do to keep from crying. "I've missed you so much."

"I've missed you." Zan's words were drawn out and slurred together.

"I can't wait for you to come home!"

My sister lifted her arm from her lap and held it straight out in front of her. Aaron joked about it being her Frankenstein pose and we all laughed, even Zan. Drool fell from her numb, swollen lips. "Hey, don't make me laugh."

Mom grabbed a cloth and wiped the dribble from her chin.

When Zan held up her arm again, I took her hand in mine. Though I would have given anything to take my sister's pain away, I hated the part of me that was grateful I was not the one suffering. The guilt swelled inside me, and I wanted so badly to hug her. Instead, I gently touched her shoulder as if to say *I know* or *It's going to be okay*, because what is there to say when nothing is okay? And because out of everyone in the room, I was the only person who understood. I understood, because it was my turn next.

—

There was a time when I thought I'd killed Zan. We were eight years old and Mom had just signed us up for softball. All our siblings had played, and it was as much about family tradition as it was about establishing normalcy.

Mom coached our team that year. She also coached our cousin Aimee's. And one afternoon, Nina, Zan, and I tagged along to the other team's practice. We grabbed a baseball bat and glove and found a spot on the blacktop nearby. Nina was catcher, Zan was pitcher, and I was up to bat. Every time I swung, I missed the ball.

"Hang on, let me practice." I circled the bat in the air as I spoke. Then I closed my eyes and envisioned a ball as I swung.

I opened my eyes the second Nina screamed. I didn't even feel the bat hit anything, but Zan lay on the pavement with blood leaking from her head. I threw the bat on the ground and cradled her head in my hands.

"I'm so sorry, sis. I'm so sorry. I didn't mean to. It was an accident. I love you. I'm so sorry." I was crying, but Zan was not.

"Please don't leave," she whispered when I said we needed to get help. Her voice was raspy and tired, and sounded like it belonged to someone else.

"Nina, go get my mom. Now! Please! Tell her it's an emergency!" I was a faster runner than Nina but I couldn't leave Zan, so every few seconds I screamed for her to hurry. As soon as Mom saw us lying on the pavement, she ran faster than I'd ever seen her run before. Nina was close behind her.

Mom carried Zan. Her eyes were now open, but only because Mom instructed Nina and me to keep talking to her. She said no matter what, Zan was not allowed to fall asleep. My sister vomited three times in the car.

Nina and I were still in shock when Mom dropped us off at home before taking Zan straight to the emergency room. After Nina left, I slipped out the back door and sat on the brick steps that connected the back porch to the garden. When Dad found me, my face was red and swollen from crying. He sat down next to me and put his arm around my shoulders. I buried my face in my hands. "I killed her." My tears were so heavy, I could hardly breathe.

"She's going to be okay. It was an accident. It's not your fault."

"Yes, it is."

When Zan got home the next morning, she had a concussion and a two-inch gash on her forehead from where her face had hit the pavement. Doctors kept her overnight for observation because they couldn't tell from scans of her head if the metal in her skull was from our surgeries or from the bat. Dr. York paid her a visit the next day just to be safe and cleared her to go home. Everyone said it was a miracle that there were no fractures and no damage to her brain. I was just happy she was alive.

As Zan recovered, I worked through my guilt by walking in the field behind our house. Walking became my distraction. I'd often just wander in circles. I'd walk to the tree, then the fence, then the barn, then finally back to the space where the pavement met the gravel. I'd loop around and do this again and again, until I grew tired of circling and wandering. I always came to the same realization—that without Zan, there was nowhere worth going.

———

After her midface surgery, Zan stopped eating. Her face felt foreign to her—like a new territory she hadn't yet learned to navigate. Her jaw was in a new place, and what hadn't been relocated was either too swollen to move or completely numb.

Every time she swallowed solid food, she thought she was choking.

One evening when Dad and I arrived at the hospital for visiting hours, Zan greeted us excitedly. "I ate today!"

"Oh yeah?" Dad looked at Mom. "What did you eat?"

"Half a noodle."

"That's great! Keep that up and you'll be out of here in no time."

Zan sat up in her hospital bed and smiled proudly. It sounded ridiculous, but it was the most she'd eaten in days.

Mom stayed positive the entire time Zan was in the hospital. She never complained. She also never slept more than a few hours at a time, if she slept at all. A little over a week after Zan's surgery, Marissa offered to stay the night with Zan so Mom could go home and rest.

Doped up on painkillers, steroids, and antibiotics, Zan was in and out of consciousness the entire time Marissa was there. She woke up every half hour or so confused and afraid, as she struggled to separate her dreams from reality. Fifteen minutes would pass and she would think it had been hours.

By three a.m., Marissa was desperate for sleep. "Let's play a game," she said lovingly. "How about we see who can fall asleep first, and then when we wake up, we'll take turns telling each other about our dreams." But fifteen minutes later, Zan would wake up again, ready to discuss.

Marissa had just given up on the dream game when Zan

became convinced there was someone else in her room and started yelling for help. The nerves in her face were tingling as the sensation in her skin came back, and she grew paranoid. "Who's touching me? Someone's touching me!"

"There's no one here, Zan. It's just me." Marissa spent the early hours of the morning holding a cool, damp cloth to Zan's face and promising not to leave her side.

Zan eventually got moved to a private room in the ICU. The room was typically reserved for bone marrow transplants or any procedures that needed a sterile environment for recovery. Even though Zan's eyes were still swollen shut and she couldn't see, Mom filled the room with Mylar balloons in fun shapes and colors. "For when she can open her eyes again," she said.

—

While Zan was in the hospital, life continued on without her as though nothing had changed. Except everything had. For the first time, I went through my days alone. In the mornings, I'd sit perched on a stool in the kitchen, eating my breakfast in silence. I'd trace my finger along the grain of the countertop, admiring the deep brown and beige hues. Lifting spoonfuls of cereal to my mouth, I'd watch as splashes of milk dripped onto the surface below.

I spent most of my afternoons alone on the ten-person sectional that occupied almost the entire living room. Across from the couch was a tall oak armoire that opened its doors like a hug to reveal a large TV. Most days Nina and Victoria would come over and we'd scroll through channels, pretending to watch whatever was on. But the shows were boring and life felt empty without Zan to laugh with. On afternoons when I was alone, I'd forget my sister's absence. If I read something funny, I'd laugh out loud to myself. And in that fraction of a moment before I remembered that my sister was not there, I'd call out to her. "Zan, you have to see this!"

Though it was temporary, I was completely unable to fathom her absence. But my sadness felt almost selfish, because I knew my loneliness was nothing compared to the physical pain she was in.

———

I didn't recognize Zan when she returned home from the hospital in early July. Her once-soft belly was now emaciated. Ribs and hip bones protruded from areas where pockets of baby fat had been. When Mom helped Zan out of her hospital gown to go home, the gray sweatpants that had once hugged her hips fell to the floor. Her once-round cheeks were hollow, and her nose was flat and pointy like a beak. Her upper lip was over two times its normal size. For months afterward, she could only move one-half of her face. She could raise one eyebrow, flare one nostril, and smile with one cheek.

Zan couldn't sleep after her time in the ICU. Every time she tried to, she would hear noises and think the doctors and the nurses were going to hurt her again. She had no feeling in most of her face, but her forehead would tingle like a thousand little ants sprinting across her skin and she would scream for me—for *anyone*—to get them off.

One night, after I had fallen asleep at the bottom of her bed, she woke crying. She yelled for me and, between sobs, begged me to get the bugs away from her. I jumped from the bed and turned on the light. My voice remained calm, but inside I panicked.

"Sis, there's nothing there," I told her. The thick, swollen skin of her cheeks was red and splotched with tears, so I did as Marissa had done, and put a cloth to her eyes and her forehead and told her stories until the feeling went away. Until she fell asleep.

———

The summer our faces changed again was the first time Zan and I really understood the helplessness in each other's suffering. Our faces had been bruised and battered before, but always at the same time. We had always been in it together. When our eyes were swollen shut, we experienced healing in tandem. It was easier that way. Seeing each other go through the surgeries we, too, would have to endure felt like an odd kind of cruelty.

Still, there was something therapeutic in being taken apart and slowly piecing ourselves back together, admiring the cracks and holes for what they were—pieces of the story. There was something dark, yet thrilling, about cheating death; about how beautiful the world looked after staring death in the face. But we knew that life meant nothing without each other in it. And like Picasso, we would spend years in darkness trying to process everything we had experienced.

TEN

"Whose cup is this?" my dad's voice boomed. He was standing in the hallway that ran from the bathroom by the back door to the living room and into the kitchen. Our home's open floor plan meant I could see him from my place on the couch. I stared at him blankly as he held a blue plastic cup in one hand and a dirty spoon in the other.

Zan and I had spent hours on the couch watching movies. Well, I watched. She listened. Earlier that morning, Zan's vision had just started to come back to her after the surgery. "I can see!" she'd shouted from bed when she woke. The skin on her face was fading from purple to green. *Progress*, I thought. The area around her cheeks was still three times its normal size, but if she focused hard enough, she could open her right eye to barely more than a squint. The left eye followed. It was painful at first. Going from days of total darkness to seeing lights and colors again was a shock to her senses. Her vision was blurred, and she couldn't hold her eyes open for more than a second without having to take a break to return to the darkness. The more the swelling went down, the wider her eyes could open.

We had put the television on as a distraction, to give the muscles in her face a break.

When Zan returned home from the hospital that summer, she'd lost so much weight you could count the ridges in her spine. Too afraid of the world and too afraid of choking, she ate little more than mashed potatoes and broccoli with cheddar cheese. I, on the other hand, did little besides eat. The anxiety I felt about undergoing the midface surgery consumed me, but food gave me something else to look forward to—something else to focus on. The more my sister wasted away, the larger I grew.

I didn't know that Zan losing weight would suddenly make the soft curves of my belly even more unacceptable. And I certainly didn't understand the constant barrage of comments from family members or friends, praising my sister's emaciated frame. I was confused when my family celebrated the moment Zan's post-surgery diet expanded to chocolate. Because whenever my sister ate a bowl of ice cream, she was praised. But if I had some, I was scolded.

"You don't need to be eating that," Mom would tell me. "If you're truly hungry, eat an apple."

But Zan was so thin, Mom was just happy she was eating at all. *She's sick*, I wanted to scream. *I am, too.*

That was how Dad knew the cup in his hand was mine. I'd used it to make a glass of chocolate milk. I'd been standing in the same place he was now standing, drinking it, until just before he arrived home. When I'd heard him open the door on the other side of the house, I rushed to dump what remained in the cup. I couldn't get to the kitchen without him noticing, so I hurried to the bathroom next to the living room instead. I licked the chocolate from my lips and shoved the dirtied cup and spoon into the drawer, hoping he would not find them. Then I returned to my spot on the couch, acting as if nothing had happened. I must have looked suspicious when he came home, because my dad never used the bathroom where he found the cup. But after he walked in and set his stuff down, he went straight to it. On the couch with Zan, I panicked as he opened the cabinet beneath the sink, and again when he slid open the drawers.

"Really?" I heard him growl.

This was the year I began drinking chocolate milk like water. When nobody was looking, I'd dump syrup and milk into plastic cups and later, reusable water bottles—the kind you could not see through—and guzzle it down as quickly as I could. The rush of sugar left me euphoric. I started doing this not long after we found out our faces would change again. I needed an escape. I lived for the brief moments of contentment when my blood sugar spiked. My habit worsened when Zan was in the hospital, when there was nothing to distract me from the stress and fear that took over my mind. My dad began monitoring what I ate and drank after I went through half a gallon of milk in one day.

"Is this yours?" he asked me again, holding the cup and spoon out in front of him.

"No." I was a terrible liar.

"Seriously?" Now he was annoyed. "So you're telling me Zan got off the couch and felt her way to the kitchen so she could drink this and then hide the cup?" It sounded ridiculous when he said it like that.

"Maybe it's an old cup." I shrugged.

Dad pointed the plastic rim toward me to show the still-wet chocolate liquid at the bottom. "This has got to stop, Ariel." He let out a sigh and carried the cup to the kitchen, where he rinsed it out and loaded it into the dishwasher. Watching him, I wondered how it felt to take up space without ever having to apologize. Zan and I could never do that. People stared too much.

Zan had fallen asleep on the couch, so I left her downstairs and went to my room. I paced back and forth for a few minutes as I stewed in shame. I could talk to my parents about most anything—anything except the one thing I needed to talk about most: food.

I slid the door open to my bathroom and stood in front of the mirror. Pressing my toes into the cold tile floor and lifting my heels from the ground, I brought myself as close to the mirror as I could without touching it. "I hate you," I whispered to my reflection. "I hate you. I hate you. I hate you." My eyes were bloodshot and my cheeks were red from crying again. "I hope you die."

———

All I ever wanted was permission to take up space—to be seen, fully. But by middle school, it felt like all my family could see was my fatness. Perhaps it was the increase in thick red and purple lines that appeared on my thighs and breasts and inner arms to accommodate my new weight. Or the way my belly poked out over the top of my jeans. Only one thing became clear: It was no longer just my face that was wrong. My body was wrong, too. *I* was wrong. Though I was always being reminded of this, it never got easier to hear. Because I never hated my body, I never wanted to hide myself away, until I learned I was supposed to.

My family discussed weight the way other people discussed sports. The obsession started early. When Zan and I were about to start kindergarten, Mom and Alexis took us back-to-school shopping. They would pull out clothes for us to try on. Since I was still struggling to gain weight, they pulled smaller-size clothing for me than for Zan.

"Can I try that, too?" Zan would ask when she saw me in an outfit she liked.

"If it fits her, there's no way it will fit you," Mom would tell her.

"You're too big, Punky," Alexis would add. Their words were not meant to be harmful, but they were.

I was now bigger than Zan. For the first time, Zan understood what it meant to have her body celebrated.

———

My oldest sister, Alexis, married her boyfriend Dave a few weeks after Zan returned home from the hospital in July 2003. Zan and I were thrilled about Dave officially becoming part of the family. They had dated for two years, and he already felt like our brother. We were even more excited when Alexis asked us to be in the wedding. With Zan still reeling from the aftermath of surgery and my procedure scheduled for the week after their nuptials, the wedding was a much-needed distraction. For the first time all summer, we could all focus on life, instead of pain.

Alexis always felt more like a second mom than an older sister. Though she and Marissa were technically our half sisters, I never saw it that way. I loved them too much. In high school, Alexis held jobs at Gymboree and GAP Kids just so she could bring home the latest styles for Zan and me to wear. She called us *her* twins and treated us like we were her own. When she and Dave first met, he thought we were her children by how much she loved us.

Since my parents worked early mornings, Alexis was often responsible for us. When my alarm went off at six o'clock every morning, it would beep and howl until she came down from her room on the third floor and turned it off. "It's time to get up, Punky," she'd whisper, shaking my body awake. Punky is what Alexis's mom had called her when she was little. She used the nickname for Zan and me interchangeably, but somehow we always knew which one of us she was talking to.

Alexis would start a bath, letting the water fill the tub while she picked out our clothes. As Zan and I took turns bathing and dressing, she'd return to her own room to get herself ready for school. Some mornings, I would wake up early and dress myself. I'd match items with neon polka dots and leopard print and floral. Alexis would walk into my room, see my outfit, and sigh loudly. "Punky, you *cannot* wear that."

In the days leading up to the wedding, Alexis took a daily dose of phentermine to lose weight. My sister was not fat, but now she'd lost so much weight, it was as though half of her had disappeared. When I hugged her, all I could feel were bones. She was proud, and I was envious of her willpower.

At dinner the night before she married Dave, I loaded my plate with chicken and potatoes and greens. When Mom saw this, she walked up next to me and patted my stomach.

"It's better to let it go to waste than to let it go to *your* waist." It was a phrase she'd learned from her own mother. Though Mom had not meant to be mean, my body suddenly felt awkward. As I took my plate and found a seat at the table next to Zan, I looked around at my brother and my sisters, and their friends. My body was round and squishy compared to theirs. I tried to focus on everyone smiling and laughing, but all I could notice was the fact that everyone had so little fat on their bones. *Is that what it takes to be happy?* I wondered.

———

Alexis and Dave got married on a Saturday. The ceremony was beautiful and intimate, and held on the lawn in front of our house. Summers in California were hot, but the yard was shaded by the giant oak trees that sat together like twins. On the day of the wedding, Zan and I stood beneath them in matching white dresses with periwinkle sashes tied around our midsections. Our dresses were identical, but our bodies were not.

After the wedding, I started writing about my need for an escape in a journal my aunt Judy gave me for my twelfth birthday. It was thick with gold-rimmed pages and a soft blue binding. At first, I used it to document each day, but after the wedding, it became less of a diary and more of a food log. At the bottom of each entry, I scribbled details about the food I had consumed that day and the foods I wanted to stop eating.

Diet was bad today. I need to stop eating for 3 days. I drew lines under my words as a reminder of my failure. *Only water and one applesauce tomorrow.* Other days, I wrote *STOP EATING* in big bold letters across the page. I never stuck to my plan for starvation, because it was never about being thin. I didn't mind the way my body curved and rolled, but everyone else did. I was used to being different—to *looking* different—but that summer I learned that being fat *and* disfigured was a double offense.

——

After her surgery, Zan's body healed and grew stronger every day she was home, but her anxiety worsened. She was scared—*always* scared. Her phobias involved normal things like spiders and earthquakes and snakes, but the specific scenarios were extreme. There was always an irrational side to that fear. If she saw a spider outside, no matter how small, she'd convince herself that it was a black widow or brown recluse. She'd tell herself that if it hadn't already, it would find its way into our house and bite someone in our family—usually me—while we slept. In the morning we'd wake up to find a giant hole carved out of our skin where the spider had bitten into our flesh. That is, if we woke up at all. Because Zan's fears weren't just related to her own health and safety. They were also about mine.

Once we passed an oleander plant while on a walk with my grandma. The thick leaves and vibrant pink flowers hung from branches, shading the pavement. During the walk, she told us a story, an old wives' tale about a family who died from oleander poisoning. They'd gone camping, Grandma said, and used sticks from an oleander bush to toast their s'mores. Within hours, all of them were dead. Later that night, Zan woke me up. It was three thirty in the morning, but she had not slept.

"I think you touched it." She was rocking back and forth in hysterics. "On our walk. I think you touched the oleander."

It took me a minute to understand what she was talking about. "No, sis, it's okay. It's only poisonous if you eat it." I thought this would calm her down, but it only made her cry harder.

"What if you ate it and didn't know?"

"I didn't, sis. I promise."

"How do you know some didn't get into your mouth?"

"Because I was very careful."

"I don't think you were." Zan's breathing was shallow now, as if she was hyperventilating. If the poison got onto my face, she said, and I licked my lip or bit my fingernail, it was only a matter of time. She feared I had but hours to live before the plant's poison took over my body. Nothing I said could calm my sister's mind. I spent the rest of the night sitting with her, because if I was awake, I couldn't be dead.

It got to the point where my mom had to bring me to the doctor on a weekly basis because Zan would convince herself there was something wrong—something requiring immediate medical attention, because I only had hours to live. Most days, it was meningitis. Every morning, before I even had time to rub the sleep from my eyes or climb out of bed, she'd run through a symptom checklist.

"How do you feel?"

"Tired."

"How are your muscles? Can you please roll your neck?"

I knew it wasn't her fault, so I tried to mask my annoyance. Each morning, with a quick sigh, I'd roll my neck. Then, to show her just how fine I felt, I'd put my chin to my chest, each ear to each shoulder, and finally tilt my head back to look at the ceiling. "See?"

"Very good."

When her fear of meningitis started to fade, she worried even more. "What if now that you're not having proper check-ups for it, you *actually* develop it?!" I told her I'd cross that bridge when I got there, but again, this did little to ease her mind.

Zan worried for the rest of our family, too. At night, she'd sneak out of bed to go check on our parents. She'd stand in the doorway and listen to Dad snore. Mom was a quiet sleeper, so Zan would gently brush her cheek with her fingers and startle her awake. "I just wanted to make sure you were still breathing."

"I'm fine, Zanny. Daddy's fine. It's okay to sleep now." And with that final reassurance, Zan would head back to bed.

There was never a way to talk Zan down from her fears, no matter how unrealistic they were. It was as if a film of tragic scenarios played on a loop in her mind. Her fears were real to her, and all we could do was validate those feelings so that she felt heard.

—

The summer our faces changed again was a summer that dragged all of us kicking and screaming into transformation. Behind my parents' hurtful criticism lurked fear and love and desperation. With so much out of their hands, the need to control something—*anything*—became overwhelming. Because it wasn't just Zan and I who suffered through each procedure. We all did. We all witnessed the aftermath, we all experienced it. We all got through it the best we could, hoping one day we would be okay again.

Even I was unprepared for the way witnessing my sister's procedures—the same ones I would be having—affected me. I'd seen her recover from dozens of surgeries, but none as emotionally or physically violent as this one. Some days, I would watch her from across the room and pray she came back soon. Because her body was there in front of me, but her soul was not. Her eyes when she spoke were hollow and lifeless.

Come back! I wanted to scream. *I need you!*

My sister was gone. And my parents knew that if they didn't do something, it was only a matter of time before I was, too.

ELEVEN

By the time Zan and I entered middle school, we understood beauty only as something we were not. Before the midface surgery the summer before seventh grade, I told myself that it would all be worth it because correcting my appearance meant strangers would stare at me less. Instead of mourning the pieces of myself that would be lost, I silenced the voice in my head that screamed *I DO NOT WANT THIS*. With each alteration, my appearance would be closer to the norm. I grew up seeing Zan and myself as subjects in Picasso's tormented paintings, and so I viewed our surgeries the way Picasso viewed cubism: Every act of creation on the canvas—on our faces—was first an act of destruction. My face had to be taken apart and reconstructed in order for me to become the person I was always meant to be— in order to become a true masterpiece.

The surgery to expand my skull and advance my forehead was scheduled for July 24, 2003, four days after Alexis's wedding. The night before the operation, I sat on the living room floor as Marissa folded and twisted my hair into tight rows of Dutch braids that sat atop my head like a headband. She was careful not to leave any lone strands behind as she separated the sections of hair in front of and behind the scar that stretched across my scalp from the last time I was cut open. When I was four, the doctors had to shave all my hair from my head to make the incision. It was bad enough that I would be returning to middle school with an altered face. I did not want to go without my hair, too. Marissa had been in seventh grade once. She remembered how cruel children could be, so she put a movie on in the family room to distract me and stayed up braiding my hair to give me hope. She said if the surgeon could easily access the center of my scalp and we could keep my hair from being in the way, maybe they would not need to shave it off.

———

The next morning, Mom and I got to the hospital just as the sun was finding its place behind the gray overhang of the Oakland fog. As I checked into the pre-operation wing of the hospital, I prepared myself. Removing my clothes, my sweats were replaced with a blue and white hospital gown.

Each room of the hospital was white, with white walls and white chairs, and the halls were filled with doctors in white lab coats. The world felt far and close and everything was so quiet. The silence screamed like a haunting voice through the white lights and walls.

Dr. York walked in, the edge of his blue scrubs scraping the floor with each step. He removed a black pen from his front pocket but never removed the cap. With the edge, he drew invisible lines ear to ear across my scalp, as if to mark where the incisions would be made. My scar tingled as he retraced the line.

"Tell me everything. I want to know exactly what you're going to do." I found it easier to go in if I was mentally prepared for what I'd wake up to.

"We'll cut from here to here." He moved his cold finger from one ear to the other. "We'll fold the skin down and insert a plate to expand the skull. Recovery shouldn't be too long."

"Well, this sounds fun." My sarcasm was in full swing. The nurse looked at me with sad, sympathetic eyes, before helping me onto the gurney.

Dr. York excused himself, and the nurse in the pre-op station placed patches of numbing cream on both of my hands where the IVs would go. "Are you afraid?" she asked after noticing my elevated blood pressure.

"No," I lied.

I watched her remove a bottle of Versed from the locked medicine cabinet and a syringe from the drawer. It was supposed to help me calm down, to make me sleepy before the operation, but the medicine tasted so bad, the only thing it made me want to do was vomit. Mom tasted it once in solidarity. She said it was so foul, she thought she was going to pass out. After that, she began slipping me a mint or piece of gum to suck on to take the taste away. The nurse always smiled and looked away as if she had not noticed. I was still on a gurney outside the pre-op station when Dad arrived.

"Look who's here, Bella." The medicine was working, and I wanted to curl up in the safety and sweetness of my mom's voice. My smile grew when I saw my dad in his Levi's and T-shirt walking toward me. My dad rarely came to see us before surgery because he always had to work. While I was happy to see him, I was scared all the same. Because I knew my dad's presence meant I was right to be afraid.

Dr. York returned to the room and began exchanging pleasantries with my parents, when another man in surgical scrubs walked in. He pulled the mask from his mouth and held his hand out toward my dad.

"Good morning, sir. My name is Dr. Kaye."

"Dr. Kaye is one of the neurosurgeons here. He'll be taking the lead," Dr. York explained. Dad shook his hand, and then Dr. Kaye turned his attention to Mom and me.

"How are you feeling?" Dr. Kaye asked.

"Delightful," I quipped.

"I'm so glad to hear that." He smiled.

After Dr. York and Dr. Kaye left to prep for surgery, my usual anesthesiologist, Kathy, walked into the room.

"Long time no see," Kathy said, half laughing, peeking over the retro blue cat-eye glasses that clung to the end of her nose. We had a similar sense of humor, and I enjoyed her sarcasm.

"It hasn't been quite long enough." It was always the joke that the hospital was my second home.

She nudged me, still smiling.

"I forgot you were the feisty one." She was looking at Mom as she spoke.

"Feisty or just generally pissed off." This time I wasn't joking.

"Do you have any questions about the procedure as we get everything ready to go?" I shook my head no. "See, I forget I'm talking to a pro!"

If there was anything I never wanted to be an expert in, it was this. Yet here I was. Part of me wondered if this surgery would have been easier had I not already had so many—had I not already seen just how many things could go wrong. But I didn't mention this to Kathy. Instead, I went over my checklist, quizzing her until I was sure there would be no pain I wasn't already anticipating.

"The IV will go in after I'm asleep?" This was not standard, but I had small veins and horrible anxiety, and instead of promising to get the IV on the first stick, Kathy would just put the IV in after I fell asleep. It was our deal. I hated needles and couldn't stand the feeling of medicine pulsing through me, so she waited until I couldn't feel anything anymore.

"Yes, I promise."

"And you won't put it in my wrists?" I already had scars on the inside of both wrists from where previous IVs had been. This made the skin more sensitive and weirded me out. It was just better to avoid the area completely.

"Not if I can help it." Kathy was a straight shooter just like me, and I appreciated the fact that even as a child, she listened to me. More than that, she *heard* me. "If it absolutely comes down to it and I cannot put it anywhere else, do you want the IV to go in your wrist or the top of your foot?"

I cringed, imagining myself waking up and kicking my legs, only to rip the IV out of my foot. It made me light-headed just thinking about it. Still, it was better than the alternative.

"My foot. Just tape it down well, please."

Kathy put her hands on the side of my hospital bed and smiled. "I'm going to go check on the others, but I think we're almost ready." Then she disappeared with another nurse—a nurse I did not recognize—through the daunting double doors.

Alone with my parents in the waiting room, the panic started to set in again. It was only a matter of minutes before I'd breathe in the chemicals and hear the hum of oblivion beating in my ears. It was only a matter of minutes until everything about me would change. I looked to my mom and dad, who stood on each side of my bed.

"I don't want to do this." My voice was deep, trying to keep the tears I was choking on in my throat.

"What's that, baby?" Mom leaned over the railing of my bed.

"I said, I don't want to do this." The tears came with my words this time.

"I know. But soon it will all be over and you won't have to worry about it anymore." My dad patted my hair lovingly.

"Besides, look at it this way, you and Zan are going to officially beat me for Best-Looking Henley." My father put his hand up to his hair and pretended to fluff it. "If anyone should be upset, it's me!" I looked at him, then over at my mom, and together we laughed. Dad was always good at making the heavy feel light.

"I hate this. I hate this so much." I pulled the blanket up to my eyes to catch the tears. I was sobbing now—big, noisy gasps escaped my body and echoed through the empty room. My parents each bent over the sides of my bed, outstretched their arms, and held me and each other. I now understood why Mom always said she didn't let herself cry for fear of never being able to stop.

"I don't want to do this." I muttered this phrase again and again as my tears soaked the edges of Mom's hair. The dreams of beauty that had eased my fears disappeared. What good was beauty if I was dead?

"Would it make you feel better if Daddy went in with you?"

"Can't you both come with me?"

Before Mom could answer, Kathy returned to the waiting area where my parents and I were huddled together. I wiped the tears from my face as soon as she entered. It was one thing for my parents to see me cry, but another thing entirely for someone like Kathy, who thought I was fearless and brave. I didn't want her to change her mind, to suddenly think less of me in my time of weakness.

Kathy stood next to Mom and placed her hands on the part

of the blanket that covered my calves. "I know this isn't fun, sweetheart. I know. But I promise it's all going to be okay. We're going to take such good care of you. And your parents, oh, you have the best of them." She touched Mom's shoulder when she said this. "We're all here for you, honey. We're all here for you."

Mom turned her head and looked at Kathy. "She wants to know if we can both go in with her."

Kathy pursed her lips and shook her head no. Before Mom could respond, a guttural sob escaped my body.

"I'm so sorry. I really am, honey. We're breaking protocol by allowing even one person in."

My body must have looked like a turtle retreating into its shell, because I pulled the top of my gown up to my eyes in a feeble attempt to hide my face. What I would have done to quietly disappear. I never cried before surgery like this. I wanted to be the brave girl. I'd had so many surgeries before. I wasn't supposed to be afraid anymore. But it wasn't just about fearing surgery or the stress of choosing who got to go into the operating room with me. It was about choosing who I would get to see last if something went wrong. I didn't want to decide which of my parents I would get to say goodbye to if I died.

I didn't want to say goodbye.

——

The operating room was filled with doctors and nurses in a sea of blue and green medical garb, with scalpels on trays in the corner and machines with the brightest lights overhead. Hands lifted me from the gurney and laid me beneath what felt like a spotlight. I wanted to run. To go anywhere else, but I stayed, frozen, as they untied my gown. The operating table was hard, and I could hear the rapid *thump* of my heart beating in my ears and in my throat as I listened to the monitors around me.

God, I'm so scared.

There were hands that lifted my head, and there were hands that put a doughnut-shaped pillow beneath it. Hands covered me, reaching across my chest and at the gown that loosely covered my body. I did not want these hands to touch me, but I did not have a choice.

Kathy lowered the gas to my face, and the hum of the nurses' talking blurred in the background. My world was spinning, so I focused on Mom standing next to me. I could feel monitor buttons being stuck to my chest, but I was fading and I didn't mind.

"I love you so much," Mom kept telling me. Her hand was warm against mine, my palm growing numb as she traced her thumb back and forth across it. Everything seemed louder, but fuzzy. Like I was in a dream.

"You're on an airplane now," Kathy said, commenting on the deep grinding I was hearing in my ears. Her voice was delayed.

"Yes, I am." I tried to smile. My words were long and drawn out. It was always like this. I'd resist breathing in the gas. But then my body would adjust and it was suddenly like nothing could hurt me anymore. It felt like freedom. It would go on like this for a few minutes. I'd resist and give in, then resist again. I forced myself to keep blinking, to fight the medicine to stay awake. To stay *alive*.

I could still hear Mom's voice as she stood next to me. She was talking and laughing with Kathy now. I squeezed her hand and she promised not to let go. "I'm right here, baby. I'm right here." I shut my eyes and clenched my fists harder, as my lungs filled with gas, but the white appeared again, like speckles in the darkness.

"I love you, Momma." My words were hard to decipher, but we'd been here so many times before, she knew what I was saying.

"Tell Daddy and Zanny and Aaron and Rissa and Lex I love them too, okay?" I wanted to list everyone I knew and loved, but I was running out of time. My world continued spinning. A vibration buzzed in my ears.

"I will, baby. We love you, too."

"I'm gonna go now, Momma." I looked up at Mom's face before shutting my eyes one last time.

"I love you, Belle."

And I was gone.

TWELVE

I woke to the rhythmic beeping of monitors and the shuffling of nurses' feet in the intensive care unit. My head was heavy and I couldn't see, but I could feel the medicine running through me. It burned as it swam through my veins. The breathing tube left a cut on the lower border of my bottom lip, where blood dried and crusted on my skin. I couldn't speak, but there was a numbing pain; the kind of pain where you forget what it's like not to hurt. *It's temporary*, I reminded myself. Our faces always healed, our eyes always opened, and eventually Zan and I were always able to resume normal life as though none of what we'd experienced had ever happened.

The surgery to expand my skull was a major operation, but I healed faster than anyone expected. On the morning of my second day in the hospital, my breathing tube and catheter were removed. By that afternoon, I told Mom I was ready to go home. I couldn't open my eyes yet, but I'd finished the antibiotics and my pain was under control.

I was anxious to get back to normal. Our lives were frequently interrupted by hospital visits, but Zan and I worked hard to establish a sense of normalcy. I was determined to keep it this way. From the minute I woke up after surgery, I channeled all my efforts into getting better and moving on.

I didn't meet the physician on duty until the next morning, when he was in my room. "I hear someone thinks they're ready to go home," he said.

When I heard his voice, I imagined he was around five-ten, with dark brown hair and olive skin. It was a game Mom and I would play in the hospital whenever I had an operation impacting my sight. I'd guess each person's appearance based on their voice, and after they left, Mom would tell me how my predictions measured up. I rarely got it right, but it gave me something to do.

"I'm Ariel. It's nice to meet you." I stuck my hand out in front of me and the doctor shook it gently.

"We usually like the swelling to go down a bit before we send patients home," he told me.

"What, this?" I jokingly pointed to my face, then waved my hand as if it were nothing. "It'll go down in no time."

The doctor laughed awkwardly. "How about this: Let's go ahead and check in again in three days."

"How about we check in now so you send me home tonight?" I tried to smile, but the swelling made it hard for my cheeks to move. Using the muscles in my face was painful, so anytime I had an operation, I spent recovery trying not to laugh, smile, cough, sneeze, or cry.

The doctor hesitated. "Let's do two days."

"Tomorrow," I countered again.

Mom had been mostly silent until now. "Ariel, this isn't a negotiation."

"Yes, it is," I told her. "I want to leave and they want me to stay. Let's compromise."

"I just don't want to send you home before you're ready," the doctor started to explain. "I would hate for something to go wrong. Then you'd just have to turn around and come right back."

"This is not my first surgery," I told him. "I can tell when my body is and isn't ready. And trust me, this body is ready to go home."

The doctor laughed again.

"Have you tried sleeping here?" I asked him.

An awkward silence lingered. "Seriously." I paused for effect. "You try sleeping here. The lights are always on. Machines are beeping every two seconds. People yell into the intercom. Like, honestly, what is with that? Do they not understand it's a microphone? I want my bed and my pillow and an actual good night's sleep. You want me to heal? Send me home. Please."

"I'll check in with you tomorrow morning. Final offer."

"Deal." The doctor shook my hand again before leaving the room.

The next day, I was out of the hospital and home before noon.

My recovery at home was much like the three days I'd spent in the hospital; there wasn't much I could do except lie around and wait for the swelling to decrease enough for my eyelids to open. The only difference between the locations was the noise and comfort levels.

Plus, we had experience. Zan and I had had several out-patient eye surgeries throughout elementary school to correct our vision and strengthen the muscles in our eyes. We had smaller procedures—like the ones on our eyes—together on the same day, because it was easier for Mom to make only one trip to and from the hospital.

At home, I spent my temporary blindness sprawled out on the couch listening to the television. Zan sat with me, describing the images on the screen as we watched.

"Who's talking?" I'd ask her. "What do they look like? What are they wearing?" I imagined every detail in my mind. When I wasn't imagining the scenes from the television, I was willing my eyes to open. I'd been trying for days. My eyebrows would move upward, but my eyelids would not budge. A week passed before I was able to open them to barely a squint. The flood of light stung my eyes, and I could only keep them open for a few seconds at a time. Everything was brighter than I'd remembered.

That morning, I went into my parents' bathroom and shut the door behind me. I stared at the floor, carefully avoiding the mirrors that hung on the wall above the vanity. I positioned myself in front of one of the sinks, and with my eyes closed, I slowly lifted my head. I wanted to see what I looked like. My eyes strained as I forced them open again.

My own reflection frightened me. My eyelids were still thick and purple, and everything from my cheeks and nose up to the top of my head was round and puffy and discolored. I looked like I'd been stabbed in the skull or beaten. *Don't cry. Don't cry*, I told myself as tears slowly creeped down my cheeks. I closed my eyes and held my breath as I tilted my head back in agony. I wasn't sure which hurt more: seeing the reality of what my new face looked like or the deep, aching pressure I felt pulsing through my head. Crying felt like a punch to the giant bruise that was my face.

———

When I think back to my temporary post-surgery blindness, I think again of Picasso. During his Blue Period—a period before cubism, when he painted his depression in all shades of blue—blindness was a recurring theme. In 1903, he painted *The Old Guitarist*, a portrait of a blind man sitting cross-legged on the ground, playing his guitar. The man is thin, his body is contorted in a way that highlights the forward slump of his shoulders and the way his head hangs downward. Art experts speculate about the meaning behind the painting and Picasso's use of blindness in his work. Some say it was a metaphor for sight—that because the man with the guitar could not see visually, he had a clearer understanding of the world around him. Others say Picasso's use of blindness was a metaphor for his own desire for deeper understanding. Picasso sought to paint what he knew, not necessarily what he saw, and so his work was often trying to examine the difference between what it meant to look at something and what it meant to see it. The theory I like most for this painting is that the guitar—the brightest-colored object in the image, the object the man is holding on to—is a symbol of what it means to cling to hope.

The day after my vision was restored, eight days after the surgery to advance my forehead, I returned to Dr. York's office so he could assess the progress of my recovery.

"Look at my masterpiece," he said when he entered the exam room. Dr. York was always admiring his work and the way he executed each procedure with such care and precision. He was an artist, and Zan and I were the canvases showcasing his life's work. He washed his hands and pulled a pair of gloves from the box on the counter before removing the thick white bandage from my head. The gauze had been wrapped so tight, I thought it was the only thing holding my head together. "Beautiful, beautiful," he said. He gently tapped each of the staples connecting the front and back of my skull and examined the scab that had already started forming. There was a slight pressure on my scalp every time he touched an area near the incision site.

I didn't know until I caught a glimpse of myself in the reflection of a picture frame that Marissa's efforts to save my hair had been only partially effective. Though Dr. York and Dr. Kaye did not shave my entire head, they did take a two-inch-wide strip. So instead of a Dutch braid stretching ear to ear, I was left with a stripe of pale, raw skin in the center of my long brown hair. I felt more like a science experiment than an art project.

———

As I recovered from surgery the summer before seventh grade, cheerleading became my metaphorical guitar—the hope I clung to. By August 8, only two weeks after my surgery, my head had healed just enough for me to start attending cheerleading practice.

Practice always started on the first day of August and was held five times a week for the first month. When school started, it dropped down to three. I'd already missed the first week, but I was grateful that the hospital cleared me to begin practice that Friday. I told myself if it didn't go well and my teammates did not like my new face, at least I would have a whole weekend to recover from the humiliation.

Mom helped coach our cheer squad that year. She did it with another woman, whose daughter Courtney was also on our team. Courtney's older sister ended up becoming one of the junior coaches, who made up all our routines and taught them to us.

Zan had her second surgery of the summer—the one to advance her forehead—seven weeks after her first surgery and two weeks after mine. So Justine and I started the cheer season without her. Justine's mom drove me to and from practice all month while Zan was still in the hospital. She was nice about picking up the slack when Mom was with Zan or me after surgery. When Zan and I signed up for cheer, we didn't understand how extensive our surgeries or the recovery would be. By the time we realized it, we needed something to look forward to, something to keep us busy, so we stuck with it. While other kids got to experience sports and extracurricular activities for what they were, Zan and I saw them as our escape. All our experiences were broken up by our surgery schedules and doctor appointments, but we were just grateful to be doing something "normal." Zan missed practice the entire month of August, and the first couple of games in September.

Justine and I arrived at our first practice to find girls lined up against the gymnasium wall, where PLEASANT VALLEY HIGH SCHOOL was written in blue and yellow letters taller than me.

"I'm feeling shy," I confided in Justine as soon as we stepped out of the car. "I feel like I'm just going to get stared at." It was clear by the appearance of my face that I was still recovering. Most of the bruising had disappeared, but the areas around my eyes and cheeks still bulged outward.

"They'll have to stare at both of us, then." Justine was good at reassuring me. She made me feel better without invalidating what it was I was feeling. "It's gonna be fun."

By the end of warm-ups, she was right. My nerves faded as

soon as the music started. I didn't have to worry about coming up with topics of conversation or trying to find ways to relate to other girls my age when we were all busy jumping up and down.

After our warm-up activities, the coaches sent all the cheer-leaders to run laps around the track, where the boys on the football team we'd be cheering for were also practicing. I ran in the outermost lane, hoping it would minimize the chances of the boys seeing me. But the boys were all Justine wanted to talk about.

"Okay, do you see number eleven?" she asked as we slowly jogged together. Since I was still recovering from surgery, I was easily exhausted and out of breath. Justine acted like she didn't notice, though. She stayed at my pace while the other girls ran laps around us.

"Yeah," I lied. I had no idea who she was looking at. The sweat from my forehead was burning my eyes. I just wanted to sit down.

"How cute is he?"

"How cute is who?"

"Number eleven! You're not paying attention!"

"Yes, I am! They all look alike with their helmets on!"

Justine stopped jogging and placed her hands on my shoul-ders, turning my body toward the blond quarterback who stood on the sidelines sans helmet, gulping water. His name was Ian. He was the older brother of one of the girls on our squad.

"How cute is he?" Justine asked me again, this time louder

than she meant to. Before I could answer, Ian looked up and smiled before giving a little wave.

"Shit," Justine said. "Run." We laughed all the way around the track.

———

At practice the following Monday, each squad met separately. There were fifteen girls on our squad. Some were returning cheerleaders, but most were new. Even the girls I recognized, I stayed away from, because I was used to people not wanting to be seen with me. Instead, I stuck so close to Justine, you would have thought an invisible thread tethered me to her.

Earlier that summer, when I'd gone with Marissa to the mall to do returns, I ran into Sadie, a girl I'd met in sixth-grade English. Sadie and I sat next to each other for much of the year and swapped stories during class every day. When I said hi and waved to her while she was shopping with friends, she pretended not to know who I was.

"Okay, why is that girl waving at you?" one of Sadie's friends asked her. "Do you know her?"

Sadie looked back at me and laughed. "Eww, no."

"What a freak," her friend said.

Why would you say hi to them? I thought, berating myself. *You are such a loser.*

Marissa was about to say something to the girls when I stopped her. "Let's just go home, please. I don't want anyone else to see me today."

The older I got, the more frequently these kinds of inter-
actions occurred. So, whenever I saw people I recognized in public places, I saved us both the embarrassment and pretended I
didn't know them. Most people seemed to prefer it this way. If
people wanted to talk to me, they would. Justine had already
made it clear she was my friend. Until the other girls on our squad
made it clear they wanted to be my friends, too, I kept to myself.

—

The next Friday, Justine and I went to a showing of *Uptown
Girls* at the local movie theater before practice. I enjoyed going
to the movies, because it meant getting out of the house without
having to be seen. The ear-to-ear scab from my incision still
throbbed, but I did my best to keep it covered. Before we left
for the theater, Marissa parted my hair down the middle and
French braided each side. Then she tied a maroon bandana over
the top of my head.

"It matches the team colors," she said happily.

In addition to the missing hair along my scar, I had bed-
sores from lying down so much during recovery. Patches of hair
where my head met my pillow fell out and were replaced by
brownish-red scabs. To help them heal, Marissa covered them
with flesh-colored bandages.

"You can hardly even tell it's there," she assured me. "The
bandage just blends right in!"

I wasn't sure if I believed her, but I didn't want to check. It
was easier not to think about it.

This worked until later that evening, after Justine's mom dropped us off at practice. It was the first day of stunting and we were learning how to lift girls up, toss them into the air, and catch them before they hit the ground. I was one of the shortest girls on the squad, but I weighed too much to be a flier. Before surgery, I'd been a base. But I couldn't risk getting kicked in the face until I'd healed more, so I mostly just watched. Watching made me feel involved without having to push my body beyond its limitations, so I didn't mind. Justine was a back spotter. She helped lift the fliers and caught them in her arms when they cradled out of a stunt.

I was watching my teammates practice the stunts with a few other girls, when my teammate Julie started to say something beside me.

"Hold still," she said. "You have something right—" Before I could stop her, she ripped the small oval bandage from my scalp and dropped it to the ground.

"Oh my God!" she screamed when she saw the patch of bare skin where my hair had fallen out. "I am so sorry!" She fumbled around in the grass for the bandage, but she was making a scene and the other girls were staring, so I told her not to worry about it. My skin stung as the opened scab began to bleed. I used the sweatshirt in my gym bag to wipe away the blood, while the other girls continued practicing. I repositioned my bandana to hide as much of the bare skin as I could.

The hardest part about healing was not my temporary

post-surgery blindness or the physical recovery, but the way it forced Zan and me to confront the fact that we were not like other girls our age. We'd put our lives on pause for surgery, only to realize that no amount of pretending could make us fit back in.

At the end of practice, our coaches sent us to do two more laps around the track to cool down. Exhausted from catching girls as they fell out of stunts, Justine groaned.

"Number eleven. Ian. Blond football player," I teased, trying to cheer her up.

Justine smiled at the thought. When she *actually* saw him, her demeanor changed entirely. She stood up straighter and softened her expression, keeping her eyes focused on the ground in front of us. I wondered what it was like to *want* to be noticed. How it felt to be stared at for something besides ugliness. I didn't want to ruin Justine's excitement over her crush, so I kept my questions to myself. On the field, Ian and his friends noticed Justine, too. But when we rounded the corner of the track and they caught a glimpse of my face, they went from ogling her to mocking me.

"Run, crazy eyes!" someone shouted. Justine and I both pretended not to hear it.

People thought they could say whatever they wanted to me and I just had to take it. As much as it angered me, I thought I deserved it. After all, cheerleaders *were* supposed to be beautiful. And as the world had drilled into me, I was not. This was my punishment. While Justine got stared at for being beautiful, I got stared at for being a freak.

Cheerleading became an act of resistance. It hurt knowing there were people who believed Zan and I did not belong on the squad. But there was nothing I enjoyed more than dancing and performing routines with choreography that took weeks to learn. It was uncomfortable being the only people to look the way we did, but there was also a sense of pride—of camaraderie—in showcasing who we were. Every time Zan and I cheered on the sidelines or performed at competitions, it was us against the world. It was a kick, a fist to the air, a middle finger to everyone who thought faces like ours should not be seen.

THIRTEEN

Friday, August 15, 2003, marked the beginning of Zan's second week in the ICU after her head surgery. That night, after cheer practice ended early, Dad drove me to the hospital to see her. As with Zan's first operation that summer, I was not looking forward to visiting her. It wasn't that I didn't want to see her; I didn't want to see *what had been done* to her. I didn't want to see her hooked up to machines, lying there in pain. This was selfish, I knew, but seeing her this way stirred an unbearable helplessness within me.

It was almost eight o'clock when Dad and I arrived at the hospital. We rode the elevator up to the third floor, where Zan was recovering in a private room in the ICU. The lights in the room were off, but a harsh brightness poured in through the windows that separated her from the other children, casting shadows all across the room. The bruises that covered Zan's face didn't seem as severe in the darkness. Though the swelling in her face was slowly decreasing, she was not yet able to open her eyes.

Zan's room was quiet compared to the chaos of the ICU. The only noise came from the heart rate monitor above her bed, where rows of colorful squiggly lines and numbers filled the otherwise black screen. *Beep . . . beep . . . beep.* The top of her bed was positioned upward at a forty-five-degree angle, with pillows to prop up her still-bandaged head. Her hospital gown hung loose over the front of her body. Cords to machines monitoring her vitals ran through the top of the gown, where they were stuck to her belly and her chest. She had a blood pressure cuff on one arm and an IV in the other. Bags of fluids hung from the pole behind her. Looking at my sister, I found myself wondering if this was what she'd seen weeks earlier when she'd visited me. *Was she as scared to see me as I am of seeing her?* I wondered. It was easier being the patient.

Mom got up and gave me a hug. "Zan just fell asleep," she whispered.

Upon hearing her name, Zan became alert. "No, I'm awake now," she said. Her voice was dry and husky.

Dad stood at the foot of Zan's bed and gently caressed her forearm with the back of his hand. "How are you feeling?" he asked her.

"I've had better days," Zan told him. "But, hey, could be worse." She coughed gently to clear her throat.

Despite my initial discomfort, I warmed up quickly. Visits with Zan reminded me that even though her physical body looked different, she was still herself on the inside. She was still my sister, my *twin*. When I sat down on the edge of her hospital bed, we didn't discuss surgery, recovery, or what our new faces looked like. We talked about *The Cheetah Girls*—a Disney Channel movie about four friends and aspiring singers that had premiered earlier that night.

"Have you seen it yet?" Zan asked me excitedly.

"I decided to come see you instead," I told her.

"Will you tell me how it is after you watch it?" she asked.

I told her I'd rather just wait for her. Since it was the Disney Channel's newest original movie, it played at various times every day or so. It didn't feel right to watch it without her. We watched all the Disney Channel movies together, but this one felt special because it was about Zan's favorite thing in the entire world: music. Zan loved to sing. She was good at it, too, just like Dad. She had a deep, soulful voice—a voice you wouldn't expect when you saw her. Sometimes when I got home after surgeries, I'd ask her to sing to me. I'd lay my head on her lap and she'd gently rub my forehead while the melody in her voice rocked me to sleep. This was the one thing I missed most about her while she was in the hospital. At home, the house felt eerily quiet without the sound of her singing to fill the halls.

While Zan and I visited, a nurse poked her head inside the room. "Is it okay if I just get some vitals real quick?" she asked.

"Sure, come on in," Mom said, moving a chair to clear a pathway to Zan. The nurse removed the empty bags of fluids connected to Zan's IV.

"How's your pain, sweetie?" she asked, as she put another bag of medicine in its place. "You're looking so good!"

"Thank you. I try," Zan replied, and the nurse laughed.

The forehead procedure was harder on Zan's body than it was on mine, just as the surgery to advance our upper jaw and midface would be harder on me. Whereas I was in the hospital for a few days, Zan was there for ten.

I don't remember much else about Zan's time in the hospital that summer, but I'll never forget her returning home later that weekend with a mess of dark brown hair that had been matted with blood and surgical ointments. Like me, she was missing hair and had a thick, white stripe of skin across her head. Her incision had already started to scab over, with areas of crusted purple, red, and green skin. If you looked closely, you could see each of the holes where the staples had been. Zan also had an inch-long piece of metal that was visible through the skin in the center of her forehead. The plate Dr. York put in our skulls was meant to dissolve, but Zan's never did. Instead, it pushed against her forehead like a baby's foot kicking inside the womb—like it was trying to find a way out. It hurt her sometimes. If pressure was applied to her forehead at the wrong angle, it would send a burning pain up through her scalp. She had to sleep sitting up because if her pillow touched her forehead, she would yelp in pain.

The afternoon Zan arrived home, Mom and Aaron helped her get from the car to the house. Her swelling had decreased enough for her eyes to open just slightly, and though she could barely see, she went straight to the downstairs bathroom, closed the door behind her, and turned on the light. When she looked at her reflection in the mirror, she was so startled by what she saw, she jumped backward. For an hour after, she sat on the floor and cried.

"How could you let them do this to me?" she shouted at Mom through the door.

Once Zan calmed down, she took a bath and put on a pair of fresh pajamas. Afterward, Mom napped while Zan and I watched a rerun of *The Cheetah Girls* in the living room. Zan kept her eyes closed because it hurt too much to hold them open, so I did for her what she'd done for me after my operation: I described every character and scene on the screen while she listened to the audio. Zan didn't need to see, anyway. She was drawn to the music and quickly memorized the lyrics to the songs. "*Cause we are sisters, we stand together,*" we'd harmonize. "*Someone's always there behind to catch us if we fall.*"

———

It took Zan one day of being home to look at her face in the mirror and four days to work up the courage to do it again.

"I'm going to do it," she told me, standing in front of the sink in the downstairs bathroom. She wasn't quite steady on her feet, so I stood behind her to make sure she didn't fall. The bathroom was dark, and with only the light from the hallway, she found comfort in knowing that when she looked in the mirror, her reflection would hardly be visible. "I want to ease into it this time," she joked. "One, two, three . . . ," she counted slowly.

With her head still lowered and her eyes still closed, she placed her hands on the white pedestal sink in front of her. "Go," she whispered to herself. The tears started the moment she got a glimpse of her reflection.

"I look like I've been attacked," she cried, and immediately closed her eyes again. "What have they done to me?" The top half of Zan's face and head were still puffy and oddly shaped. "I thought the nurse said I looked good," she said between tears. "If this is progress, I don't want to know what I looked like before."

"It's okay, sis," I said, trying to comfort her, but Zan just wanted to be alone. And with her eyes lowered to the floor, she slowly made her way up the stairs and into her bedroom. For weeks afterward, she avoided mirrors and anything reflective.

I understood my sister's shock, though the change in my appearance was not nearly as drastic as Zan's. Nothing about our surgeries that summer felt like improvement. Had our pre-operation appearances really been so bad that our now mangled faces were considered progress? Before that summer, it was the world who could not accept our appearance. But after the surgeries were completed, neither could we.

As soon as we had our vision back, our parents took us with them to run errands or eat out at restaurants. It didn't matter that the skin on our faces was still swollen and painful to touch. It didn't matter that in public, other children pointed and whispered at us, while their parents just stared. Whenever we rode in the car, Zan would refuse to sit in the front seat because she didn't want anyone in any of the other cars to see her. This always made Dad angry. I think that came from his inability to fix our pain. Our family never meant to belittle our experience by bringing us out in public. Our surgeries and recovery periods had become so normalized, our family never even considered the emotional impact that being out in public had on us. They thought it would help things feel ordinary again.

When I mentioned to Dad how much it bothered me that Zan and I were like objects on display for everyone around us to critique, he said the world did not know better. "Just ignore them," he suggested. *But why is it our job to educate them?* I wondered. Nobody else had to justify their existence or explain to others why they did or did not look a certain way. Why did we? But to my parents, it did no good to dwell on the things we could not change. Life moves on, and we had to, too.

When it comes to Zan and me recovering together—to unpacking the shape of our relationship during that time—my mind goes blank. It feels like my memories were whited out—as if my own mind was trying to protect me. Because if I had to pick one word to describe our recovery that summer, it would be *violent*. From the moment we woke up from surgery and for months afterward, we looked like we'd been physically beaten. Our faces were round and swollen. Our skin was discolored and numb on the surface, but with a deep ache that made it painful to be touched. We were upsetting to look at because it was not clear what had happened to us. The last time we'd had the mid-face surgery—at four years old—it was clear we were recovering from surgery. And there had been noticeable progress in the placement of our features. As the swelling went down, we began to look more "normal." This time, though, it was clear there was something wrong. If anything, it felt like the surgeries pushed our faces further from the golden ratio.

In some ways, our sisterhood helped our healing, because having someone else to focus on and worry about allowed us to shift the focus from ourselves to each other. It kept us from leaning into our own pain. When I talked to Alexis about this, she said it made sense, because when you love someone as much as Zan and I love each other, you could be burning up in flames but still worried about whether the other person is okay. That's what it felt like for us.

FOURTEEN

On the first day of seventh grade—the day I met Ms. J for the first time—I wore a soft pink baseball hat with a white Nike logo to cover the area of my head that had been shaved. My hair, not even half an inch long, sprouted from my head, catching the scabs of skin that fell from my scar. Under my hat, the incision that stretched across my scalp itched and ached. It had been just over a month since that first surgery on my head, and my face was still bruised and swollen.

At school I was met with swarms of students I did not recognize. Friends stood in circles, talking and laughing before class. *Keep your head down*, I thought. *Maybe they won't see you.* Who was I kidding? Of course they would.

"Damn," one boy shouted. "Do you see her?" I watched the boy slap his friend's shoulder and point to me.

"That's not a *her*, man. That's an *it*."

"Yeah, what even is that?" They laughed together.

I lowered my eyes to the ground in front of me, hoping the bill of my hat would shield me from their insults.

"I would kill myself if I looked like that."

I am a *thing*. An *it*. Barely even human. This is how they see me. It was never the surgeries or the physical pain that I hated about my condition. It was the fact that it was always there, always visible—a mark inviting the world to judge me. Some days, my disfigurement felt just subtle enough that by facing the right direction or wearing the right kind of glasses and standing at just the right angle, people wouldn't even notice. Then one person would see me, really *see* me, and then another and another, until a crowd of strangers stared holes into my soul, leaving me with an emptiness in my core. So I learned to keep my head down, walk fast, and avoid eye contact, because it's harder to hit a moving target. Though I grew up longing for acceptance, I would've settled for anonymity. I wanted to blend in, to be normal. Instead, I lived my life in reference to—and as an extension of—my ugliness.

After my first day of art with Ms. J, where the boy behind me threatened to stab a pencil through the back of my eye, and science with Ms. Cooke, it was off to French with Ms. Dupont. When I got to class, rows of desks were arranged in a U pattern. I chose a seat on the side of the room, just slightly behind where Ms. Dupont stood when she lectured. *This way she won't think to call on me*, I thought. When the final bell rang, Ms. Dupont rang her own bell to get our attention.

"Je m'appelle"—Ms. Dupont placed her hand on her chest—"Madame Dupont." As soon as we heard her name, we understood that she was introducing herself. "Je m'appelle Madame Dupont." She repeated the phrase again, this time slower and all at once.

"Comment vous appelez-vous?"

The room fell silent again.

"Comment vous appelez-vous?" Madame Dupont repeated, pointing to a girl named Bailey in the front row. When Bailey didn't respond, she moved on to the next student.

"Comment vous appelez-vous?" Nobody had an answer. When she got to me, I shrugged.

"Ariel?" I said my name, unsure of the question or the answer. Madame Dupont clapped her hands together once and removed her bag of gummy bears from the top drawer of her desk. It was always awkward being called on in class, because other students used every opportunity they could to gauge my intelligence. One wrong answer and they'd treat me like the least intelligent person in existence. But one correct answer and suddenly I was brilliant. Everything I did became a testament to my overall worth.

When I got to my intro to woodworking class later that morning, Mr. Jennings instructed me to remove my hat. His class was in a portable room on the blacktop near the field. He stood on the ramp, shaking everyone's hand as they entered.

"Hats off when you enter, please," he said, tapping me on the shoulder.

"I think my mom sent a note to the school," I said as I turned around. My voice was raspy and awkward. Like I'd suddenly forgotten how to speak. "The office was supposed to give it to you." I coughed to clear my throat. Kids were lining up behind me now, anxious to get to class. "I just had surgery on my head. I'm wearing the hat to keep it covered and, ummm, well, can I please leave it on?" I looked down at my feet.

"No problem," Mr. Jennings said without looking at me. He'd already moved on to smiling and shaking the hand of the next student.

I didn't realize he hadn't listened to a word I said until he stood in front of the classroom and asked me to remove my hat again. "I don't like to ask more than once. Take it off, please." My classmates oohed at the idea of me being in trouble.

"I can't," I mumbled. I felt myself panic at the thought of the other kids seeing the scab that crusted over my incision.

Mr. Jennings looked at me from the front of the silent classroom. "Why?" His voice was stern, almost as if he were asking a rhetorical question.

"Because my hair is gone!" I shouted. A few students laughed, others looked away. He issued me a detention slip for the next morning. Seventh grade was off to a disastrous start.

Once I left the woodworking building, I headed toward the 300 wing, where Zan, Justine, and I had our lockers. As I made my way across campus, I was greeted by the vice principal, Ms. Dodson, a young blond woman, whose daughter Cara was in my grade.

"Good morning, Ariel!"

I smiled, hoping to get by with minimal conversation.

"Can I borrow you for a second?" Ms. Dodson waved me closer.

I nodded.

"Since you were not able to get your photo taken during orientation, you will need to get one today. This way you can get your ID card and be in the yearbook!"

"I don't want to be in the yearbook." I was completely out of patience.

"ID photos are mandatory, sweetheart. Every student needs one."

"That's fine." I barely gave her time to finish her sentence before spitting my words out. My tone was harsh and I was angry. "I'll arrange to have my photo taken on the next picture day."

"Unfortunately, this is the last opportunity."

"Oh, darn," I snapped my fingers, hoping she would read my tone. "I guess I'll just need to be in even more photos next year then."

"Nice try." Before I could respond, the woman signaled to the photographer that I was next. "One more right here." The photographer waved me over.

"Feel free to go to lunch after this," she told me before walking away to wave and smile in some other poor students' direction.

The photographer was nice and pretended not to notice the tears of frustration welling up in my eyes. Marissa had given me an old dress of hers to wear for my first day. It was denim, and sleeveless, and flowed out at the waist. My eyes were still sensitive, and the lights from the photographer's equipment made it hard to keep them open. I cocked my head to the side and squinted at the camera.

"Do you want to see how it turned out?"

I cried at the sight of my picture on his screen. I didn't want an ID card. I didn't want to be in the yearbook. I didn't want to be in school at all.

———

After school that Thursday, Zan and I did our best to distract ourselves from everything we had dealt with during our first week back. Zan had undergone both procedures by the time school started, but my second operation was scheduled for that Friday. After stories about our faces had begun circulating around campus, Zan decided to take the next day off as well. Some said we'd been in a car accident. Others, that we were finishing up chemotherapy. Children we had known since kindergarten now looked at us like they were afraid of us, like we were monsters.

"One week down." Zan plopped herself at her desk and turned to face me.

"One down, forty to go." I sighed and lay down on her bed. "I wish I could just stay here forever." We had wanted to stay home longer, but we couldn't risk falling behind. Mom said homeschooling wasn't an option because there was no one to stay home and teach us. Mom needed her job to keep our health insurance, and the income from Dad's company was what our family lived on.

Zan nodded in agreement before turning on her computer and opening instant messenger. The program had just finished loading when a message from an unknown sender appeared on the screen.

You look like you had a bomb explode on your face.

Zan's shoulders slumped forward as she read the message aloud. I jumped up to see it for myself.

"Do you know who it is?" She pointed to the username that appeared in tiny red letters on the screen. I shook my head. Zan stared at the message again. "Why would someone do this?"

It didn't take us long to figure out who was behind it. After asking other friends if they recognized the screen name, everyone came back with the same response: It belonged to Carson Roche—the same boy who had threatened to stab a pencil through my eye in Ms. J's class.

For Zan, knowing who sent the message made the entire situation worse. It broke her heart to know that someone we had gone to school with for over a year, someone she'd interacted with and worked on class projects with, would say something— *think* something—so cruel. My sister's devastation made me even more enraged.

I began to rattle off insults for Zan to send back. "At least we have a reason for being weird-looking. What's your excuse?" But my sister was hardly listening. "Wait, word it like this," I told her. "Tell him it's not our fault that we have a medical condition requiring skull surgery and still manage to be cuter than him." Zan tried to smile. "Actually, just tell him he's an idiot and block him." Instead of using any of my suggestions, Zan crafted her own response.

"Thank you so much. That was so very kind of you to say. Now if you are finished and your insult has successfully made you feel better about yourself, I'm going to go." I watched my sister calmly type out each word before hitting send. She was a kinder person than I was.

That night as I lay in bed, I could not shake the idea that Zan and I had faces that looked like explosion sites. I already knew we had crooked eyes. With how we were treated, I did not need science or equations or Picasso paintings to tell me our features did not meet society's standard of beauty, but I measured them anyway. I put my hand to my forehead and used my fingers to determine the distance from my hairline to my eyelids and the top of my nose to the bottom, before moving down to the lower third of my face. The golden ratio said in order to be beautiful, the length of my face had to be divided into three equal parts, with equal distance between the features in each sector. My nose was larger than my forehead, but not as big as my chin. I was relieved that my second surgery—the one to expand my upper jaw and the center of my face—was scheduled for the following day. It meant being able to escape the torment of middle school for a while, and made me hopeful that maybe, just maybe, the second procedure would make my classmates like me again.

I looked over at Zan asleep next to me. Though Zan and I had our own rooms, we often stayed together. Her lips fluttered as air whistled in and out, and her hands were folded just beneath her chin like a prayer. I did not care about the calculations. To me, she was the most perfect person in the world.

It only took one week of seventh grade to realize everything Zan and I had been through that summer—everything we still had to get through—was nothing compared to the torture of having a face that would never meet the standards of beauty society forced upon us.

FIFTEEN

I was foolish to think my second surgery would go as smoothly as the first one did. Four days in the hospital after a major head surgery was not the norm, it was luck. Yet I told myself if I could get through head surgery that easily, a surgery to break and move my upper jaw would be no problem. They said this surgery would change my life. By rearranging my face, I would be happier, *healthier*. When I woke up from my midface surgery on August 29, 2003, part of me secretly prayed I hadn't woken up. I told myself I would have been perfectly content disappearing into the abyss of general nothingness. Too weak to sit up, I kicked my legs to get someone's attention. I needed help.

"You're okay," Mom whispered as she gently rubbed my arm. I nodded. The machines beeped loudly from every direction. I tried to speak, but the breathing tube in my throat acted as a thief in the darkness, stealing my voice. My words came out as grumbles and groans, so I moaned even louder in frustration.

"Don't try to talk right now, baby. The tube is still in."

I lifted my hand into the air and began using the sign

language alphabet—the only sign language I knew—to spell out what I was trying to say.

"I'm so sorry, baby. I don't know what you are saying."

Every time she said this, I'd drop my arm forcefully and moan loudly once more. Finally, I pushed my fingers together and waved my hand in the air, as if I were holding a writing utensil. She rushed to the nurses' station in the center of the ICU and fetched a pen and what I imagine was a yellow legal pad. But since I couldn't see the paper I was writing on, this too proved ineffective.

"You're not making any letters, Bella. It's just scribbles. I can't read it."

I finally gave up and pointed to my mouth, grunted as loud as I possibly could, and threw my thumb sideways as if to say *OUT*.

I WANT THIS THING OUT.

"I'll ask the nurse when she comes back about getting the breathing tube removed."

Mom and I repeated this scenario several times over the next few days. Still drugged and delirious from the medicine they gave me after surgery, I'd fall asleep and wake up, only to have forgotten about our entire conversation.

I thought they would finally remove the tube when a few days after surgery, I began to choke violently on my own vomit. I was always getting sick after surgery. Sometimes I'd swallowed too much blood. Other times my stomach couldn't take the harshness of the medications. My body would grow warm and

I could sense the burning panic that always started in the tips of my ears and trickled down the back of my neck. I would tell Mom I was going to be sick and she would call a nurse for an extra dose of Zofran to spare me the nausea and put me to sleep. But this time, I had no voice to tell Mom what was happening.

Nurses were doing rounds in the ICU when it started. Vomit spewed from the tube in my throat and out through the corners of my mouth. I could feel my airway getting clogged and I struggled to breathe. In a panic, I once again lifted my legs into the air and threw them onto the bed to get someone's attention. There was a button to alert a nurse somewhere around me, but I couldn't see it and I didn't have the time to search. Besides, flopping around like a fish out of water was bound to turn some heads.

I didn't realize Mom had been with me the whole time. As soon as she realized something was off, she went for help. When she returned, she held my hand while nurses unscrewed parts of the tube and suctioned it out.

The feeling of the suction was worse than the choking. Zan once compared it to having a dementor slowly suck the soul from your body, and I agreed. They only suctioned for a few seconds at a time, but it felt never-ending. Once my stomach settled and the nurses turned off their machines, I gestured to my mom again—a less-than-subtle reminder to ask about the removal of the tube.

I still couldn't sit up or move around, but I heard Mom ask

the nurses to just take the tube out altogether. They said not until I was able to breathe on my own. But how could I breathe on my own if there was a tube in my throat that wouldn't let me? I knew they were the experts, but I wanted—I *needed*—someone to be mad at. I chose them.

Later that evening, I woke again to doctors turning screws that had been implanted in my cheeks to shift the bones in my face.

Zan had warned me about this when she returned home after her surgery weeks before. One night when we lay together in her too-small bed, she'd told me how our surgeon had appeared at her bedside. "They told me they had to turn the screws." I remember examining her face as she spoke and looking to see the scars from where each screw had been. "They told me to take the pain until I couldn't possibly take it anymore." Every few seconds, she would pause her story and hold her breath, trying to regain composure. "I just . . . I remember the noise it made." I thought about the way my sister shuddered when she whispered the words, *It hurt so bad.* I knew it had changed her. Tears leaked down the sides of her face and into her ears as she relived the agony.

I recounted my sister's story in my mind and braced myself. This wasn't the first time Dr. Long had come to see me. It wasn't the first time he'd turned the screws in my face. He had done this before, but either mine had been easier to turn and I was able to sleep through it or the nurses learned from my sister's experience and preemptively offered me more medication to keep me comfortable. Either way, what luck, I thought to myself. What horror. I wished I had been so lucky again.

My cheeks stung as the metal pieces were turned, each motion slowly shifting the bones in my face forward. This was done every morning of my first few days in the hospital, until the bones were where they needed to be. My body grew tense, and I gripped the railings of my bed in pain. "Just one more," Dr. Long whispered as I screamed, the tube in my throat muffling my cries. "You're doing so well."

I gripped the blanket in my hands as the tears flooded my face, and I waited for the pain to end. It lasted a second but would haunt me for a lifetime. I wanted to die.

Zan visited me in the hospital the next day, just after the screws were removed, but I was on so much medication I didn't even know she was there. She came with Alexis and Dave, but none of them were prepared for the image of me relying on machines to keep me breathing. Even though Zan and I had the same surgeries, our bodies responded differently, and so recovery looked different for each of us. Dave comforted Alexis and Zan as they both cried. Zan had never seen me hooked up to so many cords and monitors. She feared I would not make it through recovery.

I think part of her worried she wouldn't, either. Mom once told me that the only thing worse than experiencing something horrific is having to watch someone you love suffer, unable to help them. She told me that my sister and I got dealt the worst kind of suffering, because we couldn't save ourselves and we couldn't save each other.

———

While I was in the hospital, Zan stayed at the apartment Alexis and Dave had moved into after their wedding. On days when she didn't feel like going to school, they took time off and tried to keep her occupied. I spent the next few days after Zan's visit propped up in my hospital bed. With my eyes still mostly swollen shut, I fought to stay awake for more than a few minutes at a time. On the morning of the third day, they finally removed the breathing tube.

"It might hurt a little bit," the nurse cooed. I recognized her voice. It was the same nurse who several nights before had told Mom she wouldn't remove the tube until I was able to breathe. She was the one I had decided to direct my anger toward. But once she got this thing out of me, all would be forgiven. "Are you ready?"

As soon as I nodded, I felt it ripped from my body. It was uncomfortable, like a knife scratching along my throat. It stung for several days, but I didn't care. At least it was over.

———

Being in the hospital didn't just take my voice, it took my agency. I did not get to decide or control what happened to me. There was no dignity in my experiences. Days after surgery, after the breathing tube had been removed and I was able to speak, I woke up to find my body was naked underneath my hospital gown. The underwear I had been wearing when I checked into the hospital was gone.

"Where is my underwear?" I cried to Mom. "Why did they take my underwear?" My words were slurred from the medication that the IV had been steadily pumping into me.

"They took them off for the catheter, baby."

"You mean I haven't had them on this whole time?" Mom touched my arm and promised to find me a new pair to slip on.

When you grow up in a hospital, you learn that bodily autonomy is a myth. My body was not my own. It did not belong to me. It belonged to the doctors and nurses who shaped every part of me. It belonged to the hospital personnel and to my parents, who signed their waivers, consenting to strangers touching, breaking, molding the very essence of who I was. This was what I hated most about surgery. It wasn't the idea of my body being cut open or the pain I experienced when I woke up. It wasn't even the terror I knew I'd experience during recovery. It was the oblivion. It was fading off into total nothingness. It was waking up and realizing I had no idea what had been done to me. I didn't know who saw me, who helped me, who touched me. I was helpless. I had no control over my own body.

——

Days in the hospital felt like years. With nothing but the fluorescent lighting in the ICU, there was no way to tell if it was day or night, no way to know how many days it had been or how many days you had left. It was so easy to become one with your suffering. It was lonely. The kind of loneliness where you can't even feel your own presence. And it was tiring. The kind of exhaustion that scratches at your eyelids and claws at your throat. It was the first time I remember dying. Zan and I each had so many near-death experiences during our many surgeries. But this was the first time I was old enough to remember what it was like.

I've searched my medical records to try to figure out what it was that happened in that moment, to find out what exactly went wrong inside my body, but the details of the surgeries blend together. All I know was that my body grew warm. I could feel it in my face and in my neck—like I was a furnace heating the world around me. I could feel my body shake as my breaths grew more shallow and infrequent. In the days after the breathing tube was removed, I had an upper airway edema, which was a blockage of my nose and mouth that made it hard to breathe.

"Come on, Bella, just take a few deep breaths." Mom was scared. I could hear it in her voice, but I was tired and wanted to sleep. The machines next to me began screaming, always screaming. A voice came over the speaker, and doctors and nurses rushed to my bed. And when I woke to Mom's tears, she stroked my hair, and I could hear the doctor on call say how lucky I was.

Earlier that day, the same scene had played out with another child a few beds over from mine. Machines beeped, announcements screeched over the intercom, and doctors ran to assist the child. But she was not lucky like me.

I could not see what was happening, but I prayed silently as the doctors and nurses yelled back and forth to each other, their voices simultaneously calm and panicked. Then, just like that, silence.

All I could hear was a man's voice giving orders. "We need to contact her mother."

"Is she okay, Momma?" I asked, as Mom held my hand. In my memory she died alone. [3]

———

A few days after I was stabilized, Mom told me she was going home for a shower and clean clothes but that Marissa would stay with me while she was gone. Mom had not left the

---

3   Mom says she remembers this happening with children a lot in the ICU. There were frequent emergencies with children in beds near ours and doctors and nurses rushing around trying to save them. She remembers the child in the bed next to mine having complications, and while children did die in the ICU, she does not remember if that child died that day or if it was just a close call. My memory of what happened feels so clear, but I was on so many medications I'm not sure which is true. When I spoke with Mom about it, she said, "I was too focused on you and Zan to be worrying about what was happening around us." I was just grateful I had a mom who could afford to stay by my bedside. It was not a reality for many families. I was lucky I never spent a night in the hospital without my mom or another family member. Even when there were complications, she was right there holding my hand through all of it.

hospital or my bedside in days. Still unable to see, I squeezed her hand and told her I loved her. Marissa was the only person besides Mom I would accept staying with me. Perhaps it was because she was so much like my mother. Someone who loved me so much, she was unafraid of being my voice when I did not have one. As long as Marissa or Mom were with me, I knew I would be okay.

I was still in the ICU because my oxygen levels were dropping. Every time I fell asleep, machines would beep loudly and rapidly, as if to signal panic. "A few deep breaths for me, baby," Mom would say, and I'd do it just for her. The breaths took everything out of me, leaving me dizzy and weak. When Marissa took over, she mimicked Mom.

"Just a few deep breaths for me, Bella." And like clockwork, I inhaled deeply.

After a few moments, I could hear the nurses talking in hushed tones behind me. It wasn't until I heard Marissa that I realized they were talking about me.

"This is something she *has* to do?" Marissa's voice was hesitant, and I felt her hand tighten around mine.

"Yes," one of the women responded.

Before I could ask, one of the nurses slid her hand beneath the small of my back and arched it upward as another placed what I quickly learned was a vest underneath me. Her hands were cold against my skin. The nurse lowered my body back to the bed. She unhooked my IV from the port in the wall and slid my right arm through the right side of the vest, and my left arm through the left side. She strapped it closed across my chest and hooked it up to a machine in the wall.

They were strapping a device—a high-frequency chest wall oscillator—to me because there was buildup in my lungs, making it hard to breathe. It was supposed to aggressively vibrate my chest to help loosen mucus, like patients with cystic fibrosis had to do. As soon as the shaking started, I released an agonizing groan that felt both instinctual and animalistic.

"No more," I screamed. "Please, no more." My sobs were so heavy, I choked on my words.

"Stop it!" Marissa screamed. "Stop it!" She was crying now, too.

"I'm done," I told her. "I can't do it. I can't do any more."

"It's okay, it's okay," she kept saying. But it wasn't okay. My whole body hurt.

The nurses didn't unstrap the vest from my chest. Instead, they stood next to the bed, waiting until I was ready to go another round.

"You're not doing that to her again." Marissa's rage increased as she spoke.

One of the nurses explained the importance of the vest again. If I didn't do it, they said, I'd likely get pneumonia or worse. I knew my sister's silence meant she was caving, and as much as I wanted to be angry at her for it, I wasn't. Marissa spoke to the nurses again. I couldn't make out what she said, but the nurses walked away.

"Bella," Marissa said quietly, "we have to do it again." I could hear the shame in her voice—a tone that said, *I'm sorry and I love you. Please forgive me.*

"No," I cried.

"I'm going to do it this time, though, okay?" she said. "And the minute you tell me to stop, we will." I trusted her.

We did it in increments. The vest shook me violently for seconds at a time—my insides felt like the flesh of an orange being pulsed through a blender. It was painful, but tolerable in short bursts. The nurses supervised my sister as she pressed the button turning the vest on and off, on and off, the sound of my cough and the machine's buzz filling the room.

As I lay flat against the bed, my body violently shaking from the vest, I coughed and gagged until my face turned what I imagined was a red so dark, it was almost purple. Thick chunks of mucus gathered in my throat, and I could not breathe. I panicked, crying and coughing harder and harder. One nurse held an emesis basin—one of those plastic, kidney-shaped, puke-colored bowls that hospitals always gave out—next to my head for me to spit or throw up into. Beside her was another nurse, who held a damp cloth and periodically wiped the thick slime from my face and neck and out of my mouth.

"You need to hold it longer," one of the nurses told Marissa as I worked to expel the mucus from my body. "She needs to get everything out of her lungs."

Marissa held the button longer. She started off slow, adding seconds each time. The longer she held it, the louder I cried. When the vibrations stopped, Marissa placed my hand on the button just below hers.

"We'll do it together," she told me. I almost begged her not to make me. I was running out of energy, but I knew it needed to be done.

"Ready?" It was more of a statement than a question. When I stopped being able to press the button with Marissa, she said I'd had enough. When it was over, she gently squeezed my arm and buried her head into the blankets next to me as she cried.

"I'm so sorry, Belle," she sobbed. "I'm so sorry."

I wasn't mad. I knew she didn't want to do it. In some ways, I think it hurt her more than it hurt me. I loved her even more for that.

—————

Though recovering from surgeries was hard, my family learned to make the most of it. We had to find humorous moments to get us all through it.

That night with Marissa in the ICU, a nurse forgot to place the bedpan inside the portable toilet seat next to my bed. As I sat on the commode, my urine flooded the floor. Since I was too weak to hold myself up, Marissa held my hospital gown in one hand and supported my body with the other.

"I'm so sorry. I can't stop." It had only been two days since I'd had a catheter, and I was mortified by my inability to control my bladder. Marissa could sense my distress.

"It's okay, Bella," she told me. "It can all be cleaned up. Just let it out."

Within seconds, the light-colored tile floor of the hospital room had turned yellow. Marissa's feet, only partially covered by her sandals, were soaking wet. Still supporting the weight of my body, Marissa called out for a nurse. The longer we waited, the more my urine soaked into the edges of her pants. When a nurse rounded the corner of the ICU to find the mess I'd created, Marissa and I laughed so hard, we cried again.

"Don't pee," Marissa teased, still holding me.

For the first time in days, my body hurt from laughter instead of surgery.

SIXTEEN

After Mom returned to the hospital the next morning, the lead doctor in the ICU agreed to sign off on my discharge as long as I could successfully breathe, eat, drink, and go to the bathroom independently.

When Mom told me this, I was too distracted to care. "Why is there a purple spider on the ceiling?" I asked. The skin near my eyes was still swollen and tight, but loose enough so that my eyelids were able to open.

Before Mom could answer, several more appeared. They were bright shades of blue and green, and like nothing I'd seen before. Mom and Marissa made eye contact before simultaneously looking up. There was nothing there.

"Shit," Mom muttered to herself, recognizing my behavior.

"So, uh, did he say anything about hallucinations?" Marissa laughed.

"What do you mean?"

"It's just the medicine, baby. I promise you if there's something there, we will tell you." Mom scooted a chair closer to my bed.

"But um, Belle." Marissa leaned in closer. "Don't mention this to the doctor just yet?"

"Why not?"

"Because they'll want you to stay longer to run the same tests they've already run," Mom explained. "We just have to wait it out."

I nodded. I was ready to leave. I didn't want to stay any longer than I had to. "Oh God, they're moving." There were now spiders running across my legs. I squeezed my eyes closed to try to get the image out of my mind.

"You're okay," Mom said. "Just try to focus on us."

"Easy for you to say. They're not crawling on *you*." My heart was racing. Being in the hospital, I understood what it meant to have no sense of agency, but the hallucinations made me feel like I'd lost my mind as well.

I'd had hallucinations before, violent ones. After the first midface surgery, when Zan and I were four years old, I'd lie in my hospital bed and nervously pick at my fingertips, removing pieces of my fingernails until they were so short, they bled. I was prescribed Ativan for my anxiety spells. The medication calmed my spirit. At first, the doctors thought the medication they'd prescribed for my anxiety was the hallucinogen, because after every dose I took, I was haunted by visions of everything I feared.

The first time, I saw snakes. They were everywhere, inches from my face, slithering up the legs of my pajamas and wrapping themselves around my waist, then my arms, then my neck. Their grip quickly becoming stronger . . . *tighter and tighter.* Mom brought me back to the hospital, where I was admitted and kept in a safety bed in the ICU—a bed with tall railings all around it like a cage.

I was petrified, unable to breathe. I brought my knees to my chest and kicked my legs back and forth, up and down, trying to get them away.

"Get them off me! Please get them off me," I begged, but Mom saw nothing.

"There's nothing there, baby," she told me repeatedly as she stroked my hair and called for the nurses, but I didn't believe her. They *were* there. They were everywhere. How could she not see them? After that, Mom slept in the caged bed with me, holding me as I tried to wrestle fact from fiction.

The next vision was dinosaurs. As Mom slept peacefully next to me, I saw a large *Tyrannosaurus rex* stomp through the hospital floor and enter my room. It had scaly skin and teeth as sharp as razor blades. Blood dripped from its mouth, and it had claws like knives. I swore I saw people in the halls running, arms flailing, voices shrieking, fearing for their lives. I called for my mom to wake up, to run, to get away while she could, but she didn't hear me. I watched as the dinosaur ripped Mom's head from her neck, blood spraying the walls around me. My sobs turned to screams. At almost five years old, I knew dinosaurs were not real, but my young mind could not refute what I had just witnessed with my own eyes. It was only when I shut my eyes tight and opened them to see her next to me, one hand on my cheek, that I could begin to believe it was not real. The hallucinations continued off and on for the next several weeks, even after I returned home. The doctors didn't understand that it wasn't the medication causing my hallucinations. It was a psychosis caused by the stress and trauma of the surgeries I'd had and the surgeries that were coming.

At home, I'd see mice in the wood grain on the doorframes. I'd see snakes on the floor of the car as I sat strapped into my car seat in the back and spiders covering the walls around me. At night, I'd see the dinosaurs again—always coming for the people I loved. Even when my visions tried to take me away from reality, Mom was always there to hold me and remind me that no matter where my mind went, no matter how hard the darkness tried to swallow me, I would never be alone.

Marissa could see the fear on my face as I closed my eyes to escape the visions that were now haunting me again. "Belle, tell me where they are and I'll get them for you. Just point and I'll kill them," she said.

"On the wall," I said. "By the light switch."

"Right here?" Marissa pointed.

"Lower. To the right."

"Here?"

I nodded.

Marissa made a fist and smacked the wall. The body of the spider was flattened into the wood, before disappearing altogether. She and Mom did this every time I saw one near me.

"I'm glad nobody else is here to see how ridiculous we look," I told them.

"What?" Marissa said casually. "We're just killin' some spiders!"

When a nurse stopped by my room later that morning, she said I had to pass the food test before the hospital would send me home. I hadn't had much of an appetite during my stay, but I'd forced myself to eat small amounts of whatever meals the nurses brought me each day. But the final test felt impossible. In order to leave, I had to consume a large bowl of blueberry yogurt—the kind with chunks of fruit at the bottom. Repulsed by blueberries, I mentally accepted defeat.

"Just eat as much of this as you can and I'll tell the doctor you're ready to go home." The nurse pushed the tray of food closer to me. When she left the room, Mom and Marissa both laughed at my disgust.

"Come on, Belle." Marissa was smiling as she spoke. "Just take, like, three big bites and swallow it superfast. You won't even taste it." She scooped the clumpy purple mixture onto the spoon as if to demonstrate.

"Absolutely not."

Mom was laughing as she packed my belongings into a large plastic bag.

"Belle, you have to do it. The nurse is going to come back, and then you won't be able to leave."

"She's right," Mom added. "You don't want to stay here another night."

"I would rather stay here than eat *that*," I said, only half joking. I'd had an aversion to blueberries for as long as I could remember, and with the added nausea from the medication they'd pumped into my system, I couldn't make myself do it.

As the three of us bantered back and forth, we could hear my nurse's booming voice from down the hall.

"Belle, hurry and eat the yogurt," Marissa said, once again sliding the bowl closer to me. "She's coming."

As the woman's voice grew louder, Mom grabbed the spoon and in two bites, shoved an entire bowl's worth of yogurt into her mouth and swallowed.

"Water," she pleaded, gagging. Mom dramatically squinted her eyes and held out her tongue.

"Okay, drama queen," Marissa teased as she handed Mom one of the many half-empty bottles of water from the bedside table.

"Seriously," I added. Mom immediately stopped chugging the water and cocked her head to look at me.

"You have no room to talk, Miss I Refuse to Eat Anything Blue," Marissa added lovingly.

Before I could quip back, the nurse came in. "Hooray! You finished it all!" She proudly removed the bowl and spoon from the table. Behind her, Mom pretended to lick her hand, as though she was still trying to get rid of the taste.

The hallucinations didn't stop, but I got better at ignoring them. I watched the purple spider on the ceiling as the nurse removed my other IV and helped me out of my hospital gown and into my clothes. *It's all in your head*, I told myself when the spider was joined by another bright green one. Then a pink one. *It's all in your head.*

According to my medical records, I was discharged from the hospital on September 2, 2003, just four days after the operation to move my jaw, but again, that is not what I remember. In my memory, I was there for two, maybe three weeks. It was this way in Mom's and Marissa's memories, too. Perhaps I was discharged from the ICU on September 2, or perhaps in the stress of recovery, we were all losing our minds.

Zan was waiting for me on the steps of the garage when I first arrived home with Mom and Marissa. As soon as we parked and turned off the car, Zan opened the passenger door. I was weak and tired but happy to see her.

"Hi, sis," she said, as she took my hand in hers. She stood like that for a few minutes, while Mom went inside to get Dad to carry me in from the car so I did not fall.

Zan grabbed my hospital bag from the back seat, as Dad gently hoisted me up into his arms and carried me into the house. Inside, Mom started drawing me a bath.

We thought the hallucinations would stop by the time the

medicine was out of my system. But after getting into the bath, I yelled for Mom, who had disappeared down the hall to fetch a towel.

"You got me kittens!" I squealed, as I flung myself out of the tub and crawled across the floor to pet the two orange tabbies I saw curled up in the corner. When Mom returned, she found me lying on the floor, lovingly petting the carpet.

It's all in your head.

PART II

After

SEVENTEEN

My first day back to seventh grade was the start of a section on abstract art. Ms. J showed us images of paintings by Jackson Pollock and colorful, shapely creations by Wassily Kandinsky. It was in Kandinsky's *Composition* series that I once again saw Picasso. This was how each class went: Ms. J would introduce the unit by explaining the type of art and show us examples. Then we would have a week to think about and create a rough draft of our assignment. We were required to sketch out our ideas to show we'd thought critically about each project. We'd spend the second week working on the final draft. Ms. J would put out a large stack of the high-quality, professional art paper for us to use, along with any supplies we might need.

Ms. J made art feel like a safe place for nonartists and artists alike. Because it wasn't about being better than anyone else in the room. It was about learning and growing and being better than we were yesterday. It was about learning how to use our creativity to convey our emotions.

"Feel free to use any of the resources in the back to get

inspired," she announced. "Raise your hand if you have any questions. I'll be wandering around the room."

I was stuck and unsure what to draw, so I walked to the back of the classroom, where Ms. J had a small shelf of art-related books. I thumbed through the titles before selecting one with drawings and paintings by Picasso.

I flipped through the book, vivid colors and bold shapes on each page. I stopped when I reached a painting called *Girl Before a Mirror*. On one side of the painting was a woman made of geometrical shapes. Her distorted reflection took up the other half. I stared at the painting and thought of the many hours I'd spent in front of my own mirror. The blurb next to the image commented on how others had a face they showed to the world and a face—a side of them—they kept for themselves. Reading this made me angry. Not because of the woman in the painting or even Picasso. My anger went deeper than that. Because my face was how others defined me, and I could never hide it. The woman in the painting was physically beautiful but in a self-critical moment, saw her reflection as ugly. But I was *actually* ugly on the outside. When others looked at me, this was all they saw, all they would ever see.

I studied the image for a moment before turning the page to find an etching of a Minotaur. My gaze was locked on the drawing when Ms. J appeared next to me. I could see her from the corner of my eye as she lowered her elbows to the top of the bookshelf and leaned forward.

"Some say the Minotaurs in Picasso's work are supposed to

be him." I could feel Ms. J watching me examine the creature in the image. "A sort of abstract self-portrait."

I knew what a Minotaur was. It was a mythological monster who had the body of a man and the head of a bull. It was said to be a vicious beast who devoured humans and was forced to live hidden away in a labyrinth.

I flipped through the pages to find more of Picasso's Minotaurs. Once I knew to look for them, I saw them everywhere. They appeared on page after page, some blended into the background, others the central focus of the piece.

"Why did he paint himself as a Minotaur?" I asked Ms. J. "Was he a monster?" I regretted the question almost immediately. Because him being a monster would have made the comparison even worse.

"There are theories." Ms. J tidied a stack of books next to her as she spoke. "He wasn't known for being the . . . nicest to the women in his life." I could tell from her tone and the way she chose her words carefully that there was more to the story. "It depends on the specific piece. Sometimes the Minotaur is violent. Other times he's victimized. Some say the Minotaur represents the two sides of his personality." Ms. J could tell from my expression that I was confused. "Picasso was abusive toward women, but one can be a monster and a victim. Perhaps monstrosity stems from suffering." She shrugged. "Hey, maybe it's something for you to explore." In retrospect, I never got the feeling she was talking about Picasso. I always believed Ms. J saw my own anger. She had a no-nonsense attitude, but she believed it was important to understand why people were the way they were. Because people's behaviors could be explained without being excused.

As I turned her comments over in my mind, Ms. J walked to a table across the room, where a student sat with his hand waving impatiently in the air. I was so focused on what she'd said, I hardly even noticed she'd left.

That afternoon, I returned to core class to discover my teacher had divided students into groups for a unit on medieval times while I was gone. When I entered the classroom, students' desks were pushed together to make six clusters of five. Each of the six tables represented a fictional medieval house, all from different socioeconomic classes. There were lords and peasants, and the students in each unit would spend months completing assignments together. Since I had been absent and had never been assigned a group, my return to class was awkward. Everyone knew where to sit and what was expected of them. I did not.

"Which group am I in?" I asked Mr. Lawson quietly. He stood at the front of the room going through his notes for the day while students finished shuffling in. I could tell by the look on his face that he hadn't remembered if he'd assigned me one.

"What group is Ariel in?" he asked my classmates as the final bell rang. The room fell quiet and everyone turned their eyes to where I stood, nervously shifting my weight back and forth between each leg.

"Where did she come from?" one of the students yelled. "Since when is she in this class?" A couple of students snickered, but Mr. Lawson shut it down.

"That's enough. Worry about yourself." Mr. Lawson scanned the room once more. "Ah, a table of four." He snapped his fingers and pointed to the right side of the classroom. "Go ahead and join Jacob, Christian, Shelby, and Anna."

Jacob groaned. "Way to assign us the girl nobody wants."

Mr. Lawson shot him a disapproving look. "You. See me after class."

I had been going to school with Jacob for as long as I could remember. We were never really friends, but until that moment, there had never been any indication that he didn't like me. It had been talked about all over town that Jacob's dad committed suicide years earlier. I knew he was hurting, so my initial reaction to his words was shame, but not anger.

I walked over to my new group and placed my backpack on the empty desk between Jacob and Christian.

"Hi." I tried to smile, but the skin on my face was still swollen and hard to move. Everyone responded except for Jacob, who, the second I sat down, stood up to retrieve the bottle of hand sanitizer from Mr. Lawson's desk. When I made eye contact with him as he made his way back to his seat, he pretended to gag.

"Sorry," Jacob said, looking only at Christian, Shelby, and

Anna. "I have to make sure I don't catch anything." He gave a slight nod of his head in my direction to show he was referring to me, but I pretended not to see it. The other group members didn't join in his ridicule, but they did not defend me, either.

After school, Mom heard me telling Zan about Jacob and core class, and she called the school. I didn't know of this until the next day at lunch.

As I sat eating my sandwich, our vice principal, Ms. Dodson, approached Zan and me. She swiped a strand of blond hair from her face and removed the walkie-talkie from her hip before squatting down among our group of friends. "Are people being mean to you?" Everyone around us was staring.

Embarrassed and ashamed, I lied and told her no.

"Are people being mean to them?" This time Ms. Dodson asked our friends, pointing to Zan and me. "Because I want you all to tell me if you see that happening. I'll put a stop to it."

I wanted to be defended, but not like that. I only felt more like a loser.

When Mom picked us up from school that afternoon, I questioned her about it.

"Hi, Bella!" she said excitedly as I opened the car's passenger door and climbed in. Mom was always so happy to see me—as if the mere sight of me made something inside her spark—but I was too upset to feel it or reciprocate.

"Did you tell the school people were mean to me?" I didn't

even give her a chance to respond. "Now everyone knows I'm a freak!" Mom's expression turned to sadness as tears welled in her eyes. "Just stay out of my life!"

We spent the rest of the drive home in silence.

"I wish people would just decide," I told Mom once. "I wish the world would just come to an agreement on whether Zan and I are acceptable or not, and let it be." The back-and-forth and intense extremes in opinions surrounding our faces was confusing. Because as soon as we felt okay, as soon as one person made us feel like we were worthy of kindness and compassion, five more told us we were nothing.

Instead of dealing with the experiences I wanted so desperately to escape from, I turned to anger. Zan was the object of much of my misdirected emotion. For as much as I loved her, part of me resented her. Because when Zan and I were together, we were treated even more terribly. As if the fact that there were two of us with our condition—our faces—meant we were truly defective. We never talked about it, but I knew in some ways she resented me, too.

So when we returned to school for seventh grade, we alternated between wanting to spend every moment together and keeping our distance. This was hard to do when we were in the same science class. Zan and I were always paired together. But sometimes during experiments, our classmates would tease us, sending rubber bands flying at our heads.

"I hate you," I would tell her. When we sat next to each

other, I would kick her under the table as hard as I could. When she'd rise from her seat in an effort to hide the tears in her eyes, I would stomp on her toes. "I said sit down."

"I don't know what you want me to do," she would say. Her eyes would turn glassy and her bottom lip would quiver, and I'd hate myself more after each outburst.

I want you to make it stop, I wanted to tell her. "I'm so sorry," I would cry instead. I wanted her, someone—anyone—to make everything stop hurting.

"It's okay, sis," Zan would tell me.

But it wasn't.

I read once that abusers are often people who were abused themselves. I abused the people I loved most in the world because the world had abused me. But this realization didn't undo the terrible things I had done.

———

After my run-in with Ms. Dodson, I was determined to spend core class avoiding Jacob as much as I could. The other people at my table seemed nice, I thought. Maybe I could just talk to them instead. I decided this was a good plan when I arrived the next day to find my group talking about animals—something I could contribute to.

"I got a new dog yesterday," Christian told us. Christian was a tall, lanky kid with a mop of blond, curly hair.

Shelby squealed, and in her best trying-to-be-cute whine, asked for a picture.

"He's a Lab." Christian pulled a cell phone from his pocket and flipped it open to reveal an image so pixelated, it was hard to make out what the object on the screen even was.

"Looks like that dog from the World's Ugliest Dog contest," Jacob joked.

Christian played along. "Did you see the dog that won?"

"Aww, yes," Anna said.

"It was so ugly it was almost cute." Shelby gave a slight frown and laughed.

"Aww, that's so sad," I added. "What kind of dog was it? What did it look like?" I knew immediately I should have kept my mouth shut. I never learned to stop giving those around me material to use against me.

"I mean, it was the world's ugliest dog." Jacob looked at me like I had asked the dumbest question imaginable.

"So—"

"So, it looked like you in dog form."

Shelby gasped and Anna let out a single cackle.

Jacob smiled across the table at Christian, whose face had turned an alarming shade of red.

Before the first half of our core class ended, Mr. Lawson got a call from the office saying someone was there to pick me up for an appointment. As I gathered my belongings, he handed me a copy of the lecture notes for history and since the second half of our class was dedicated to English, instructions for our first writing assignment: a short story on the topic of our choosing. Finally, an assignment I could have fun with. But the story would have to wait.

I could see Mom's car from the hallway as soon as I left the classroom. She was parked in front of the office, flipping through the pages of a magazine while she waited for me. She smiled when I got into the car, but I was still upset about Jacob and ready to fight.

"Do I have a doctor's appointment?" I asked aggressively, as I threw my backpack down on the floor of the passenger seat. I slammed the door behind me for added effect.

"No." Her voice was quiet.

"Then why are you here?"

Without responding, Mom started the car and left the school's parking lot. A moment later, she pulled over onto one of the side streets and removed the key from the ignition.

"I don't know what to do," she said, still staring at the steering wheel. "Tell me what to do. How do I make this better?" As soon as she turned to look at me, I could tell she had been crying.

"What do you mean?" I asked, even though I already knew.

"Your anger, Ariel." Mom released an exasperated sigh. "You are so hateful all the time."

"I'm sorry." It physically pained me to know I made Mom cry, but I was selfish and lost in my own suffering.

"I don't know how to help you. What do you need from me, Ariel? What can I do?"

"I don't know." And that was perhaps the most maddening truth of all. I knew Mom was right about my anger being a problem, but I didn't know how to switch it off. Bringing others into my pain with me was the only thing I could do to keep from losing my mind. It wasn't right or okay. It was weak. *I* was weak.

"I love you." Mom and I were both in tears as we leaned over the center console to hug each other through our seat belts.

"I'm so sorry," I cried into her shoulder. "I want to be better. I don't know how to stop hurting." I wiped the tears from my cheeks and sat back in my seat.

"Belle." Mom turned her head to look at me for a moment. "You would tell me if someone hurt you, right?"

I didn't understand her question at first, and so I shrugged. "Yeah, sure."

"Has anyone ever touched you . . . *inappropriately?*" Mom paused, and I could tell from her silence that she was carefully considering what to say next. "Sometimes after people hurt others, they make threats to try to keep them from telling anyone. But Bella, even if someone told you that nobody would believe you or if they threatened to kill me or Daddy, you tell us, okay?" I nodded.

Mom's knuckles were white as she gripped the steering wheel. She thought I had been *violated* because both anger and bed-wetting are signs of sexual abuse, and I peed myself most nights until I was well into being a teenager. Though we did not know it at the time, these were also signs of PTSD.

"Momma, did something happen?"

"No, I just want both you and Zan to know that you can come to me. Always." The car stayed in park but her focus on the road in front of us remained trancelike. I could tell she was deep in thought—lost in a memory or a nightmare, I could not tell which. "I will never doubt you."

These conversations happened periodically for the next several years and always ended the same way: with me nodding and making a promise that no matter what happened, I would always go to her for help. But my response to trauma meant my cries for help were not easy to decipher. I didn't know how to explain to her that I was always being hurt. That every time they cut me open, they took parts of me I could never get back.

The next morning, I arrived at room 101 excited to continue mapping out the art project Ms. J had assigned. With scratch paper in front of me and a pencil in hand, I began to think about the abstract work Picasso had created. How I could use lines and shapes and colors on the page to represent my rage and my sadness.

If Picasso saw himself as a Minotaur, what would I be? I sat with this question for several minutes. I thought of the look on Zan's face when I told her I wanted her to die and of watching

Mom cry into the steering wheel of her car, begging me to tell her why I hated her, to come up with an answer that could explain the insults I hurled at the people who loved me the most—the people *I* loved the most. In that moment it hit me: Maybe in comparing me to Picasso, the *Marie Claire* journalist was not as wrong as I had hoped. Maybe I was Picasso, the abusive artist, instead of his world-famous art.

EIGHTEEN

Cheerleading was a minefield of toxic beauty standards, but it made me an expert in refusing to hide my face. That's not to say I didn't want to. At games, Zan and I stood on the sidelines with the rest of our squad, facing stands filled with people, most of whom we did not know. During our cheers, I'd watch as people in the audience—usually children and young boys—openly mocked the shapes of our eyes. A quarter of the way through the game, it was customary for our cheerleading squad to line up and march and chant our way to the other side of the track. When we got there, we would introduce ourselves to the cheerleaders rooting for the other team. We would give them favors—little goodie bags with treats and bubbles, and they'd sit on the ground beneath the bleachers as we performed a friendly "hello" cheer. After we finished and returned to our side, they'd march over and do the same for us. It was a game-day ritual for every team in the league. The girls on the other squad would often not notice our facial differences right away. But slowly, one by one, they'd see us. It would've been easier to look away. To hang my head so low, they couldn't catch a glimpse. Nobody on our team ever stood up for us. People never put a stop to the children's comments. In their silence, they agreed.

I started cheerleading again the weekend before I returned to school in October 2003. Zan had missed the first month of cheer practice that year, and the first few games in early September. By the time we were both back to regularly attending practices and cheering at games, it felt like years had passed.

My first game back was held at the same high school where we practiced. Though it was the same team, routines, and location I was already familiar with, I felt more out of place than ever before. My face was still awkwardly shaped from the swelling and my body was round and curvy in a way that set me apart from the girls on my squad. Some of it was from the steroids I'd been given to prevent infection, but mostly it was because I still could not stop eating. Everything about me felt wrong in some way. Before the surgery, I was told I didn't look like a cheerleader. Now, for the first time, I felt it.

I was made more self-conscious by people's constant obsession with Zan's skeletal figure. Our teammates, coaches, and even other parents came up to her and congratulated her on her weight loss. "You are so thin now!" the mom of one of the football players told Zan. "You look fantastic! Congratulations!" Zan never knew how to respond, so she just smiled and said thank you.

Our cheerleading uniforms consisted of skirts that sat mid-thigh and shell tops that covered most of our collarbones down to our midriffs. *Panthers* was embroidered in cursive white letters across the front. Gold and black stripes lined the bottoms of both the shell and the skirt. Everything else was a deep shade of maroon, like the flesh of dark cherries before you bite into them. Even our spankies—the thick, high-waisted underpants we had to wear under our skirts—were the same deep reddish-purple hue. On days when it was cold out, we wore spandex liners beneath our shells. The long-sleeved garments were cropped at our rib cage and did little to keep us warm, but they were better than nothing.

It had been decided earlier on the morning of my first post-surgery game that we would all wear our maroon crop tops, but when we reached the bleachers where the rest of our team was gathered, we were told to switch our maroon liners for our white ones. Bathrooms on campus were not open on week-ends, so we all moved from sitting on the bleachers to standing beneath them as we strategically replaced one uniform garment with another. Justine had a large towel in her cheer bag, so we alternated holding it up in front of each other so that we could each have a bit of privacy to change. When it was Zan's turn, she lifted her arms and I helped her gently pull the spandex over her head. I was focused on helping her do this without hurting the skin on her face. I didn't even notice the other girls ogling her body. They saw her rib cage and each knob of her spine, and she instantly became the source of their envy. When Zan noticed the others noticing her, she no longer worried about being careful of her head or her face. She quickly threw on her other crop top and the shell that went over it.

———

Justine was constantly torn between her friendship with us and her desire to fit in with the rest of our team. At practice, the other girls on our squad tried to get Justine to join their clique. "Justine, come sit with us," they would say.

"Come on, guys," she would tell us, as she waved for us to follow. But the girls would make only enough space for one person to join their circle. Though it hurt to be left out, we never held it against Justine when she took the opportunity to be included.

My family did their best to offset our rejection. Mom signed up to be one of our coaches that year, and Aaron and Dad always came to our games. I particularly liked when Aaron came, because he was still in high school and the girls on the squad had crushes on him. Even our teenage coaches begged me to give them my brother's number, but I never did. I liked feeling as if I had something they wanted. Like I was in control. Before Aaron started attending our games, most of my teammates just pretended Zan and I weren't there. Aaron never noticed the girls fawning over him. That made them love him even more. Me too. Because now, thanks to my brother, the other girls on the squad had a reason to talk to me.

———

Panthers made a big deal of homecoming every year. All the local teams did. We even had a homecoming court, where each cheer squad voted for a princess and each football team voted for a prince. The winners were crowned and celebrated after the game at an evening dance. I had been looking forward to missing it, because with my face the way it was, the last thing I wanted was to be stuck in a large room with other teenagers. But Justine and the team were excited about the festivities, so I tried to keep my negativity to myself.

"Do you think Ian will be there?" Justine asked after practice that Friday. "Maybe I'll get a dance."

That night, we slept over at her house, and as Justine climbed into her bed and Zan and I into our sleeping bags, we rattled off our guesses as to who would be crowned homecoming royalty.

"I voted for you," we all told each other.

"How cool would it be if I could be princess and Ian could be prince?" Justine squealed.

"That would be so cute," I told her, and Zan agreed. And I meant it, I did. But as much as I wanted the boy Justine liked to like her back, I wanted things like that for Zan and me, too.

That night, before I closed my eyes and drifted off to sleep, I said a silent prayer asking for Zan and me to have a chance at winning princess. *God*, I said to myself, *even if neither Zan nor I win, I pray the day comes when we can be seen as beautiful, too. Please help others not to see us as ugly anymore. In your name I pray. Amen.*

At the homecoming game the next afternoon, the stands were decorated with our team colors. Maroon and white streamers flapped in the wind, and a balloon arch decorated the track near the end zone.

The first part of the game was the same as every other game, but by the end of the second quarter, the excitement was palpable. After our halftime routine, we were told to join the football players beneath the balloons on the other side of the field.

"Wait, do we get to be *escorted*?" my teammate Amber asked salaciously. Amber was the most boy-obsessed girl on the squad. It helped that she and a handful of the others went to school with most of the guys on the football team. Some of them were even dating.

"I'm not sure what the plan is," Courtney's mom said. "Just finish your water and head over there."

The girls tried to play it cool as they sprinted off toward the field. Zan and I locked eyes and, without a word, could sense each other's discomfort.

"I do *not* want to do this," Zan groaned.

"You think if we walk slow enough they'll just forget to call our names?" I asked.

Zan laughed nervously. "I wish."

"Ughh. Let's just get this over with."

Zan nodded and together we ran to meet up with the others.

Some of the girls had already started being paired up with

football players by the time we reached the field. It was supposed to be a special moment. Moms of the boys on the football team even purchased a single red rose for each football player to give to the cheerleader they'd been assigned.

"You're going to be right here, girls," a woman told Zan and me. "Which one of you is Alixandria?"

Zan raised her hand just slightly.

"Okay, perfect. Then you will walk out first."

"Great." Zan was polite even when trying to be sarcastic.

The woman called over two boys. They kept their helmets on, so I never even saw what they looked like. It quickly became clear that my partner was unhappy about being my escort. I could tell by the way he went back and forth between looking at me and arguing with his coach. I smiled at my sister and looked around awkwardly.

"Stop it," his coach said sternly. "Partners have been assigned. All you have to do is walk together."

The boy finally joined me in line as the MC finished thanking our team's sponsors and prepared to begin introductions. As soon as the football players heard their names, they were supposed to hand their partner a rose and link arms, before escorting each cheerleader across the field.

When it was my turn, my partner handed me a rose, but when we went to link arms, he would not touch me. Instead, his arm hovered inches away from mine, as though I was contagious. When we reached the end of the field, we separated.

Football players lined up behind the cheerleaders, and I listened as the other players teased my partner.

"You got through it, man," one of them said. Another just slapped his jersey and laughed.

I wanted to disappear. It was easier to ignore the constant humiliation than confront it.

After the game, Zan and I went back to Justine's house to get ready for the big dance that evening. Zan wore a soft blue strapless dress with a thin, pink zip-up sweatshirt over it. Then she tied a bandana in her hair to cover her scar. I wore a black velvet dress with red roses that went down to my ankles. After our dresses were on and our hair was done, Justine, Zan, and I piled into Justine's mom's Suburban and she drove us back to the school where we continued the celebration.

———

The homecoming court announcements went quickly. There were four princesses and four princes. Winners were announced by division, starting with the youngest. After names were called, winners went to the podium to collect a bouquet of flowers and a plastic crown.

When the announcer got to our squad, some of the girls held hands. Courtney had convinced herself and everyone around her that she'd won, and she was anxiously waiting for the crown to be hers.

"And this year's princess is . . . Alixandria Henley!"

Zan's cheeks flushed pink as she looked around the room.

I clapped loud and hard and smiled wider than I'd smiled in a long time.

"Go up there!" Justine told her excitedly. "Go get your crown!"

Zan became shy whenever she was the center of attention, so she lowered her head to the floor as she made her way to the stage. The DJ placed a crown on her head and a sash over her dress, and Zan looked proud. It had been a hard few months, and Zan winning homecoming princess felt like that bit of hope I had prayed for.

I was busy watching my sister accept the award when Justine gently tapped my arm. "They're mad." She pointed to the corner of the room where Courtney stood with Amber and a couple of the other girls. They all had serious expressions on their faces.

After accepting her crown, Zan was led to a makeshift photo station on the side of the gymnasium. There was a white trellis background with fake flowers woven through the wooden openings.

Courtney watched with her arms folded across her chest, as the photographer snapped portraits of the winners. "I guess it helps when your mom is there to change the votes," Courtney shouted over the applause.

Zan looked at her, shocked, like she had just been punched in the stomach.

"Put your arm around her. Get a little closer," someone told the boy who won homecoming prince. He smiled and looked at Zan but didn't move. After Courtney's comment, Zan assumed they were making fun of her, and out of embarrassment said, "Don't you dare touch me." The photographer took one final picture of Zan and the boy each holding their crowns, and the two went their separate ways.

The DJ went back to his music station and everyone resumed dancing, but Courtney could not let go of her loss. She bumped through the crowd, finding as many girls from our squad as she could. "Who did you vote for?" she asked each of them over the music. She wrote the responses on the back of a receipt she found in her purse and tallied up the votes.

"It just doesn't make sense that she won when nobody voted for her," Courtney said, showing the list she'd made documenting everyone's responses.

"Are you serious?" I snapped. "Our entire squad isn't even here right now."

"Well, everyone said they voted for me. I should have won."

I was disgusted. "Of course they would say that. They're afraid of you."

Zan interrupted before Courtney could respond. "If you want the stupid crown, you can have it." She chucked the plastic headpiece toward Courtney. "I don't want it. I don't even care about this. You've already ruined the entire experience anyway."

"Oww." Courtney rubbed her arm dramatically, as if she

had been violently assaulted by the edge of the plastic that had barely brushed her skin.

"You totally hit her with it," I told Zan, laughing as we made our way out of the auditorium.

"Good," Zan said. She did not laugh or crack a smile.

NINETEEN

Everything that happened at the homecoming dance showed me the way truth could change depending on the speaker. And it made me realize that the person telling a story was not always the person who *should* be. The more I thought about it, the more I could not help but wonder if Courtney and the others would have responded the same way if someone else had won the crown. Would Courtney have doubted the other girls on our squad the way she doubted Zan?

Courtney took her desire to be crowned homecoming princess all the way to the director of the organization. Bullying Zan was not enough for her. Soon, Courtney's mom and sister joined her crusade to strip Zan of the title. We found out the night before our next practice, when the director called Mom and told her we would be having a team meeting to discuss the issue. The director then contacted every person on our team and their parents and told them that attendance was mandatory.

At practice the next evening, Mom and Courtney's mother were both in attendance, but there was a clear divide among our teammates. Courtney sat on the pavement, pouting. A few of the other girls sat with her and spoke shamelessly about how Zan had not deserved to win. Justine, Zan, and I moved away from them so we did not have to listen to their insults. Mom was appalled by the blatant disrespect and couldn't believe Courtney's mother not only allowed her daughter to openly harass Zan, but also supported her accusations that Mom had changed the votes.

"That does not make any sense," Mom said to her. "You are the other coach. You were right there with me. We collected all the votes together and turned them in *together*. When . . . *how* would I have changed them?"

Courtney's mom did not respond.

"Okay, listen up, everyone," Mom said to the group. "I want to address what happened at homecoming. Let me assure you that no votes were changed by me or anyone else."

"Of course they weren't," Courtney muttered, and rolled her eyes.

"The girls and I were not even supposed to be in town for homecoming," Mom explained. "I didn't even know Alixandria had won until the director contacted me about it to make sure she would be in attendance."

"How convenient," Amber commented.

Mom ignored the rude remarks. "Let's not waste any more practice time on this issue."

Most of the girls on our squad told us they disapproved of

the way Zan and Mom were being treated but were afraid to say anything because they feared being subjected to Courtney's abuse. But Courtney took their silence as support and continued calling Zan a cheater and Mom a liar every opportunity she could.

"Can you stop?" Julie finally asked her. "Why won't you just let it go?"

"Because she was supposed to win," Amber answered, pointing to Courtney.

"No, she was not!" Julie snapped. "If she was supposed to win, she would have!"

When it was clear our practice was turning into a verbal sparring match, Mom called the director's cell phone and told us to grab our stuff and head to the bleachers.

It was mid-October and the sky was gray and dreary as we made our way from one end of campus to the other. I was trying not to focus on the shock of the cold metal bench against my thighs when the director arrived. She started the meeting immediately.

"Never in all my years of being involved with this organization have I seen such terrible behavior." The director was about the same age as Mom and had a daughter on one of the younger cheer squads and a son who played football. She was well versed in the organization and league policies. "You should be ashamed of yourselves." She was stern and straightforward and spoke in a way that demanded both attention and respect.

Courtney raised her hand.

"What?" the director said.

"I just don't think it's fair to say we should be ashamed when a coach changed the votes so her daughter would win."

"Oh, *enough*!" the director snapped.

Courtney's cheeks reddened, but she did not back down. "I'm just saying."

"Nobody changed any votes." The director sighed and scanned the bleachers, looking at each one of us. "Are we really this insecure, girls? That we have to lie and spread rumors about people because we can't handle not winning? This is a *team*. You are supposed to support one another, not turn against each other."

Amber raised her hand now. "Well, we took a vote at the dance," she said, looking at Courtney, who was seated to her left.

"What are you . . . what do you mean you took a vote?" It was clear from the tone in the director's voice that she was beyond fed up.

"When we realized Zan won, we didn't think it was right, so the three of us went around and asked everyone at the dance who they voted for." Amber pointed to herself, Courtney, and Elyse. They were like the Three Musketeers of cheerleading bullies. "Everyone said they voted for Courtney, so that means the votes were changed."

"Some of us weren't even at the dance," Michelle blurted out, as she turned her body to look at them. "*I* didn't vote for Courtney."

Zan, Justine, and I stayed quiet as the girls bickered back and forth.

"The fact that your teammate was crowned princess and instead of supporting her, you went around the dance to try to prove she did not deserve it . . . Have you no shame?" The woman's voice echoed through the stands.

Finally. Someone to put Courtney and her friends in their place.

"Fine, Courtney. You want to know who all voted for you?"

Courtney, Amber, and Elyse all sat up.

"We are going to go through and read the names of every single vote. Do you want a piece of paper so you can tally them up again? Because gosh, I don't want you thinking I'm withholding any information."

I love this woman, I thought.

The director opened her bag and took out the closed envelope that contained the slips of paper we had each written our votes on and read the names one by one. Courtney had only received one vote.

"If you want to examine them for handwriting, have at it," the woman said, tossing the envelope onto the steps in front of her. "Because after tonight, I do not want to hear another word about any of this. Is that clear?"

Everyone nodded.

"And from where I stand, every single one of you—*especially* you three—owe Alixandria and your coach a huge apology." The director kept her eyes on Courtney, Amber, and Elyse as she spoke. Without a word or a goodbye, Courtney, her mom, and her sister left.

When Zan and I had expressed frustration over Courtney's behavior, Courtney and her friends would not hear of it. It was only when the president of the organization—someone in power—voiced the same thing, that anything was done, that anyone cared.

Zan had not said a word the entire meeting, but when I looked at her seated next to me, I saw her bloodshot eyes and the subtle tears leaking down each cheek. My sister always avoided conflict and did not like attention, and now she was at the center of both.

"Are you okay, sis?" I whispered.

Zan nodded and wiped her tears on the back of her hand.

After that, all the girls on our squad besides Courtney apologized to Zan, but Zan just wanted it to go away. She wanted to move on and pretend none of it ever happened.

—

If there was one thing I learned in seventh grade, it was the power of a voice—rather, the power of a voice when listened to. When I got home from cheer practice the night of the meeting, I sat down at the round dining table in the family room and prepared to write my short story for Mr. Lawson's class. I placed my school books in the center of the table and laid my papers out in front of me. Then I stared blankly at my notebook before picking up my pen to write.

I started with a description of a bandaged head. I detailed pulsating pain deep within the skull, stolen vision, and waking up in a hospital bed. *It's supposed to be fiction*, I reminded myself, but every time I wrote a sentence, I realized all I wanted to do was tell my own story. At twelve years old, my worldview was limited and writing was the only power I had. All I could speak to were the things I'd experienced myself. I decided to build on this for the assignment.

I wrote from what I knew, turning lines about head trauma and hospital stays into a story of twin sisters who were in a life-shattering car accident. In my story, one twin was killed and the other woke up with a face she could no longer recognize. The surviving twin spent the story mourning the loss of both her sister and herself. At the end, she learned her sister was not dead but simply had a new face like she did. Like the aftermath of the surgeries I'd had that summer, the character's recovery from the accident was about learning to grieve what was lost but finding hope in what mattered: that her sister, though unrecognizable, was still there.

I liked writing because when I spoke about my experiences, I had to choose my words carefully and filter what I said. Once I said something aloud, I could not take it back. In life, when I found myself being too real, too honest, *too* much, I was always left trying to comfort others. But when I *wrote* about my experiences, I could be honest. When I put words on the page, my soul sang. I was finally free. I was finally allowed to scream all the things that were killing me to keep inside. I was finally allowed to speak my truth without having to worry about it making other people uncomfortable. I finally had a voice.

———

The morning after the meeting with our cheer squad, Courtney's mom called the director and said they would not return until Courtney was acknowledged as the real winner. The director responded by giving them the opportunity to step down— Courtney from her place on the squad and Courtney's mom and sister from their position as coaches. Otherwise, she told them, they would be formally removed. It was a good thing Zan and I had already finished our surgeries, because with Courtney out of the picture, Mom became our only coach.

The director's handling of the homecoming situation gave me hope that our feelings and experiences would not always come second to those who looked "normal."

TWENTY

Public school was not designed for people like Zan and me. We missed so much school for surgeries and doctor appointments, there were things everyone but us seemed to know. We did not have the exposure to the material the way our classmates did. We did not have the mental and emotional energy to dedicate to learning. But we did our best to fill in the gaps in our knowledge as we went. It only got worse when we got to seventh grade, because people assumed from the appearance of our faces that we had a "cognitive impairment." I learned this after I overheard Jacob calling me retarded.

"Don't you see her eyes and the way her head is shaped?" he asked the rest of my table. "That's why she's so stupid." Jacob didn't realize I had been standing right behind him, until I threw my backpack in my seat and sat down.

"Honestly, no wonder your dad killed himself," I spat back. "I would too if I had to live with you." Jacob's smile fell from his lips. "What?" My body shook from the adrenaline rushing through me. "You can dish it but you can't take it?" I had dealt with Jacob's abuse for weeks, and it was his turn to deal with mine, to see how it felt. At least that was how I justified it to myself. I just wanted him to leave me alone.

Students weren't the only ones who treated Zan and me this way. Teachers did, too. Especially Mr. Jennings. Soon, the assumption that Zan and I were intellectually inferior became a self-fulfilling prophecy. We stopped studying and never did homework, because no matter how hard we tried, people looked for ways to prove what they already assumed. It was easier to fail on purpose and let everyone believe they were right than risk trying and fail anyway. It continued like this until my woodworking grade was so low I begged my mom to let me drop the class, but she refused. I was at risk of flunking because I never did the homework. And since I never did homework, I rarely passed the quizzes. But the work was all math-focused. Mr. Jennings said this was important because part of building was understanding angles and measurements, and how to calculate them. And so we always had to show we understood *how* to build something correctly before we were allowed to begin our actual projects. But how could I focus on learning measurement conversions and calculations when I was so distracted by the fact that my own reflection was a stranger to me? It all felt meaningless. School. Homework. *Life.*

My teachers made me get tested for learning disabilities—everything from dyslexia to auditory processing disorder—because they thought I belonged in the special education program. I think it was easier for them to blame it on me not understanding the material than actually deal with the fact that my absences had caused me to fall so far behind—and they didn't know how to help me catch up. Being doubted only motivated me. I didn't care about school or completing homework until I was at risk of failing or being held back. I'd just needed a chance to catch my breath. I spent my second month back at school focused on passing Mr. Jennings's woodworking class.

One day, Mr. Jennings called me to his desk right as the second bell rang. As students trickled out of the room, a handful of my classmates lingered behind to chat as they packed up their bags. "Ariel, I need to see you for a minute."

I usually met Zan right outside the classroom. When I wasn't there, she poked her head inside to see what was going on, then waited by my desk.

"I'm missing all these assignments from you." Mr. Jennings pulled out a list of all the homework we'd been expected to do over the last month. But I knew he was lying. I had done it all. And I'd photocopied it so I'd have proof. I'd been keeping track of my work each day, having been so proud of myself for sitting down after school and getting it all completed. So proud of myself for functioning like a normal middle schooler—or at least trying to. When I told Mr. Jennings I'd done those assignments, he denied ever receiving them.

"But I have photocopies of everything right here." I pulled my binder out of my bag to show him.

"How do I know when you did those? Just because you have them there doesn't mean you turned them in."

"Are you serious?" After everything I'd been through, I wasn't in the mood to deal with him, too.

"Yes, I'm serious." He kind of scoffed as he spoke.

I was angry. I wanted to scream and cry and bang my hands against the floor. Instead, I stood in front of Mr. Jennings and looked him square in the face and said, "I'm not doing it again, so *whatever*." I hadn't meant to be so disrespectful. The words just came out.

Mr. Jennings's mouth fell open just slightly and he stood there for a second with his eyebrows raised so high, his forehead became one giant wrinkle. "Don't talk to me like that."

"I will talk to you however I want." If Mom had seen my behavior, she would've been mortified. But I didn't care. What did I have to lose?

"Ariel!" Zan snapped at me. "Stop it!"

"I'm so sorry," she said to Mr. Jennings.

"Don't apologize to him!" The students who had stuck around after class stared at us: me and Mr. Jennings ready to face off and Zan in the middle—the levelheaded one just trying to keep the peace. It was clear from their awkward glances that the other students weren't sure whether to stay or leave. Without another word, I grabbed my binder and my bag and left.

Outside, once we were far enough away from the door of Mr. Jennings's classroom, Zan snapped, "Why would you do that!" It wasn't a question.

My body shaking, I stopped walking and let out a quiet scream. "Why are you never on my side?!"

"I'm always on your side! He's a jerk! You know he's a jerk! I know he's a jerk! HE knows he's a jerk! But what do you honestly expect to happen from that?"

I stomped my shoe down against the blacktop, sending sharp tingles up my leg. "I just hate everything," I whispered. I was on the verge of crying now. I was fighting back tears and people were staring. As if I hadn't already drawn enough attention to myself. "I'm so sick of this. I'm so sick of people treating us this way."

"I am too, sis. But yelling at people is just going to make it worse."

"I'm not going back there. You know I did those assignments. You know I did."

"I know, sis. I know."

―――

That afternoon in Mr. Lawson's class was the first time Jacob did not talk to or about me. *Finally*, I thought. I still felt guilty for commenting on his dad's suicide, but at least it got him to leave me alone. I thought about telling him I was sorry and asking his forgiveness, but I decided to keep to myself instead. *He probably prefers it this way, too*, I told myself. I was distracted with trying to justify my actions when Mr. Lawson began passing out everyone's short stories.

"These were fun to read," Mr. Lawson said as he wandered the room, handing us back our assignments. "Some of you got very creative with this." He passed Christian his paper as he said this, and we laughed.

"What?" Christian said, playing along. "You said it was *creative* writing."

I squirmed in my seat as I anxiously awaited his comments on my story. *What if he hated it?* I worried. *What if it was actually really terrible?* I was lost in my negative thoughts when my story appeared facedown on my desk. My heart raced as I picked up the paper and slowly turned it over. There was a giant A in red ink in the top right corner.

"This is great," the comment below it read. "I think you might have a future as a short story writer."

I smiled as I read my teacher's note and wondered if he knew everything I'd written was about Zan and me.

"Nice work, Ariel," Mr. Lawson said when he saw my excitement.

I was in a great mood for the rest of the afternoon. Maybe I'd found my *thing*, I thought.

—

I got home from school that afternoon just as the phone in the family room began to ring. I ran to pick it up.

"Hello?" I said into the receiver.

"Ariel?" It was Ms. J. "I spoke with the office and they gave me your number. Can we call Justine? I want to talk to you both."

Ms. J went on to explain that the school had suddenly let

her go, claiming that students had complained about how much homework she assigned. Justine and I were shocked into silence.

"Thank you for everything," we told her after it sank in. "We'll miss you."

Ms. J wished us well and hung up. She cared so deeply about her class and her students. Compared to Mr. Jennings's woodworking class and core class with Mr. Lawson, art with Ms. J was my safe place. Without her, school would just feel like another place I did not belong.

———

When Zan and I told our parents about how people treated us, they would sometimes try to make light of the situation. They would try to see things from the other person's perspective. When we got stared at or made fun of, they would say it was because we were beautiful. Or because people were curious. Or because they did not know any better. My parents meant well in teaching us to assume the best in those around us. They did not want us to take the way others viewed us personally, so they tried to teach us to be understanding and tolerant. But their well-meaning system of empathy instilled self-doubt.

When I'd first told my dad about what had happened with Mr. Jennings, he chalked it up to a misunderstanding. Even so, after Mr. Jennings and I had that fight about my homework assignments, Mom tried to get me and Zan moved from his class. Rumor had it that Mr. Jennings was already on thin ice. He had a habit of being too friendly with the pretty girls in class. "You look very nice today," he would say. When he went around the room checking everyone's work, he would sometimes stop and take a whiff of girls' hair. "You smell good," he would tell them. Too many students were transferring out of his class. Or trying to, anyway. So the guidance counselor said my request to transfer into another elective course had been denied.

I continued attending woodworking that week. Every morning when I entered the classroom, Mr. Jennings would lock eyes with mine. His face was strong and his expression was cold. *Fine*, I thought. *This is how it's going to be.* I knew how to handle him. I'd been stared at my whole life. Every time his eyes met mine, I refused to look away. I was used to bullies of all ages. He did not scare me.

By Friday, there was so much tension in the air, I could hardly focus. All week, his hard glares had not intimidated me, but that morning, he had the vice principal sit in on our class.

"Just pretend I'm not here," she said, standing in the back of the classroom.

Mr. Jennings took every opportunity to call on me that day.

"Ariel, come do this problem up on the board," he told me. He tapped the cap of a dry-erase marker against the whiteboard, where he had written down the one homework problem I'd left blank. I'd left a note in the margin of the assignment when I'd turned it in the day before, saying it was the one I did not know how to do.

I closed my notebook and stood from my desk. *Of course he*

gave me this one, I thought. Standing in front of the room with my back to the other students, I awkwardly fumbled through the equation. When I finished, I stepped back and pretended to examine my work. I knew my answer was incorrect, but I had no idea how to fix it because I had no idea what it was even asking me to do in the first place. I placed the marker back in the tray and returned to my seat. I'd made it halfway down the aisle when Mr. Jennings called me back up to the front of the room.

"Hey, hey, hey," he said. "Not so fast." He smiled, and I knew he was loving the fact that I'd gotten it wrong and that the vice principal was there to witness it. That was, after all, why he had chosen the equation. I was sure of it. "Walk me through your process."

My process? I thought as I went back to the board. *Write down a bunch of numbers and pray nobody can tell I have no idea how to do these calculations. Keep a low profile until I can get out of this class. Beg my dad to show me how to do everything, because your teaching style makes no sense. That's my 'process,'* I wanted to tell him. "I'm not sure what I did," I said instead. "This problem confused me. Can you please teach me?" I smiled sheepishly for good measure. If he was putting on a show for the school's administrators, I could, too.

———

Our new art teacher, Ms. Holden, was short and thin, and always mentioning just how short and thin she was. I was insecure with my own physique, so her constant mention of her slender frame bothered me. She was young—probably midtwenties—and wore cotton shirts and skirts that flowed from her body. Some of the kids called her a Berkeley hippie behind her back, as if it were something to be ashamed of, but I never noticed her clothes. All I could see was that she had Bell's palsy, which caused the muscles on one side of her face to be paralyzed. For once, I was not the only one in the room with a face that was different.

On her first day, Ms. Holden told us to stop working on the project we'd been doing for Ms. J and instead begin to think about our next assignment, which involved sketches of buildings and horizon lines. Unlike Ms. J, Ms. Holden focused mostly on landscapes and perspectives. Whereas Ms. J believed in sharing the beauty of art, Ms. Holden was more interested in mechanics and techniques. In class, we did numerous drawings of street corners and landscapes, all from different perspectives.

"Make a dot somewhere on your paper," she'd tell us. "Now connect every building to this vantage point." This was important, she explained, because everything looks different depending on where you are and what you see. Perspective. I thought buildings were boring and I was not good at drawing them. Mostly, I missed Ms. J.

"My building is ugly," I commented to Justine, and we laughed together at my uneven angles and crooked lines.

Ms. Holden overheard my remark and seized the

opportunity for a teachable moment. "Nothing is ugly in art. Everything has a purpose," she commented loudly. I rolled my eyes.

Later that week, Ms. Holden brought up ugliness again. She started by asking the class what beauty meant, what it was. Students gave variations of the question as their answer.

"Beauty is being attractive," one student said.

"Beauty is something that's pretty," added another.

"Okay, but how do you *know* if it's pretty?" Ms. Holden asked. Nobody had the answer.

She then asked the same thing about ugliness. "What does it mean for something to be ugly? Who decides?"

"It sort of just depends on the person and what they do or don't like," a boy named Justin commented.

"Okay, so personal preference?" Ms. Holden said.

"Yeah." Justin nodded his head to confirm.

"What else?" Ms. Holden looked around the room. "The meaning of beauty and ugliness has been debated for centuries." She stretched her arms out and leaned back dramatically as she spoke. "What have we learned about ugliness from that? What *is* it?"

I read once that ugliness is simply the opposite of beauty. When looking at standards of beauty and ugliness throughout history, all we have to go on is art—the pieces created and revered by society during those times—but I did not share this with the class.

A girl in the back of the room raised her hand. "Well"—she paused, trying to find the words—"when people are messed up." My body grew tense and I looked at Justine, holding her stare as if to say *you have got to be kidding me*.

"Okay." Ms. Holden gave a slight laugh, as if she were surprised by the girl's statement. "Messed up how?" I was hoping she would say the comment was inappropriate, that those of us who were different were not ugly. It was one thing for me to say it, but another when it came from a classmate.

"Like, deformed, I guess," the girl said.

I hated these discussions, because it always came back to the same thing: Ugliness meant asymmetry. Ugliness meant disfigurement. Ugliness meant faces like mine. Finally, when it was clear the discussion was not going anywhere productive, Ms. Holden put an end to it.

As students returned to their projects, I headed to the back of the room to revisit the book of Picasso paintings Ms. J and I had been discussing before she left. I turned to the page where I'd first seen the image of a Minotaur and then flipped through until I reached *Girl Before a Mirror*. As I examined the Picasso painting, I could not get Ms. Holden's question about ugliness and how it was defined out of my mind. I looked at the asymmetrical shapes that made up the woman's face and body. *What does it mean for something to be ugly?* My face was disfigured and asymmetrical, and so the only answer I could come up with was me.

After school, I told Mom about Mr. Jennings having me do the calculation on the board and the girl in my art class equating ugliness with disfigurement. It was not the first time one of us had been targeted by teachers, so I didn't think much of it. We were often marked down in class for missing school due to our medical procedures. Teachers would have an attendance policy that said students could not miss more than three classes without receiving a grade deduction, so they would give us an F in participation with no way to make it up.

"We cannot give you special treatment," they told us. "It would not be fair to the other students." As though our absences had been a choice we made, and failing was the consequence we deserved.

But the other students are not having their heads cut open and their faces rearranged, I wanted to explain. It wasn't that I wanted sympathy or pity—I didn't. I just wanted to stop being punished for having the surgeries I needed to keep me alive.

To my surprise, Mom set up a meeting with Mr. Jennings, the guidance counselor, and the principal without my knowing. I only found out when Zan and I were called to the office one afternoon. School was almost over when their meeting ended, but since my parents were already on campus, they were taking Zan and me home early.

At first my parents would not tell me exactly what had been said during the meeting, but I knew it was bad, because the first thing my dad did when he left the conference room was tell us to grab our stuff, that we were leaving. Mom was right behind him, and from the look on her face, she was just as angry.

I made eye contact with Mr. Jennings as he stood with our principal, Mr. Tomlinson, in the center of the office, but neither of us flinched or looked away. Everyone at the front desk stared as we left through the main door.

"What happened?" I asked Dad in the car.

"That guy is an idiot," he told me.

"Well, I know that, but why are you so upset?"

"We're getting you out of this shithead's class."

My dad rarely swore. Hearing him curse was like witnessing someone else's voice take over his body.

"Did you know they were friends?" he asked Mom.

She shook her head. "Of course not. Why would I know that?"

"Who?" I leaned forward from the back seat, trying to get more information. "Who is friends with Mr. Jennings?"

"Your woodshop teacher and your principal are buddies." Dad was fuming. "That . . . that *jerk* is going to go unpunished. Thinks he can say whatever he wants and treat people however he wants." My father shook his head and tightened his arms, lengthening the distance between himself and the steering wheel. "Asshole."

Eventually they told us that Mr. Jennings had said Zan and I needed more help than our teacher could provide. We were behind, he said, and we needed extra attention—something that was not fair to the other students. I could tell there was more to the story. Mom said Dad stayed quiet for most of the meeting while she gave her spiel, then Mr. Jennings, then Mr. Tomlinson, while Mrs. Hardy took notes. He listened and took in everything that was being said before responding. Mom was passionate and outspoken, while my dad had a quiet strength about him. He understood that real strength was shown through patience, kindness, and empathy. Zan was like him in that way. But they both had their limits. And though he was quiet and reserved, people listened when he spoke.

"It's a shame you can look at someone, at children, and judge them like this," he told Mr. Jennings, "especially as an educator." My father knew our teacher's issue was not with our lack of talent when it came to building wooden objects, but with our appearance. He would never tell me exactly what Mr. Jennings said about our faces, only that I should not worry, because he put my teacher in his place.

"No, I get it," my father told him. "You like the pretty students, is that right? And what? My girls are not pretty enough to deserve your attention?" I imagine Dad laughing maniacally. "Well, let me tell you something, you do not deserve to have them in your classroom." Mom said Dad delivered these lines calmly. He did not yell at or threaten our teacher. He simply spoke the truth. After which, he sat back in his seat, looked at the principal, and said, "You need to put my girls in another class. Today."

It felt good to know our parents were angry on our behalf, because it validated the feelings I had been taught to question. After the conference, Dad's demands and my parents' dramatic exit seemed to have worked, because the next morning I was called to the guidance counselor's office and told I would be switching to a different class.

"Let's try to keep this between us, please," the counselor told me. "We can't be having everybody switching classes."

By then, word had gotten around about my issue with Mr. Jennings. When a student asked why I wasn't in class that day, Mr. Jennings told everyone Zan and I had been transferred out of his classroom, because our faces were too distracting and not conducive to their learning.

I didn't tell my parents about this, because I didn't want Dad to get upset again. He was right. Mr. Jennings *could* say whatever he wanted with no repercussions. But Zan and I were out of his class, and that was all that mattered.

TWENTY-ONE

Seventh grade felt like one long, bad dream. The kind where you tell yourself to wake up but can't. By the time spring rolled around, I was relieved to soon be out of my nightmare.

I was still seeing Beth, my therapist, every Thursday for our weekly appointment. "I know it's been a difficult year for you," she said at one of our sessions late in the spring. "How do you feel like you've been handling things lately?"

I shrugged. "Okay, I think."

"How is your anger?" she asked me.

"Still there." I smiled, hoping to make her laugh. I was not good at acknowledging the severity of everything I had been through.

"Can you tell me about that?"

I paused, trying to think of what to say. I wanted to tell her that I was always scared and anxious. That every time I spoke to someone in my family, I had to tell them I loved them at least six times, because time was never a guarantee. That I hated myself for being so angry. I wanted to tell her that I cried myself to sleep most nights and dreamt I was back in the ICU, recovering. I wanted to tell her that I was thirteen years old and still waking up in pools of my own urine. Instead, I told her I didn't want to talk about it. "Can we maybe go into that stuff next time?"

"Of course we can." She smiled. "Thank you for saying that. I'm proud of you for identifying what you are comfortable with and setting those boundaries for yourself." Beth was the first therapist I really connected with. She respected my limits and I trusted her for it. "What would *you* like to talk about?"

"Hmm." I crossed one leg over my knee and tapped a finger against my bottom lip.

"Anything you want." Beth put her notepad on her desk and took off her glasses, rubbing the top of her nose between her eyes. "We can take it easy and just chat about whatever is on your mind. How's school? Are you feeling good about the end of the school year approaching?"

"School is good." I told Beth about the upper-level French class returning from their weeklong trip to Paris. "My goal is to get better at French and maybe go with my class next year. It looks so beautiful."

"So you want to travel?" Beth's eyes lit up.

"I do. Life is so short," I explained. "I want to see everything."

"Do you think about that often?" she asked me.

"About what? Traveling?"

"About how short life is."

"All the time," I told her.

"What does that look like for you?"

I thought about her question for a moment before answering. "I just feel like I don't have much time. Sometimes it gets overwhelming. If I think about life and death and time for too long, it feels like I'm being sucked into a vortex. Or like I've been thrown into a black hole." I closed my eyes. "I try not to let my mind go there."

"What do you do when you have these thoughts?"

"Well, sometimes I sit with the panic for a little while. It sort of eats away at me from the inside, so I just sit with it until it passes."

"How does it make you feel?"

"Scared. Sometimes angry. Almost always sad."

"Why sad?" Beth seemed genuinely curious by the emotions I'd described.

"Because there's so much I still want to do," I said. "That's why I try to channel my energy into something I can look forward to, like traveling." The midface surgery was over, but it didn't magically take the Crouzon syndrome away. We weren't suddenly healed and made to be like everyone else. There were still more surgeries hanging over us. There were still more opportunities for things to go wrong inside us.

Beth could tell I was trying to change the subject to something lighter, so she followed my lead. "If you could go anywhere in the world, where would you go?"

"Somewhere in Europe. I'd love to see its history in person. It seems like there are stories on every corner."

"Have you ever been to Ireland?" Beth asked me. "I'm going on a trip there next week."

"Oh!" I exclaimed. "So that's why our appointment for next week is canceled!"

Beth nodded.

We spent the rest of our session talking about the places we dreamed of going. She told me of her Irish heritage and how eager she was to share her favorite places with her husband. Before the end of our appointment, she pulled a small swatch of fabric from the top desk of her drawer. "This is what I got during my last visit," she said, handing it to me. Printed on the top of it was an old Irish blessing.

May the wind always be at your back. May the sun shine warm upon your face, and rains fall soft upon your fields. And until we meet again, May God hold you in the palm of his hand.

"I like that," I told her.

"I thought you would." Beth placed the fabric back onto her desk. "Well, Miss Ariel, our session has come to an end."

I stood and gathered my belongings. "Thank you for telling me about you," I said as I turned to leave. "And have a great time on your trip."

"Thank you," Beth responded. "And until we meet again, May God hold you in the palm of his hand."

I smiled and closed the door to her office behind me.

A few days after Beth left for Ireland, I got a letter in the mail inviting me to the end-of-year awards night at school. I hadn't even known our school had an awards night, but my heart raced as I read the invitation. It did not mention what awards recipients would be receiving, but at the bottom of the page was a list of categories that would be presented at the event. Most were related to academic achievement and athleticism, along with one surprise category. Zan and Nina got the same invitation I did. Since none of us were scholars or school athletes, we spent the rest of the week trying to figure out what we were being awarded and why.

"It's probably for being so fabulous." Nina flipped her hair playfully.

"Well, obviously," Zan added.

I laughed.

The days leading up to the ceremony passed slowly, but Friday evening finally arrived.

"Look who pulled out all the stops," Nina said when we walked into the school auditorium. The wooden bleachers had been pulled out from the wall, and there were rows of plastic chairs set up in the center of the room. Nina's sense of humor had always been sarcastic.

Mr. Tomlinson and Ms. Dodson stood together behind a wooden podium in the front of the room. On each side was a single row of chairs, where teachers sat facing the audience. Nina, Zan, and I all sat together with our parents in one of the first rows of bleachers. One by one, the awards were presented. The principal and vice principal took turns announcing each one individually, explaining what it was for and why each student deserved it. Nearly two hours passed before they got to the final award. Nina, Zan, and I had yet to have our names called, so we knew we were next.

"Now this is a special award," Mr. Tomlinson announced, as he slowly looked around the room. "We are giving these awards out tonight to people we think overcame a lot this year."

Zan leaned over and whispered into my ear. "I swear if he announces our surgery to the entire room, I will lose it."

"I know," I mouthed.

Without stating what we had done, Mr. Tomlinson called Nina, Zan, and me up to the podium. "Tonight, we are presenting these young ladies with an award to commend their inspiring behavior." He thanked us for being examples of kindness and resilience, for inspiring our school community to be kinder toward one another.

The three of us stood nervously next to each other at the front of the room, as our teachers handed us paper certificates with the words *Most Inspirational* printed on them. Standing in front of everyone made me feel shy and exposed, but I smiled proudly as I accepted my award. It felt good to be recognized for something other than my face.

"But wait, why are we inspirational exactly?" Zan asked quietly when we returned to our seats.

Nina and I both shrugged.

As I reflected on Zan's question, I realized she was right to critique the underlying message. It was a nice gesture and I didn't mean to be ungrateful, but I was confused as to how I had been inspiring. What had we done to deserve such recognition? It all felt like mixed messaging. Society rewarded beauty. Zan and I knew this. We had been ridiculed all year because we were not beautiful. But if the award was not valuing our beauty, was it valuing our ugliness?

———

After the awards ceremony, I was eager for my next appointment with Beth. So eager that when Mom dropped me off for my appointment that evening, I raced up the steps and burst through Beth's door without knocking. Normally she waited outside to greet me, but when I did not see her, I swung open her door and stepped into the room, where a balding man in a brown suit was sitting in my seat. Beth looked startled, and the man seemed offended by my intrusion.

"Ariel, I am still with a patient," Beth said. "Please wait outside until I come get you."

"I'm so sorry," I said, inching backward toward the door. I was embarrassed and out of breath from running from the car.

When the man left a few minutes later, Beth invited me inside.

"How was your trip?" I asked her.

"We'll get to that." Beth waved her hand toward me. "I want to hear about you first."

I told her about the awards ceremony and how Nina, Zan, and I were all praised for being inspirational.

Beth cocked her head at me. "They did not explain why?"

I shook my head. "It was sort of implied that Zan and I got the award because of our surgeries, but they just lumped Nina in there with us."

Beth frowned and scrunched her eyebrows, then let out a long *hmmm*. "How do you feel about it?"

"Confused," I said. "I am not inspirational. Zan and I are just trying to live our lives."

"You *have* been through a lot," Beth said. She was always trying to get me to not be so hard on myself, but I did not need or want things—the truth—sugarcoated.

"I know. I just don't understand why having surgery is inspiring. Like, what about that is inspirational exactly? It's not like I *chose* to have it," I said. "It's not like Zan, Nina, and I gave each other our vital organs or sacrificed some part of ourselves so the other could live."

Beth listened and nodded.

"I don't mean to sound like Nina and Zan don't deserve an award," I explained. "They are amazing and should be celebrated. It just feels . . ." I paused, trying to find the perfect word. "Empty. It feels empty."

"I'm confused," Beth said. "Did Nina get an award because of you and Zan or was it just announced together?"

"That's the thing," I said. "We don't know." I stared at the wall behind Beth's head while I gathered my thoughts. "I don't mean to sound self-centered or make Nina's award about me," I explained. "It didn't even occur to me that Nina got the award *because* of Zan and me until she made a comment about it."

"Until *Nina* made a comment about it?" Beth clarified.

"Yeah." I nodded. "We were standing outside the auditorium while our parents chatted, and Nina made a comment about how she thought the principal was confused."

"What did she say?"

"'Do they think I had surgery, too?' She said it jokingly," I told Beth. "But there was some truth there also. Then she said, 'Oh my gosh! Did we get awards because they felt bad for us? Did I get an award for being friends with you?' And it was like it suddenly all clicked. Then we were all laughing, of course, because it was so absurd."

Beth still looked like she wasn't completely following what I was trying to explain, so I broke it down further.

"If Zan and I had gone through what we did without ever missing a homework assignment, while maintaining a perfect grade point average, joining clubs, and fostering friendships, *that* would have been inspirational. But we didn't. If I had been able to handle recovery without lashing out at those around me and saying hateful things to the people I loved, maybe I could have felt worthy of an award. Did other people find us inspiring because they were grateful they weren't like us?"

"And what about Nina?" Beth asked. "How does she play into it?"

"Exactly," I said. "Was Nina given an award simply for being friends with Zan and me? Because befriending the *ugly* girls who everyone else treated as lepers was inspiring?" The more I analyzed the situation, the more worked up I became. "Zan and I did not go through everything we did just so other people could hear our story and witness our struggle and use it as a reminder of how good their lives are. We do not exist to help non-disfigured people feel better about themselves. That's crap."

"You're right," Beth agreed. "That is crap."

Then she took a small gift bag from her desk. "I brought you something," she said. "And this seems like a good time to give it to you."

I smiled and removed the tissue paper from the bag. It had been wrapped tightly into a square. I carefully unfolded each layer until I reached the object in the center—a square stained-glass ornament of a field with green hills and flowers, with a gold rim. "Wow." The top corners were connected with a thin thread that hung over a small transparent suction cup.

"So you can hang it in your window," Beth told me.

I held it up in front of the light and stared at the object as the brightness poured through it. "It's so beautiful." The thoughtfulness of the gift made me teary-eyed. "Thank you."

Beth smiled. "Of course. It's good luck for light to shine through it."

Part of me wondered if she'd made that up, but I didn't care. I loved her gift. Besides, I was a girl with a disfigured face in an appearance-obsessed society. I needed all the luck I could get.

TWENTY-TWO

We live in a world filled with Picassos: men who believe it is a woman's duty to serve as their muse. Picasso once claimed he did not believe in beauty. "I love or I hate," he said. "When I love a woman, that tears apart everything, especially my painting." But in both his art and his life, he was drawn to classical beauty and was heavily inspired by his obsession with sex and the female form.

In this way, women were either goddesses or doormats, a sentiment that mirrors our society's current attitude. Beautiful women are to be worshipped and those who are not beautiful are to be cast aside. Yet art historians describe Picasso as passionate and intense instead of abusive. Many fail to mention that he was a sexual predator. While married to his first wife, Olga Khokhlova, a former ballerina, Picasso had affairs with several women, including Marie-Thérèse Walter, who at seventeen years old was underage when their "relationship" began. Picasso was forty-five. One summer, he rented a house for his family—for Olga and their son—near a summer camp Marie-Thérèse was attending. Every morning, he would take his young mistress to a cabana he'd rented on the beach and have sex with her. For years, he kept it hidden—not because he was married, but because she was a child and the affair was illegal at its beginning. The only evidence of their relationship were the erotic portraits he painted of her. By 1932, the affair with Marie-Thérèse served as his main source of inspiration, and the majority of the work he produced focused on the female figure. Writer Lara Marlowe called it "Picasso's most erotic year."[4] In *Le Rêve*, Picasso painted half of Marie-Thérèse's face in the shape of a penis. In January of that year, he also drew *The Painter Before His Model*, a sketch in which the painter's penis is holding the paintbrush.

Before the end of his affair with Marie-Thérèse, he began another with an artist named Dora Maar, a surrealist photographer and painter. Picasso loved pitting women against each other, and once, during a visit to his studio, he told Dora and Marie-Thérèse to battle it out. He would later say that the memory of their physical altercation was one of his "choicest memories." Forcing Dora and Marie-Thérèse to fight each other over him was a distraction, and only prevented the women from discovering the real problem: Picasso. And just as society casts aside those who do not meet superficial aesthetic standards, when he stopped finding inspiration in their beauty, he left them both.

Picasso was never faithful to any woman, but he used any

---

4   Lara Marlowe, "Sex on the canvas: Picasso's most erotic year laid bare." *The Irish Times,* February 17, 2018, www.irishtimes.com/culture/art-and-design/visual-art/sex-on-the-canvas-picasso-s-most-erotic-year-laid-bare-1.3392315.

means necessary to ensure control over his partners, to keep them coming back. He withheld money, used his influence to threaten their reputations, and even portrayed them a certain way on his canvases to influence how they were viewed by the public. After Olga discovered Picasso's affairs, she wanted a divorce, but Picasso refused to provide spousal support. Though separated, Olga was forced to stay legally married to him until she died in 1955. In 1943, sixty-one-year-old Picasso began seeing twenty-one-year-old artist Françoise Gilot. In 1961, six years after Olga's death, Picasso, who was now seventy-nine, married thirty-four-year-old Jacqueline Roque. They stayed together until Picasso's death in 1973. The effects of Picasso's predatory behavior, manipulation, and abuse had a lasting impact on the women who loved him. In the early 1940s, when Picasso left Dora for Françoise Gilot, Dora had a nervous breakdown and, for years, stopped showing her work. In 1977, Marie-Thérèse hanged herself. In 1986, Jacqueline shot herself.

———

By the end of eighth grade in 2005, I wanted more than anything to know what it was like to go from being a doormat to being praised for my beauty—to being a goddess. To prove to society there was value in my existence. But I felt about my body the way I felt about my face: I hated it. Not because I thought my fatness made me ugly or my disfigured face made me wrong, but because everyone else did.

Whereas Zan's anxiety had left her too empty to eat, I ate until I was so full there was no room for the emptiness that had taken up residence inside me. Food was the one thing in my life I could look forward to. The one thing I could depend on to never change. No matter how much my face changed, the sweetness of sugar would always be there to comfort me, to satisfy me, to fill me up. Every binge, every bite made me feel like the empty cracks inside me were closing. But the relief was temporary. The bigger I grew and the further I got from the beauty standards society expected women to live up to, the more shame I felt. Though our methods differed, Zan and I were chasing the same thing: the desire to exert control over our own lives.

Worried for my health, my parents tried everything they could think of to help me. They tried telling me I couldn't have dessert. They tried refusing to buy me new clothes—ones that fit—hoping I would use it as motivation to change my ways. My father, praying the rising number on the scale would scare me into changing, started forcing me to weigh in. I told myself I hated him for this, but I didn't. He was only trying to help me.

That March, he even asked a doctor to tell me I *had* to lose weight, that it was not a suggestion, but a demand. Mom was still at work, so Dad took us to our appointment. It was just a checkup with one of the practitioners I did not know well. The three of us—Zan, Dad, and I—sat together in an exam room as the doctor looked into our ears and listened to our hearts. As the doctor finished his exam and prepared to leave the room, Dad turned to him and asked for another moment of his time.

"She's going to be angry I'm doing this, but Ariel is at *least* thirty pounds heavier than Alixandria," my dad said to the doctor.

The man looked at me, then at my dad, before awkwardly opening my medical chart. "Yes, that is correct." I could feel the blood drain from my face.

"Can you *please* tell her she needs to lose weight?"

"Well, a healthy weight range would be a bit lower."

"See? Now you have doctor's orders." My father laughed, trying to make light of the situation.

"Little changes can help—diet, exercise, plenty of water, and lots of rest. The receptionist can help connect you with a dietician if you'd like."

How was it possible to feel so big and so small—so *ashamed*—all at once? I wondered. Being shamed did not inspire me to want to change my eating habits. It made me want to disappear.

The next week, during an appointment with my orthodontist, I was told that in order to get my braces off, I had to start wearing rubber bands on each of the brackets. Dr. Zimmerman leaned me back in the chair and had me hold a mirror above my mouth so he could show me how to put them on. He looped one end of a rubber band through the hook on the inside of my bottom teeth and attached the other end to a bracket on the top. He did this several times until my mouth was no longer just a mess of metal, but a mess of metal tied together with beige rubber bands.

"You need to wear these at all times," Dr. Zimmerman told me. "You should only take them off for meals and to brush your teeth. Then you should put new ones right back on."

"What happens if I don't wear them?" I asked. "Or if I forget?"

"We'll have to wire your mouth shut."

I laughed along for a moment, thinking he was joking.

"He's serious," one of the dental assistants said.

"What?" I was shocked. "How do you eat?"

"You don't," he said. "It's a liquid diet. It's really not fun, so just wear your rubber bands."

Dr. Zimmerman's honesty was meant to scare me into doing as I was told, but I was too distracted by the thought of the weight I would lose if forced to be on a liquid diet. It was the perfect plan. With a mouth that could not open, there was no way I could fail.

When I returned to Dr. Zimmerman's office a month later and he realized I had not worn my rubber bands, that my teeth had not shifted at all, he did what he'd warned me he'd do: He fastened metal wires to each bracket, wrapping each strand around the bottom and the top until my jaw was stuck closed. Though I'd planned it this way, having my jaws tied together was more painful than I'd anticipated. By the end of my appointment, my mouth was sore and my teeth ached.

For the next two weeks, I drank my calories. Mostly through small bottles of Ensure, the chocolate ones. If I drank them quickly enough, the empty ache in my belly would be replaced with nausea. I was weak and light-headed from hunger, but too proud to care. I focused instead on the way my body was changing. I was losing one pound per day. *I'm so close*, I thought. *Fifteen more pounds and I'll be beautiful. Twenty more pounds and I'll be happy.*

Dr. Zimmerman removed the wires and evaluated the shift of my teeth when I returned to his office later that month.

"How does it feel?" he asked me as I slowly opened and closed my mouth.

"Weird," I told him. "Nice to be able to talk normally again." I smiled and began massaging the area below my ear.

"Are you ready to wear your rubber bands now?" he asked me.

I shrugged. "Can you actually just tie it shut again?"

Dr. Zimmerman looked surprised. "You'd rather do it again?"

"I'd rather just get it over with," I told him. I didn't know how to tell him that I wanted to keep my mouth forcibly closed because I liked the way starving myself made me feel like I was strong and, for once, in control of my impulses.

Dr. Zimmerman agreed.

———

That April, with my jaw still fastened together, I attended cheerleading tryouts for the high school Zan and I would be attending the following year. I wasn't expecting to make the team, but I hoped I would, because part of me believed it would be my way of getting back at everyone who'd made fun of me in middle school, everyone who'd said I didn't *look* like a cheerleader. High school cheerleading was more elite, more selective. Making the team would prove a point: that I would never be limited by my ugliness.

During tryouts, the high school gymnasium was crowded with girls all vying for a spot on the freshman, JV, or varsity cheer squads. It was easy to spot the eighth graders. There were dozens of us, mostly shy and not quite out of our awkward phases, all hoping we would be one of the thirteen girls to make the freshman squad. The audition was exactly as it had been years before when I tried out for the Bulldogs. It was a weeklong process. The first three days were spent learning a dance and cheer and the fourth day was a practice day to prepare for the Friday afternoon tryouts.

I attended the clinic with Justine. Other girls stared at me, but the coaches never seemed fazed by my differences.

That Friday, Mom picked me up after school and, on our way to the tryouts, took me to the craft store for a green shirt and gold ribbon for my hair. When we got to the high school, a crowd of teenagers in cheerleading shorts and hair bows were practicing together. Girls auditioned two at a time and since Zan had no interest in being on the squad, Justine and I chose to go together. Before our turn, the coaches stepped out of the auditorium to make an announcement. Shouting through a megaphone, the woman thanked us all for working so hard and told us that no matter what happened, we were all talented. My nerves fired all at once when they told us a list of everyone who made the squad would be posted on the wall of the gymnasium late that night. I immediately looked at Mom with equal parts terror and anticipation. I couldn't remember anything after my audition, only that Justine and I both thought we'd done well. In all my nervous excitement, it was like I'd blocked it from my memory.

The hours after the audition passed slowly. After Justine and I hugged goodbye, I went home and tried to distract myself. It was nearly eleven p.m. when Justine's mom called and told Mom the names had been posted.

"Was my name on the list?" I asked Mom.

"She didn't say. "I think we need to drive up there."

"Let's go!" I shouted excitedly as I barreled down the stairs of the garage and into the passenger side of my mom's Escalade.

When we pulled up in front of the gymnasium, I could see a white paper taped to the door—a paper with what I knew would be a list of only thirteen names.

"I can't look." I pulled my knees to my chest and shielded my eyes.

"Want me to go and tell you what it says?" Mom took off her seat belt and got out of the car. When she got to the door, she motioned for me to come to her. My heart sank as I rolled down the window.

"It's a no?" I shouted from the car.

"Come read this with me. I don't think this is the list for cheerleading."

She probably doesn't see my name because I didn't make the team, I thought.

I didn't even make it all the way to the door when Mom cracked a smile. I screamed when I saw both Justine's name and my name in small bold letters. Not only was I one of the thirteen freshmen to make the squad, I was one of the captains.

———

After cheerleading auditions were over, Zan started to feel like herself again. She stopped waking up every night with pain in her forehead and started eating more than ice cream and broccoli. She was still thin but no longer dangerously so. Despite my weight loss, I was still larger than Zan, but I was proud of my shrinking figure.

Dr. Zimmerman removed the wires from my mouth in late July, just in time for the start of the cheer season.

Practice officially started on August 1 and were held for two hours every morning until school started. My parents both worked and I was not yet old enough to drive, so I woke up early and rode my bike the four miles each way. While Justine arrived to practice looking beautiful, I did not. Every morning when I parked my bike in front of the gymnasium, I was sweaty, frumpy, and ready for a nap. I told myself it didn't matter, because it was an extra workout. Riding my bike *and* attending practice meant I'd burn more calories. Everything centered around my appearance, around losing weight.

During one of our practices that summer, our coach—a twenty-three-year-old woman named Karly—made a comment to Justine about her beauty. Karly had jet black hair on the top of her head, but the layers underneath were various shades of pink. Just before our season started, she'd gotten breast implants so that her chest would be larger than her belly. She was always talking about appearance.

At practice, Justine wore a pair of black cotton shorts and a loose T-shirt strategically tied to cinch her waist. As we practiced on the sidelines, Karly studied her. "You're super gorgeous, Justine," she said during a water break. "You could be a Playmate."

"You really think so?" Justine asked, almost starstruck. Justine had always been pretty. She was tall and thin with vibrant red hair and perfectly white teeth. But she was more than that. She was kind, funny, and smart. She loved animals and art and interior design. She was more than her beauty. She was my best friend.

"A playmate?" I was fourteen and had no idea what they were talking about. Karly pretended she hadn't heard the question.

"*Playboy*." Justine's explanation was short, but at least she responded to me.

The rest of the girls on the squad joined in, telling Justine and each other how beautiful they were. How many boys liked them. How popular they were going to be in a few weeks once the school year started. And then there was me. I was like an awkward fly on the wall as they fantasized about the months ahead. They didn't ignore me per se, but I was not a part of their conversation.

After Coach Karly told Justine she could be a *Playboy* Playmate, things changed. It didn't happen all at once. Perhaps it would have been easier if it had. Instead, it was a gradual change—a shift that made me aware, even as it was happening, that I was losing my closest friend.

That September, the week before the first game of the season, Justine and I spent an entire afternoon in her driveway, decorating posters to hang in the stands. Justine was more artistic than I was, so I wrote the words and she drew our mascot. She played music from a radio station in the garage so we could dance and sing along as we worked. It was moments like these that made me forget I was different. I could forget about all the summers before this one that had been spent in a hospital bed. For a moment, our appearance didn't matter. There was only happiness.

I was still in between writing *GO LIONS!* and *RC CHEER* in black paint when the song ended. Justine walked to the garage and turned down the music as the next one came on.

"Can I ask you a question?" She studied the ground while she spoke.

I put the paint down and stood up. "Yeah, sure. Go ahead."

"Is it hard to be my friend?" She looked nervous.

I fumbled over my words, confused by the question. "Of course not."

She nodded and seemed satisfied with my answer, but it was clear there was still something bothering her.

"Is it hard being mine?" I hoped asking the question back to her would get her to tell me why she was asking in the first place. I never expected her to say yes.

"It's just that people ask me all the time why I'm friends with you, and it gets a little old, ya know?"

"Oh. And what do you say back?" I asked.

"I tell them I don't know."

I stood barefoot in her driveway, the bottoms of my feet blackened from the pavement. I knew the constant stares and comments were hard to deal with, just like I knew in that moment our friendship would never be the same. Like Picasso pitted the women in his life against each other, toxic societal standards pitted me against Justine. I was different and she was not. That was when it hit me: If my own friends could not define my worth, there was no hope that other people would learn to accept me. People would never see me for anything more than what I was, a freak.

In hindsight, I do not blame Justine for not wanting to be friends. I was jealous. Everything seemed so effortless for her, like she never even had to try. She was just naturally beautiful. I had spent so long killing myself trying to be like her, trying to fit in and be accepted, but it never worked. I was angry at myself for being unable to change my face and heartbroken that my differences were too much even for my best friend. I'd thought cheerleading would be the thing that made others realize I was just like them, but all it did was show me that beauty was a moving target—one I could never seem to reach.

As weeks passed, I didn't know how to say that I missed her, that I didn't want to lose her, so I pushed her further away instead. When she posted a photo online of herself in a cropped sweater and push-up bra lying on the ground to emphasize her cleavage, I left comments that were rude and judgmental. *Wow, you're cool?* When she posted another with a necklace of a Play-boy Bunny icon, I left a sarcastic *classy*. I wanted to make her feel the way I did. I wanted her to hurt like me.

I've come to view Picasso as a symbol of the toxic beauty stan-dards that plague women, and his relationships as the way we've been taught to internalize the male gaze. Picasso's partners were left abused and belittled, forced to believe that without him they'd be nothing. Just as I was taught to believe that with-out beauty, I had no purpose. I grew up believing that being a woman meant adhering to patriarchal beauty standards, because the belief that a woman's value lay in her appearance had been passed down for generations—for centuries. I told myself that the beautiful women around me were the standards against which I should measure myself.

What I didn't realize was that Zan and I were in an abusive relationship with the world around us. We were mocked and humiliated and put down. We faced near-constant criticism from people, some of whom we didn't even know. When people weren't openly mean to us, we were often ignored and excluded. The one thing we could not change about ourselves—the one thing we were most insecure about—was always being used against us. And like with many abusers, we were made to believe it was our fault. That we deserved it. We were the ones who were unable to live up to the beauty standards that had been set by society. It did not matter how impossible they were. Our differences made us unforgivably flawed.

At fourteen, I succumbed to this belief. Whereas I had once been driven by my need to show that my life, and the lives of others who were different like Zan and me, was of value, I now felt controlled by my desire to obtain beauty and acceptance the way Picasso's lovers were controlled by him.

PART III

Healing

TWENTY-THREE

If Dr. York had been a sculptor, Zan and I would have been his clay. Leaving our major surgeries behind in middle school meant high school was about finding—creating—the faces we wanted for ourselves. The procedures in seventh grade—the ones that shifted the bones in the middle of our faces—altered the shapes of our features in ways we had not anticipated. Our noses were flatter and my chin appeared underdeveloped. So, feature by feature, Zan and I spent all four years of high school having our faces "fixed" to look more like they had before the operation.

After surgery, Zan and I were constantly mourning the pieces of ourselves, of each other, that we had left behind. I was always comparing my current face to what I had looked like in the past. Referencing my previous appearance allowed me to become my own benchmark in some ways. My understanding of beauty was rooted in the symmetrical faces of those around me, but it was also measured in the progress I made back toward myself. It was my way of holding on to who we had been while also dreaming of who we could become.

On March 10, 2005, toward the end of eighth grade, Mom took Zan and me to the hospital for a panel evaluation, where we spent the day sitting in an exam room while doctors and surgeons from every department stopped by to evaluate our progress and determine what else we needed, both medically and aesthetically. We did this once a year. The style of the appointment was meant to be convenient for patients and their parents, a sort of one-stop shop in one afternoon kind of deal. For Zan and me, these appointments meant hours of doctors discussing our asymmetrical faces and explaining how they could get our appearance closer to a normal ratio.

"It's a little flat now," Dr. York said of my nose. "I can fix it." Then he cupped my chin and studied it. "This can be made more prominent as well." I don't remember the conversations going much further beyond that. He saw something that needed fixing, and just like that, the plan to do so was in motion. In my medical record after our panel visit, Dr. York wrote:

Ariel is 14 years of age. She is the twin sister of Alixandria. Her issues and concerns are similar to her sister's. She is concerned about her nose and her eyes. She did have a negative experience with her most recent anesthetic and is not overly enthusiastic about additional surgery. Examination reveals downward mongoloid slanting of her eyes. There are nasal irregularities with septal deviation. I discussed the procedure of rhinoplasty. This will be done in the near future. We will also correct the downward slant of her eyes.

In other words, I needed a nose job. The golden ratio stated that in order for a nose to be attractive, the width of the nostrils when measured from one alar crease to the other should be the same as the height of the nostril, and the area from the nostril to the top of the nose needed a 2:1 ratio. I didn't want another operation, but I wanted my face to be acceptable. I wanted my face to blend in. After Dr. York and all the other doctors pointed out the flatness of our noses and the difference a chin augmentation could make, I became obsessed with correcting my perceived flaws—with being remade into society's image of how we should be.

———

That November, just months into our freshman year of high school, Zan and I took time off from school to have the appearance of our noses corrected. The operation was Dr. York's attempt to reduce the width and change the shape of its tip from flat to lifted. He did this by cutting the alar crease on each nostril, eliminating excess skin, and moving each side of our nose inward and closer to each other, before reattaching them to our faces. For two weeks afterward, we had cotton tubes placed in each nostril, all the way up to our eyes, to control the bleeding. The procedure went well, but recovery did not. On December 13, 2005, two weeks after the cotton was removed, Marissa and I were in the checkout line at Target when my nose started pouring blood. The cashier handed me a plastic bag when I could no longer hold all the blood in my hands. Marissa and I spent thirty minutes in the bathroom trying to stop the bleeding before we drove to the emergency room to have them shove packing back up my nostrils. It didn't hurt, but I was nauseous and light-headed. Mom drove me back to the emergency room the following night when the blood began seeping through the packing that had been put in place the afternoon before. There, the nurses threw away the soaked cotton and examined my nose for any sign of infection or post-surgery trauma. When they found nothing, they packed it again and sent me on my way. The nosebleeds stopped just in time for Christmas.

After the packing was removed, Zan and I lifted our heads back and examined our noses from the base. Our nostrils, where Dr. York had cut each side and reattached them, were now different shapes and sizes on each side. While we never reached what we thought at the time was our perfect aesthetic ideal, the surgery on our noses brought us closer. My new nose suited my face and reminded me of how I'd looked before the second mid-face advancement. Though still imperfect and asymmetrical, my nose felt like mine again.

Despite the physical nature of Zan's and my healing, recovery was more mental than physical. From November until January, we rarely left our house.

When it was clear our bodies and our minds needed more time to heal, Mom contacted the school to see what options they had for how Zan and I could finish out the semester without being physically present. They told us the school district had home teachers available for students on medical leave. We'd been attending school in the same district for ten years, but this was the first we'd heard of this option. While Zan and I stayed home and focused on recovery, school came to us.

Our teacher was a man named Bill. He was in his early fifties and rode a Harley. The sound of his bike was like the chime of a school bell. Every time we heard the rev of his engine as he tore down the boulevard, we knew class was almost in session. We worked with him one-on-one every day for the rest of the semester. Bill was nice at first, but he was impatient and had a fiery temper. The more comfortable he got, the more hurtful he became.

"It's not rocket science, girls," he would say when Zan and I did not know the answers to his questions. "Try it again." He would tap the paper in front of us, then walk to our refrigerator in search of leftover cookie dough. "Come on," he would say if we got the answer wrong again. "Did you take a stupid pill this morning?"

Our parents were at work during the day, so they did not witness the way Bill acted when Zan and I didn't understand something. Though his comments were inappropriate, I liked to believe his tactics were rooted in tough love. At least he did not speak to us like children. I told myself Bill understood our strength and was only frustrated by our current show of weakness. Because there was a certain power in the fact that our surgeries had stretched our bodies and minds to their limits. And Bill knew death. He'd lost his wife years before, and like me, his sadness was cloaked in anger. He understood how harsh the world could be and wanted to toughen us up. As he always liked to tell us, "You need to develop thicker skin, girls. The world will eat you alive just to spit you back out if you let it."

Dealing with Bill was better than the alternative. The way he treated us was nothing compared to the abuse of our peers at school. Even on Bill's worst days, Zan and I had fun staying home together. When we weren't doing homework, we marathoned movies and television shows. As the holidays approached, we spent hours decorating the inside of the house with Christmas lights and garlands. When it was just the two of us together, there was no beauty or ugliness. There was no pressure to conform. We were ourselves and that was beauty enough.

When Zan and I returned to school in the middle of January 2006, we made a deal with our parents and the school district. We would attend the local high school part-time and complete the rest of our coursework through Westview, an independent study school in the next town over. This gave us time to attend doctor appointments and schedule surgeries so we could continue correcting our faces—putting ourselves back together one piece at a time.

———

Our high school had been under construction while Zan and I were under the knife. The campus was getting a new library and cafeteria. On our first day back at school for our second semester of ninth grade, entire areas were blocked off to make room for the new additions. I was relieved to find that the original library—the *old* library, as it came to be called—was still standing.

The old library was a dimly lit room with rows of outdated books and computers. It was small and uninviting, but I liked to spend the first few minutes of my lunch period looking through the books on the shelves because it was easier to keep my nose buried in a book than to try to make conversation. It was here that I found a copy of Françoise Gilot's 1964 memoir *Life with Picasso*. It was sitting on a table near a stack of papers next to the printer. I picked it up and examined the front and back cover, but there were no library stickers or bar codes on it anywhere. I opened the book and turned to the front page, but again there was nothing tying it to the school or the library. Secured to the inside cover, students could always find worn and yellowed book due date slips with unfamiliar names scribbled next to dates ranging from the early 1990s to the 2000s. On the first blank page, librarians marked books with a stamp that read PROPERTY OF REDWOOD CREEK HIGH SCHOOL. When this book did not have any of these markings, I decided someone had probably left it behind.

I put the book back down on the table and looked around the room to see if there was anyone there it could belong to. Aside from the librarians at the desk and the four or five students working together at a study table, the room was empty. I could have brought the book to the circulation desk to find out whose it was and where it came from, but I knew not to ask questions I did not want answers to.

It had been years since I'd found the article that said Zan and I resembled Picasso paintings. Finding the book felt like fate. I wanted to know how disfigured faces in Picasso's paintings could be viewed and valued for being different in their beauty, while those of us living with actual disfigurements were still treated as subhuman. I told myself that Françoise Gilot's memoir held the answers I needed. By reading the story of someone who had once been close to Picasso, I could better understand the artist himself. I looked around once more. Then I tucked the book into my backpack and made my way to the exit.

I did not look at it until I got home from school. Then I read far enough to learn that the author was a French painter and writer who met Picasso in 1943. She was just twenty-one years old at the time, and Picasso was in his sixties. Françoise was Picasso's muse for several portraits. They stayed together for a decade and had two children.

I continued skimming through the chapters until I reached a section on cubism. In her book, Françoise Gilot said Picasso once explained cubism by differentiating between a bowl that was painted and a real physical object. "When the Cubist painter said to himself, 'I will paint a bowl,' he set out to do it with the full realization that a bowl in painting has nothing to do with a bowl in real life," she wrote.

I was struck by Picasso's explanation of cubism and wrote about it in my journal. The analysis did not sit well with me, because it ignored the very real existence of individuals with disfigured faces both in life and on the canvas. To say that cubism did not reflect reality or real life or real people meant erasing people with faces like mine. To paint a beautiful woman as though she was disfigured and say it had nothing to do with those of us who were actually disfigured felt ignorant and cold. Picasso, I wrote, was just like kids who tormented me in school. I was sure of it. To people like Picasso, those with faces like mine did not exist unless it served them or their work.

I did not think about the book again until the next morning in Ms. Gilbert's English class, where in addition to reading works by Shakespeare for the main course curriculum, we had to read a handful of books independently and write about them. For these assignments, we were allowed to read whatever we wanted so long as Ms. Gilbert approved our selection. Some days, she gave us time to read from our books in class.

"Go ahead and get out your materials," she told us. "You have fifteen minutes." Students chatted with each other as they unzipped their bags and removed their books. I'd decided the week before that I would read *Normal Girl* by Molly Jong-Fast, about an "It girl" who longed for normalcy. It was on a list of books Ms. Gilbert had recommended, so I chose it based on the title alone. My parents bought a copy of it from a bookstore that weekend, but after reading the first several chapters of *Life with Picasso* instead, I accidentally left the book I'd been supposed to be reading on the desk in my bedroom.

"Do you have an extra book with you?" I leaned over and asked my friend Savannah. "I forgot mine."

"I don't, sorry," she said.

"It's okay." I pulled my backpack onto my lap and pretended to rummage through it in search of the book I knew I'd forgotten to bring.

I considered pulling out *Life with Picasso* but hesitated. *What if it belongs to someone in this room?* I thought. *What if they know I took it and they tell on me?* I could feel my breathing quicken and my heart race. Even the palms of my hands started to dampen with sweat. *Everyone is going to think I'm a thief.*

I was lost in my panic when Ms. Gilbert told everyone to quiet down. "This is a silent *solo* activity," she told us, "so I'm not sure why you are all talking right now." She scanned the room to make sure everyone was on task.

I could feel her lingering stare, so I grabbed the stolen book from my bag and slapped it onto the desk in front of me, quickly opening it to where I'd left off, before my teacher or anyone else could get a view of the cover. The edges of the book were soft and the corners of the pages were folded in several areas.

Fifteen minutes turned to twenty-five, as Ms. Gilbert lost track of time. I did not mind, though. I quickly skimmed the pages of Françoise Gilot's memoir, trying to inhale as much of her story and Picasso's history as I could. Much of what I read felt confusing and unfamiliar, but each time I found a paragraph I liked, I read it two or three times until I could make sense of what it was saying.

Cubism, I learned, grew out of Picasso's fear of people who were different, people who looked like Zan and me. Picasso once told Françoise Gilot that when he was a child, he dreamt his limbs grew to be huge and shrank until they were small again. "And all around me, in my dream, I saw other people going through the same transformations, getting huge or very tiny. I felt terribly anguished every time I dreamed about that,"[5] he explained. After this, Françoise understood more of Picasso's work. "They had started through the recollection of those dreams and been carried on as a means of breaking the

---

5   Gilot, *Life with Picasso*, p. 111.

monotony of classical body forms,"[6] she wrote. This again made it sound like people who looked like this did not exist in real life—like disfigurement had been made in *his* image instead of God's or nature's. Once again, people who looked different were not the norm, but something abnormal, something to be feared—something from a nightmare.

Picasso's use of disfigurement spoke to how society viewed faces that were asymmetrical and different. "When I paint, I always try to give an image people are not expecting and, beyond that, one they reject. That's what interests me. It's in this sense that I mean I always try to be subversive. That is, I give a man an image of himself whose elements are collected from among the usual way of seeing things in traditional painting and then reassembled in a fashion that is unexpected and disturbing enough to make it impossible for him to escape the questions it raises."[7]

When I got to the part of Françoise's memoir where she wrote of meeting Picasso and seeing portraits he had done of his mistress Dora Maar, I thought of Ms. J. *He wasn't known for being the nicest to women*, I remembered her telling me.

Françoise described the work as being tortured and said it was meant to be more a symbol of tragedy than a simple disfigurement.

---

6   Gilot, *Life with Picasso*, p. 111.
7   Gilot, *Life with Picasso*, p. 64.

Though I did not know it then, my reading that morning forever shaped my views of Picasso and his artwork, because it validated what I'd felt all along. My reading confirmed my belief that being compared to Picasso was not, nor would it ever be, a compliment. For me, Picasso's cubism was not revolutionary. Picasso was not a visionary. He took what he wanted from women and cultures and people with disfigurements and tried to make them his own. He exploited the most vulnerable and portrayed them as "other."[8]

I did not listen to a word Ms. Gilbert said after reading time ended. I was still unpacking all I had read of Picasso's and Françoise's lives. This and the guilt of taking the book from the library hung over me for the rest of the morning. Though nobody in Ms. Gilbert's class called me out on it, I told myself it was only a matter of time. So when the bell rang for lunch that afternoon, I walked straight to the library. I smiled at the librarian behind the desk and pretended to busy myself on one of the computers. When the librarian was out of sight, I unzipped my backpack and removed the copy of *Life with Picasso* I'd taken the day before. When I was sure nobody was looking, I placed it back on the table where I'd found it. Then I closed my backpack and rushed to the door before anyone could question me.

---

8   Picasso's early experimentation with cubism was also inspired by his appropriation of African tribal masks.

I got my braces removed that spring. They'd been put on just after we discovered the tooth in my nose, so by the time they were removed, I'd had them for seven years—nearly half my life. Dr. Zimmerman was as ready to be done as I was. When braces were removed, every patient got balloons and a treat bag to celebrate the transition. Pictures were taken and a Polaroid was added to the wall of smiles at the back of the office. When my braces came off, I did not get balloons, a treat bag, or a photo with a perfect smile. Instead, I went back to having a flipper and no front teeth.

Having front teeth on a retainer was less amusing as a teenager. As a child, it was odd but acceptable. As a teenager, it just made me seem strange. It didn't help that anytime I ate food, I had to remove my retainer and my teeth. I would try to be subtle by holding a napkin in front of my mouth while I did it, but at lunch, people tended to notice when my teeth were there one minute and gone the next.

One afternoon, I called Dad from the Starbucks next to the high school and asked him to pick me up early. I'd been having a hard day, so I snuck off campus. While I waited for him, I bought a croissant and ate in the car on the way home.

"I'm going to fill up the tank while we're out," he told me, as he pulled into a gas station. I finished my food while he hooked the pump to the car. When he was done, he collected the trash that had accumulated in the center console and tossed it into the garbage bin. It wasn't until we were almost home that I realized my retainer was among the items he'd thrown away.

"It's gone!" I shrieked as I felt around the floor of the car and looked in each of the cup holders. "My teeth are gone!" I ran my tongue across the gums in the front of my mouth in panic.

"You put it in a napkin again, didn't you?" I could tell my dad was trying not to be annoyed, but he was.

When we got back to the gas station, I watched as he reached his hand into the trash and dug around to retrieve my retainer. I gagged at just the thought of it. I could not fathom the idea of putting something so filthy back into my mouth, but I also could not let more people realize my secret—that unlike most other teenagers, I did not have front teeth. When we got home, I called Mom and told her what happened and how Dad saved the day. That afternoon, she arranged for me to begin the dental implant process.

Conforming to the world around me felt like my only hope of survival. I was grateful for the surgery on my nose and I looked forward to getting dental implants, but what I most wanted corrected were my eyes. Not a day went by that I did not pray, asking God to give me eyes that were symmetrical— eyes that did not angle downward so drastically. In December 2006, after years of asking Dr. York to make them look like everyone else's, he thought he'd found a way. The plan was to surgically lift the outer corners of our eyelids to give the illusion that they were in the correct place on our faces.

"If this for some reason does not work, we could try a more invasive approach," Dr. York told me at our following appointment. He lifted my cheeks up toward my eyes with his hands. "But let's cross that bridge when—*if*—we come to it."

I was a Picasso painting in reverse.

TWENTY-FOUR

My feelings about surgery contradicted my intense desire to be beautiful; I hated the procedures but I wanted the results. Each operation made me believe I was being remade—reborn— into the ideal me, the person I was always meant to be. The more surgery I had, the more I wanted. It was like I believed that beneath the layers of who I was lived a beautiful woman who just needed to be carved out.

In early December 2006, the week before the procedure to straighten our eyes, I informed my teachers that I would have to miss school for the operation and recovery. "I'm not sure when I'll be back," I told my sophomore art teacher, Mr. T. "But someone from the school district will be in touch with you, so that I can keep up with all my assignments."

Mr. T was a small man with dark hair, glasses, and a playful sense of humor. He was kind and funny, and often joked with the class by singing pop songs to get everyone's attention.

"Is everything okay?" Mr. T asked.

"Oh yeah," I said casually. "They're going to straighten my eyes. Well, that's the plan, anyway." It felt good to say it out loud. To tell a teacher what was going on and share my excitement without fear of some strange reaction.

Mr. T wished me well and said he would send home the work I'd need to complete while I was gone. "Take your time, though," he told me. "Just focus on feeling better."

I appreciated his kindness.

The night before the operation, Zan and I sat on the floor of her bedroom with a mirror and took turns imagining what our eyes would look like. Nina and Victoria came by later that evening with a plate of congratulatory cookies and a card. Though they didn't think we needed to change ourselves, they understood what the surgery meant to us. It was the operation we had always dreamed of.

———

Fixing our eyes was supposed to be a simple outpatient procedure. Zan and I were scheduled to have it on the same day, just hours apart. I went first. Checking in for surgery, trading my clothes for a hospital gown, and moving onto the operating table felt less terrifying than all our surgeries before. Zan and I were too excited about what we were going to look like when we woke up to think about what could go wrong.

Marissa met Mom and Zan at the hospital while I was in surgery. While my operation was underway, the nurses prepped Zan. She had just taken the preoperative sedative and climbed onto the gurney when Dr. York returned to tell her that he could not move forward with her surgery. Mine had not gone well, he told them. He'd had to stop midway through the procedure because my body was not responding as he'd hoped. There was too much scar tissue preventing him from lifting the outer corners of my eyelids as he had planned. Every alternative he tried either lifted my bottom eyelid so much it obstructed my vision, or simply would not hold.

At first, Zan was worried about me. Her disappointment turned to anger as she listened to Dr. York explain there was nothing else he could do. Officially out of options, we had gotten our hopes up for nothing.

Marissa and Mom sat together with Zan while she cried tears of hopeless frustration. They waited with her while the medicine wore off, then helped her change back into her normal clothes. After, Marissa took Zan out to lunch while Mom stayed with me in the recovery unit.

When I woke up a few hours later, my eyes were swollen and sore. When my eyelids flickered open, my vision was blurred by an object too close to make out. Mom caught me as I lifted my hands to my face. She stopped me before I could touch my eyes.

"There is something there," I told her. "There is something in my eyes."

"They're stitches, baby. Don't touch them."

"Oh, that is so gross," I whined. "Did the surgery go okay? Are my eyes straight?"

Mom paused, not knowing how to break the news. I'd been expecting my eyes to be swollen shut, so I should have known something was off.

"They couldn't do it, Bella."

I cried before Mom even finished her sentence.

"I know. I know. I'm so sorry. He tried, baby. He really tried." Mom gently wiped my bloodstained tears with a thick cloth.

"Where is Zan?" I asked. "Is she okay? Did it work on her?"

"No. They didn't do it. Marissa took her home."

I thought my sister was perfect as she was. I did not think she needed to change a thing about herself, but I understood her desire and she understood mine. Zan and I already had such little hope that things would get better, but now the bit we had been clinging to was gone. I cried to myself until the nurse came to take my vitals and remove my IV, until it was time for me to be discharged, to return to life as it was before. I was angry that the operation hadn't worked and even angrier for allowing myself to believe that it would.

After the operation failed, Dr. York's inability to fix my eyes, to meet my expectations, felt like betrayal. At our follow-up appointment a few days after surgery, Dr. York told us again that he had done as much as he could to help us, but that his hands were tied. "The technology is always changing," he told us. "We can revisit this in the future, but right now, there's not much else I can do." I'd had so much faith in his ability to change me, but I left all that remained of it in the operating room that day.

Our relationship with Dr. York changed after that. To him, we probably seemed ungrateful. After all he had done for us, after all we had been through together, Dr. York felt like family. I loved him. I trusted him. I was so consumed by my own hopelessness, I could not see things from his perspective. We'd lost so many years to surgeries and so much time to our perceived ugliness, and for what? I would never know what it was like to have a face society did not deem unacceptable.

In the days following the appointment, the swelling in my eyes increased so much, it was hard to close my eyelids. As the skin expanded, the stitches held my eyelids together and prevented them from being stuck open. It was physically painful and emotionally exhausting, and I was glad Zan did not end up having to experience the recovery too. She started to agree when later that week she found me with blood dripping from my eyes as I rested in our parents' room.

"Can you help her?" Zan cried as she woke Mom, who was asleep in bed next to me.

"She's fine. She's fine. It's just drainage," Mom assured her.

"It looked like you were dead," Zan told me later.

———

During our junior year of high school, Zan stopped going to school altogether. She'd had surgery to reattach a chain to her tooth in order to move it to where it needed to be. When it was clear the procedure was not working as planned, Mom gave the okay for Dr. Long to do whatever he felt was necessary. He pulled the tooth out for good and moved the rest of her teeth over in order to hide the gap.

Marissa had plans to move to New York the same week Zan returned home from the hospital in October 2007. Her boyfriend David had been accepted to the business program at Columbia University, and he asked her to go with him. Marissa's job had an office in New York, and she requested a transfer so they could be together.

Zan knew when she left the hospital after her operation that her body was not ready yet, but she could not tolerate the feeling of the IVs in her arms anymore, so she convinced the nurses she was okay to leave. Our family knew it was a mistake, too. She could not even swallow sips of water on her own. She was in so much pain, and there was nothing we could do but listen to her agonizing cries.

"We should never have brought her home," Marissa told Mom between tears, but Zan refused to go back to the hospital.

For Zan and me, recovery at home had always been painful but never scary. Being able to leave the hospital meant we were out of the woods, that we just needed to give our bodies time to heal and adjust. Before this, I had never been so afraid that Zan would go to sleep and never wake up.

Still on painkillers, Zan struggled to adjust to the changes that had been made in her mouth and at home. She was heartbroken at the thought of Marissa leaving. "Please don't go," she begged our sister. "Please don't leave." Had Zan not been on medication, I doubt she would have asked Marissa to stay.

Neither of us wanted her to move, but we understood our sister had her own life to live.

The night before her flight, Marissa sat on the floor of her old bedroom and contemplated staying. "I'm not going," she told Mom, who was adamant that Marissa not alter any of her plans.

My parents knew she had a life waiting for her on the other side of the country and told her she could not put her life on hold for Zan and me.

"I don't know what to do," she said, as she buried her hands in her face.

"It's okay, Riss." I sat down on the floor next to her and draped my arms around her shoulders. "Zan is going to be okay. And we will visit you as soon as she heals."

She cried while she sorted through more of her belongings to decide what to bring and what to leave behind. The next day, Mom made sure Marissa got on the plane.

"I've got it from here," Mom told her. "Now go to New York."

After Marissa left, I'd wake up to find Zan sitting on the edge of my bed, watching me as I slept. We'd been sleeping in separate rooms while Zan recovered.

"What are you doing, sis?" she would say, smiling. The glow from the clock on the nightstand would illuminate the room just enough to make out her expression.

"Are you okay?"

"I can't sleep," Zan would say.

"Did you try?" I'd pull back the comforter and scoot over to offer her a place to lie down, but she did not want it.

"I'm not tired," she would tell me. I didn't understand how that was possible, because she never seemed to sleep.

"You should lie down, sis." Whenever I told Zan I was worried, her demeanor would shift.

"I'm sorry. You're right. I'll go get in bed right now."

It was usually after three o'clock in the morning when Zan would leave my room to head to sleep, but Dad would find her hours later sitting in the darkness of the living room, staring at a television that had not even been turned on. At night, I started sleeping on the edge of the twin-size bed in her room. I would spend hours in that zone between being asleep and being awake, forcing myself up every hour to make sure she was still there next to me. When she used the bathroom, I waited outside the door. When she ate or drank or watched reruns of shows on the television downstairs, I stayed with her. Some days she hated me for it. Other days, she was thankful. The failed operation felt like the loss of every dream we'd ever had. My sister needed to grieve. And so did I.

In the three years since middle school, I gained back the weight I'd lost when my mouth was wired shut and then some. At only five feet, I weighed 170 pounds; my chin was like a fold that morphed into my neck. I'd thought that once the downward tilt of my eyelids had been straightened, my chin would be the last thing to need tweaking. In the months leading up to the operation to straighten my eyes, I'd begged my parents to schedule the chin augmentation, too. I wanted a date on the calendar, an end in sight. I told them I would happily deal with the pain of the final surgeries if it meant seeing the results I wanted. But after the disappointment of the failed eye surgery and witnessing the emotional effect of Zan's oral surgery complications, I decided I no longer wanted surgery—not on my eyes, not on my chin, not anywhere. I didn't want to go through surgery and recovery, only to wake up and discover it had not worked, that I was still me.

TWENTY-FIVE

Surgery hurt but high school was hell. I was jealous of Zan after the operation on her mouth, because Mom stopped making her attend classes there. Instead, she became a full-time student at Westview. When not on medical leave, I only ever took one or two courses at Westview, but Zan begged Mom to let her attend full-time, and after enough pleading, she caved. I'd run the idea by my parents that summer, but my dad told me I had to continue taking most of my classes at the public high school, because it was important to keep structure and stick to a routine. My dad thought if I stopped attending public school, I'd become a recluse and slowly lose my mind.

"Having that social aspect is good for you," he told me.

Dad would not budge on his decision to make Zan and me continue traditional education, so Mom did not tell him when she pulled Zan out of school for good.

"Is he going to be upset?" Zan asked.

"You let me worry about that," Mom told her.

He didn't discover the arrangement until weeks later, when

he came home from work unexpectedly and found Zan listening to music on the third floor.

"What are you doing home?" he asked. "Did you leave early?"

Zan froze in panic, unsure whether to admit to getting caught or lie to keep the plan in place.

I'd carpooled to school with Nina that morning but cut my second-period class and waited at the bus stop across the street instead. When I got home, I found Zan and our father sitting together in the kitchen. I panicked.

"It's okay," Zan said, waving me inside. "He already knows."

I slowly tiptoed into the kitchen and smiled at him.

"Are you serious?" Dad said when he saw me. He shook his head and laughed to himself. Had he understood the magnitude of our struggles, I think he would have been supportive of our desire to pursue a nontraditional education. He genuinely believed that by keeping us enrolled in school, we would have a reason to get up and out of the house every day. We would have friends to lean on and something besides our pain to focus on.

Once he understood why we didn't want to go back, he supported Zan's desire to switch high schools and my desire to take fewer classes there. By spring, I was taking only two classes at school and was home before noon every day.

———

Victoria was envious of our nontraditional school schedule. She was thirteen and in eighth grade at the same middle school Zan and I had attended years earlier. One afternoon, after leaving school early, she came over crying. In front of the entire class, a boy had told her to "lay off the Twinkies" when she accidentally sat down on a broken chair in science class.

"The whole thing collapsed to the floor," she wailed.

Zan and I comforted her while she told us how the other girls in her class, the ones she'd been friends with, laughed at her. I thought of Picasso again, and of the pressure to be beautiful that followed girls and women at every age.

Victoria had always had many friends, but when she reached middle school, she found that suddenly, all anyone cared about was being cool. She tried to fit in, but like Zan and me, there was a part of her that always felt like she was on the outside.

That Halloween, determined to shed her new "Twinkie" nickname, Victoria went trick-or-treating with a large group of kids from school. It was the popular crowd, and Victoria wanted to make a good impression, so Zan and I pulled items from our closet and helped her get ready. Victoria and her friends spent the evening going door to door in Blackhawk, an upscale community near Danville. The year before, rumors had spread that instead of candy, families were passing out iPods. This year, instead of electronics, one of the houses in the neighborhood had shots of alcohol on a tray on the porch; candy for the children, vodka for the parents. Victoria's group took turns downing alcohol, but Victoria opted out. Instead, she walked back to her friend's house, called her dad, and went home. Our friendship showed me that even girls without disfigured faces felt pressure to look and act and *be* a certain way.

Victoria's struggles in middle school reminded me of my own. The idea of anyone else experiencing what Zan and I had made me want to scream. But it also made me want to do something, anything, to help break the cycle of abuse teenagers upheld. After Victoria told me about the incident on Halloween and the comments people made about her weight, I decided to reach out to the middle school and offer to start a mentoring program for girls. It would be a chance to bring them together to discuss things besides each other, I thought. I had no idea how to run a mentorship program, but I found a program called Girl Talk, a nonprofit organization with peer mentoring programs for young women all across the country. Much of the curriculum was already made and offered the kind of structure I needed to get started.

That fall, I sent an email to the guidance counselor, Mrs. Hardy.

I'm not sure if you remember me, I wrote, *but I was hoping to talk to you about the possibility of starting an after-school mentoring program for girls in grades 6-8.*

She responded quickly and asked me to come in to discuss my ideas with her and the principal—still Mr. Tomlinson—the following week.

The morning of my meeting at the middle school, I regretted my decision. *What was I thinking?* My anxiety sat with me the entire way there and worsened when I arrived. After parking in the front lot, I stared at the school for several minutes. Everything looked exactly the same. Inside, the office was as I remembered it. I greeted the woman at the desk and sat down in one of the chairs by the door.

"We're just getting organized," Mr. Tomlinson said, sticking his head out of his office. "We'll be with you in just a moment."

I smiled politely. "Take your time." The last time I'd seen his office, my father had practically yelled at him.

As I waited for Mr. Tomlinson, I saw the one person I'd hoped I wouldn't run into: Mr. Jennings. When our eyes met, I did not smile or look away and neither did he. Looking away would have made him feel as though he had won, as though he still, after all this time, held some sort of power. Like all those years before, I held his gaze unapologetically.

"All right, Ariel. We are ready for you," Mrs. Hardy called cheerfully. As I stood and walked toward her, she put out her arms for a hug. "It's so great to see you."

Well, this is going better than I thought.

Inside Mr. Tomlinson's office, the three of us sat at a round table in the corner. I told them about my plan, about how I hoped to hold hour-long meetings once a week after school. "As you may remember, I did not have the easiest time in middle school," I explained. "My goal here is just to create the kind of space I wished I'd had."

They nodded sympathetically.

"We'll talk about issues facing women and girls, things like bullying and body image," I explained. "And once a month, I'd love to hold a fundraiser to raise money for whatever cause the girls are interested in that month. We can do local charities to start off and then widen our net." I handed them each a sample meeting itinerary and program to review.

"This all looks very promising," Mr. Tomlinson told me. "How will you recruit the girls?"

I removed a stack of flyers from my bag. "Is it okay if I hang these up?" He reviewed them and gave me his approval. "Can you also include a memo in the weekly email newsletter?" I asked Mrs. Hardy. She agreed.

At our first meeting two weeks later, there were eight girls in attendance, including Victoria. We gathered around the table in the conference room and took turns introducing ourselves. Since it was my first time meeting most of them, I kept my expectations low. I was pleased when they quickly began opening up to one another. We spent that hour talking about the pressures we felt as young women. We talked about weight and the hair on our heads and on our bodies. We discussed whether or not it was "cool" to wear glasses, and how the standards of beauty always seemed to be changing. We ended the meeting by writing and decorating cards for hospice patients at a nearby medical center. Focusing on the bigger picture—that beauty was subjective and life was temporary—was a reminder for myself that regardless of what I looked like, being alive was a privilege.

When our meeting ended that evening, I met Zan and my parents for dinner at our town's only Mexican restaurant.

"You remembered to cancel my chin surgery, right, Mom?" I asked as I flipped through the menu. The chin augmentation had been scheduled for months, but I assumed that after telling her I'd changed my mind and no longer wanted to have it, she had relayed the message to the hospital.

"No." Mom paused. "Everything has been scheduled for months."

"Well, I changed my mind," I said. My tone was sharp and aggressive.

"I really think after you have it you're going to feel better," she told me. "You are so angry all the time." She thought that by changing my face once more, I'd finally be happier. She thought it would help me to feel better about myself. But it was no longer just my body I was angry about. It was the fact that to everyone around me, I was simultaneously too much and yet not enough.

My dad reached his hand into the chip basket and offered me a concession. "After you recover, we can get you a new Toyota or Honda or whatever you want," he told me.

"I don't want a car and I don't want the surgery." I sat back in my chair and folded my arms across my chest. *What will I tell the girls about my surgery?* I wondered. My father had thought making me go to school full-time would give me something to focus on besides my own pain, but it was staying home and getting involved with Girl Talk that ended up being my saving grace. Meeting with them to talk about self-esteem and building each other up gave me a sense of purpose but made me feel like a fraud. How could I tell other girls to accept themselves and their bodies when I hated mine?

—

Dr. York was the one who had suggested the chin augmentation, but it was Dr. Long who performed it. Had I voiced an ounce of hesitation, Dr. Long would have stopped the operation immediately, but I kept my feelings to myself. Once I was sedated, he made an incision inside my mouth along the bottom of my gums and inserted a silicone implant. It was supposed to be an outpatient procedure, but my entire face swelled up like an allergic reaction. I was kept overnight for observation to make sure my airway was not obstructed.

Zan, Nina, and Victoria were at the house waiting for me when I returned from the hospital the next afternoon. When they saw me, they burst out laughing at my temporarily altered appearance. When I looked in a mirror to see what they saw, I laughed, too. Most of the swelling was down within a month, but the stitches lingered. For weeks I could feel each individual piece of thread in the front of my mouth. Whenever I was bored, I moved my tongue to the fold at the bottom of my gums and felt the weblike pattern the scar tissue had formed. When the swelling disappeared completely, I was pleased with the surgery's overall results. I refused to admit it to my parents, but I was grateful they'd made me get the operation. My new chin gave shape to my jawline and eliminated the excess fat underneath it. I went from having a double chin to a thin, angled jaw. The bottom half of my face was beautiful.

When it came to my mental health during recovery, it did not matter that I liked the change in my appearance. I was driven and ambitious, and always focused on achieving my next goal. But my days spent at home recovering allowed for few diversions. I was forced to lie there and think about my appearance and my surgeries. Without the distraction of working toward something, my recovery was marked by an overwhelming depression. I spent the afternoons in my family's library—a small room in the front of our house with a desk, chair, and stacks of books as high as my waistline. I wore the same pajamas—plaid blue pants and a yellow T-shirt—for days at a time. Once the facial swelling went down, I got dressed and pulled myself together long enough to return to running weekly Girl Talk meetings. And every week, the girls welcomed me, never once mentioning my altered appearance. As was always the case with my operations, I existed as two people: one who was determined, and well-adjusted, and one who was depressed and in isolation. The more time I spent at home, the harder it was to want to go back to existing in the real world.

When I returned to eleventh grade after weeks of recovering from the chin augmentation, I found myself still stuck in such a deep depression, I rarely spoke. I did not know what to talk to people about anymore. Other kids my age were worried about their grades and going to a good college. They went to parties and got drunk together and had sex for the first time. But me? I was worried about when my next surgery would be and how long the recovery process would take. Nothing about my life was a good conversation starter.

Art was one of the only classes I continued taking on-site at the high school. When I returned after being away, Mr. T was often the only person I spoke to. I think he knew this, because every day, he would come to my desk and check on me. One morning, he walked over to my workstation, where I sat at a tall black table with a metal stool.

"How was your weekend?" I asked him.

"It was really good, actually," he said as he dragged an unused stool toward my table and sat down.

"That's great." I smiled. "Do anything exciting?"

"My wife and I found this really neat antique store," he told me.

"I love antique stores," I told him. "Everything has a story."

"Yeah, but I will admit they always make me feel gross." Mr. T smiled at his own comment, but I didn't get it. "I love digging for items, but the dust and the dirt." He shuddered. "Makes me want to go home and immediately take a shower."

I laughed and told him I knew exactly what he meant. "Find anything cool?"

"Oh, that's what I was going to tell you." Mr. T put one finger in the air, as though he'd just flicked the switch to his memory. "Do you know what your name means?"

"The meaning of *my* name?" I shook my head no.

"My wife and I found this super-neat book," he said. "It was old, very vintage-y looking, and of course like everything else in that store, super dusty."

I smiled and nodded along again.

"Well, we were flipping through it and discovered it was an old anthology of names, their origins, and their meanings."

"That's really cool," I said.

"As my wife and I were flipping through the pages," Mr. T continued, "I thought of you. Your name is unique and not one I hear often, so I was curious what it meant." He paused.

"Yeah, I've never really thought about it," I told him, "but now I'm curious."

"Ariel means Lion of God," Mr. T explained. "It's a Hebrew name."

I smiled. "I really like that."

"I thought you would. I was telling my wife about you, and when we saw the meaning, she was like, 'You have to share this with her!'"

Mr. T could see in my face that his comments sparked something in me. "I just thought you should know that," he said as he stood up. "I think it fits." He knocked on the table with his fists and wandered away to check on the other students.

I spent the rest of the morning thinking about his comment. Symbolically, lions are known for two things: their brutality and their bravery. It was like I'd suddenly been reminded of my strength and the fact that high school was temporary. Though things were hard at that moment, they wouldn't be forever.

TWENTY-SIX

I always knew I would go to college. It was expected. Never even an option, really. My parents' lack of higher education made them want more for their children. They always said that if Zan and I could get into college, they would figure out a way to pay for it. But by the end of high school, I rarely went to school anymore. I had already dropped down to part-time, but even that felt unmanageable.

Zan and I never gave much consideration to where or what we would study. We had so much going on, it wasn't our priority. All I knew was that I wanted to go somewhere far away from the town I grew up in. For me, college meant starting over. It meant a chance to be whoever I wanted to be. My classmates had seen too much. I wanted to go somewhere new, somewhere that did not remind me of home or surgeries or the standards of beauty I did not meet. I wanted to go somewhere where I no longer felt limited by the appearance of my face.

At the start of my senior year of high school, in fall 2008, students were told they had to set up an appointment with the guidance counselor to make sure we were on track for graduation and discuss our postgraduation plans. Since I was taking only a couple of classes on campus, I went by the office one morning before heading home.

"Is Mrs. Keene in?" I asked one of the women at the front desk. Mrs. Keene was one of two counselors at the school. She was petite and had hair cut into a bob.

"Do you have an appointment?" The woman at the desk wore glasses that sat on the tip of her nose and did not look up from her computer when she spoke.

"I don't," I started to say, when Mrs. Keene poked her head out of her office.

"I thought that voice sounded familiar!" Mrs. Keene smiled and stretched out her arms to give me a hug. "Come on in." She pointed to a chair in the corner of the room and closed the door behind us.

Mrs. Keene's workspace was tidy and organized, with everything always in its designated place. Looking at her, this did not surprise me. She was always put together. Her office, her demeanor, even her physical appearance. She was in her fifties and did not have a single wrinkle in her forehead. Her lips were full and her eyebrows were lifted to maintain a perfect arch. I had to find the humor in the fact that I'd had more plastic surgery in my seventeen years than she'd had in her entire life, but she still looked more fabulous than I ever would.

"What can I do for you?" Mrs. Keene asked me.

When I told her I was there to check in and make sure there

was nothing else I needed to do before graduation, she thanked me for being so on top of my academics and assured me I was on track. "I was also wondering if you could maybe write me a letter of recommendation for college," I said nervously.

"I can double-check the requirements," Mrs. Keene told me, "but I don't think you really need a letter of recommendation for a junior college."

"Oh." I paused, confused by how surprised she seemed at my request. "I'm actually not really thinking of a junior college," I explained. "There's nothing wrong with them, I've just been planning to go straight to a four-year school."

"Let's take a look here." Mrs. Keene pursed her lips as she pulled up my transcript on her screen. "I'm not sure that's the best idea."

"What do you mean?"

"I'm not sure where you would get in." Mrs. Keene was still staring at her computer, scrolling through my transcript. "I think your best bet is to go to a two-year school and transfer."

I stared ahead, trying to think of how to respond. I knew she was only being honest, but I had asked for her support, not her opinion.

"I just don't want you to get disappointed, sweetheart," she told me. But the only thing I found disappointing was her lack of faith in my ability to succeed. I left her office torn between accepting that she was right and wanting to prove her wrong.

Zan and I were still attending Westview School. Since the curriculum used an independent study model, we would meet with
our teacher, George Davis, once a week. Mr. Davis was a small,
gray-haired man who Zan and I quickly grew to love. He only
had two other students besides Zan and me, so he got to know
us in a way most of our other teachers had not. Every week, we
met with him to turn in our homework and take exams. We
would spend our hour taking turns interrupting the curriculum
to share stories and tell jokes.

Mr. Davis was in his sixties and had spent most of his career
working as a guidance counselor before retiring and deciding to
teach instead.

"Have you started thinking about college?" he asked me
that September.

"I'm not sure," I told him. "I don't think so. I don't really
think I will get in."

Mr. Davis looked more offended than surprised. "But you
have so much to offer," he assured me. When I told him about
what Mrs. Keene had said, he told me he would write me a
letter of recommendation instead.

That October, he asked for a list of the schools I planned
to apply to.

"I don't know where to apply," I admitted. Since my parents
had not attended college, the entire process baffled me.

"Next week, there's a college fair happening at the high
school next door," Mr. Davis told Zan and me. "Representatives

from institutions all over the country will be there to give information to prospective students."

"Are we allowed to go if we're not students there?" Zan asked.

"Absolutely," Mr. Davis assured us. "It's open to the public."

The following week, my parents, Zan, and I piled into the car and headed to Westview. Mr. Davis met us out front and walked us over to the auditorium of the high school and showed us how it worked. Once we got the hang of it, he left us to look around.

Zan and I collected information from dozens of colleges. We talked to representatives from schools that were public and private, secular and non-secular, in-state and out of state. Though the college fair introduced me to schools I would not have otherwise known about, I still was not sure what I was looking for or what I wanted to study. I clung to Mrs. Keene's words and assumed I would not be accepted anywhere I applied, but I applied nonetheless. I began listing the University of every state and looking at the pictures of each school online. If the campus seemed picturesque and the town was somewhere I could see myself being happy, I decided I would apply. After I narrowed my list down to just over a dozen schools, I signed up to take the SAT and ACT.

My GPA was average and my test scores were okay, but I hoped the admissions office would take my individual circumstances into account. In my personal essay, I explained what high school had been like for me and what I'd learned from balancing my education and life while in and out of the hospital. I wrote about Girl Talk and how during my time at home, when I was done recovering physically but not mentally ready to go back to school, I would work with the girls to organize volunteer efforts throughout the community. We collected Halloween costumes for children who were otherwise unable to afford them. We held bake sales benefiting local animal rescue organizations. We even collected pencils and school supplies for schools in underfunded districts. I wrote about how helping others gave me something to do and allowed me to place my purpose in something outside of myself.

Dad wanted Zan and me to stay close to home for college. "Why don't you guys apply to some of the schools around here?" he asked us over dinner. "Berkeley has so many great programs." He had not had a home without kids in it for thirty years, and the thought of an empty nest broke his heart.

I nodded and told him I would look into it.

It was November by the time I went to submit an application. Until then, I hadn't realized the SAT and the SAT subject tests were entirely different exams, and I missed the deadline. When Dad asked me about it later, I told him I had applied to state schools instead. He was just happy I was considering staying in California at all.

Despite my father's wishes, I approached college the way I'd approached entering kindergarten: Wherever I went, I wanted to do it alone, to experience it for myself, away from Zan. I wanted it to be a time when I could focus only on myself. I wanted to be selfish in my healing. We had been through so much together, I needed to know it was possible to do something on my own. When I mentioned to Zan that I thought we should go our separate ways for college, she seemed taken aback. "Fine, I don't want to go to college with you anyway," she told me.

We still applied to many of the same schools: University of Maine, University of Connecticut, Gonzaga University, University of Oregon, and a handful of state schools in California. We each had a school that was off-limits to each other—one we promised each other we would not apply to. It guaranteed us the opportunity to go somewhere on our own if we wanted. For me, this was the University of Vermont, a medium-size public school in Burlington. For Zan, it was University of the Pacific, a small private school in Stockton, California. Zan upheld her end of the agreement, but I did not. She never applied to go to Vermont with me, but just before the deadline, I applied to University of the Pacific. Though it was my idea to go our separate ways, I held on to the possibility of staying together.

I applied to half a dozen schools before I realized I could not afford the cost of attendance. I was used to getting what I wanted. My parents never talked about money, so I had no concept of what things cost and what we could afford. It was 2008, and in the midst of the recession, money was tighter than it had ever been before. My parents wanted to give their children everything we could ever dream of, but with college costing nearly $40,000 per year, I knew it was not feasible. Dad was already putting in extra hours at the office to bid on more jobs, and Mom was working well into the night. I knew they would do their best to honor their agreement to help me pay for college, but with Aaron, Zan, and I all working toward a degree at the same time, I wanted to lessen our financial load.

The next week at school, I popped into Mrs. Keene's office again.

"I was just wondering if you know of any scholarship opportunities, or how I can go about finding them."

"Of course, Miss Ariel," she said. "Come with me."

Mrs. Keene led me to the career center, a room full of tables with study materials and college pennants covering the walls. At the back of the room was a map with pins poked into every state where a graduating senior had decided to attend college. I wondered where my pin would go, where I would end up.

The two women who worked in the center were kind and helpful. They showed me a binder they kept up to date with all the local and national scholarships high school students could apply for. I read through each description and wrote down the details for the ones I qualified for. When I got home that afternoon, I completed an application for each one. I did this every week for months. I went by the office, got the application information for as many scholarships as I could, and immediately applied.

Each application I filled out asked me what I planned to study in college and what my long-term career goals were. I had no idea. I hardly knew anything about college, except that it was my escape from the painful memories I'd spent so many years reliving. I thought about the people who had gotten me through high school, the teachers who had helped me, and how rare it was to find ones who were understanding of what Zan and I had been through. I decided it made sense to go into education. When I wrote this on my scholarship applications, I told them I wanted to be the kind of teacher I had needed when I was young.

When I told Mr. Davis of my new life plan at our next meeting, I half expected him to tell me I was being unrealistic or comment on the irony of someone who hardly went to school becoming a school teacher. He had been nothing but supportive and encouraging the entire time I had known him, but I was used to being told that I did not measure up. I was relieved when he gave me his approval. "I think you will make an excellent educator."

"You really think so?" I asked.

"I really do."

After submitting my application to the University of Vermont in December 2008, I looked at the website and pictures of the campus every day. The brick buildings and beautiful grounds were everything I had imagined for college. Photos of smiling faces hiking the Green Mountains and playing hockey filled the screen. I wanted to be like the students in the pictures. Every time I envisioned my life beyond high school, my mind wandered to thoughts of my family and friends, and the girls from Girl Talk that I got to see every week. On one hand, I told myself I was chasing a version of me, of my life that did not exist. On the other, nothing in my life would change unless I changed it. I could be whoever I wanted to be, I thought. Even a teacher. Mentoring girls on self-acceptance may have made me a hypocrite, but going to college was my attempt at believing I could do anything I set my mind to.

TWENTY-SEVEN

"There's a fifty percent chance of brain damage, blindness, or death," Dr. York told me. My heart sank to my stomach as I sat back in the exam room chair. Two years had passed since the failed eye surgery, but our desire to correct our faces was stronger than ever. After the success of the chin augmentation, I still wanted to correct the one thing that was left: my eyes. Zan and I wanted our eyes straightened and moved closer together before we went off to college in the fall. We thought Dr. York was going to tell us that everything we'd been through, the dozens of surgeries we'd had, was about to finally pay off; that this would be the surgery to end all our surgeries.

This procedure was our last hope. It would tie the outsides of our eyes to our skulls with wire and use fat and tissue grafts to fill our cheekbones, making the bones and the tissue deep within our faces more malleable and easier to move. The procedure was experimental and dangerous, but I no longer feared being cut open, because the nerve endings had long been destroyed. I was already numb in the places where pain had once lived.

Dr. York placed his hand on my chin and tilted my head

upward toward the light, as if to examine his work. "There's really nothing more I can do. Besides, I think you look great."

"No, they don't," Mom practically shouted.

I felt the skin on my face grow warm the moment her words left her mouth, and I lowered my eyes to the floor in shame.

I knew Mom only wanted to protect us; that this was her way of advocating for us. Though she'd never say it, she knew the pain our faces—our perceived *ugliness*—caused. She'd spent years watching the cruelty of the world tear us apart from the inside out. And she saw how the world limited people who were not beautiful like her and my dad and my older siblings. My mom only wanted to protect us. She was doing what we asked. Still, there was a part of me that had wanted her to agree with the doctor, to say that she, too, thought I was beautiful just as I was. I wanted it to be okay to exist *with* my condition. To carry my experiences with me like they were a part of me, without having to be defined by them.

Dr. York continued looking intensely at my face, studying it. As if he was looking for something to trigger a new idea. Still, he did not speak.

"Is there anyone else who can help us?" I finally asked. "I don't need to be beautiful. I just want to be normal."

Dr. York paused and looked down at the floor, before nodding toward my mother, as if to say, *We knew this day would come.* But after her outburst, Mom remained silent. She had always been my biggest advocate—my voice when I didn't have one—but the time had come when the doctors had done all they could. And there was nothing she could say to change that. Dr. York nodded again, this time toward me—an unspoken *I'm sorry*. Then he left the room, closing the door behind him.

After we left Dr. York, we rode the elevator one floor up and decided to see if Dr. Long was available. When we got to his office, the receptionist informed us that he was with another patient.

"Oh, that's okay," my mom said. "We don't have an appointment. We were just downstairs and thought we'd stop in." Before we could leave, the woman asked us for our names.

"I knew you looked familiar," she said. She told us to have a seat and disappeared down the hall. When she came back, she said Dr. Long wanted us to wait.

"He'll be out soon," she said.

The waiting room was filled with warm, neutral colors. On the walls were pieces of artwork Dr. Long's wife had created, and I admired the curves of the lines on each canvas. I traced the images with my eyes to distract myself from the disappointment that still raged inside me.

As we sat there, I closed my eyes and with the tip of my index finger went from mentally outlining the paintings on the wall to tracing the features of my face. I traced the skin around my nose, mouth, and eyes, where surgeons had spent years breaking and re-breaking my bones, using screws and titanium plates to shift my face up, down, and around until I was no longer recognizable. I traced the skin, trying to visualize the details of who I was, to understand the ugliness others saw when they looked at me. But I'd had so many faces, I could no longer remember them all.

Zan, my mom, and I sat in silence, until Dr. Long came walking toward us. He wore a fitted black suit and black shoes the same shade as his hair. When he saw us, he smiled and let out a warm, lengthy "Hello," as if the *o* at the end of his greeting had gotten caught in his throat. He was surprised to see us but pleased all the same. He shook our hands and gave us hugs, before leading us to a small exam room at the other end of the hall.

Once settled in, we told him about the appointment we'd had with Dr. York. We told him of the hope we'd had and the desperation we now felt. We asked him for advice. Surely there was someone else who could help us.

Dr. Long stood with his elbow resting upon the counter in the exam room as we spoke. When we finished, he hesitated. He was sympathetic to our desire to finally shed the emotional weight of having a disfigured face but said that if Dr. York said something was too risky, then perhaps it was. Because even though Dr. Long understood my belief that life would be better once I was beautiful, he was also realistic. He knew all too well the risk associated with what I was asking him to do. There was danger in the kind of beauty I was desperate to achieve.

"Who's to define beauty?" he'd asked me once. "Who says when enough is enough—that it's time to be happy just as you are?"

I never had an answer for him. Enough would be enough when *I* was enough.

Dr. Long opened a drawer behind him. When he turned around, he held a business card in one hand and pushed his glasses up the ridge of his nose with the other. On the back of the card, he'd scribbled a name and telephone number.

"There's a doctor in Paris," he said, handing my mom the information. "Perhaps it would be worth a consultation."

Before we left, Dr. Long encouraged us to listen to what Dr. York said and have patience. The medical field was always evolving, and perhaps years down the line, there would be a less risky procedure that could help us. But I didn't *have* patience, because I was running out of time. I'd spent my entire life waiting to live. After eighteen years—eighteen years of living with a disfigured face—I needed this hope. I needed to believe things could and would get better. That I could go to college and not spend the rest of my life with a face society refused to accept.

Later that night, after we returned home from our appointments in the city, I told Dad that I wanted to go to Paris to have surgery on my eyes. When I told him that I wanted to finally be beautiful, he told me I was selfish. Even at eighteen, Zan and I were his babies. He could not understand our willingness, our *desire*, to undergo a procedure so painful and so risky.

"I feel like I'm dying," I said. "I don't want to hate myself anymore."

Dad was furious at the very thought of the operation, and even more so with Mom for entertaining the idea. But since Zan and I were both eighteen, we no longer needed our parents' approval or consent. We were determined to have the surgery one way or another, and Mom knew this.

"Joe," I heard her say to my dad one night, "this isn't our decision."

Though she was right, he was unable to fathom her willingness to support us. But my mother's involvement wasn't her supporting our desire to have the procedure. It was her way of doing everything she could to help keep us safe. Because like him, she was heartbroken. Like him, she was terrified.

Mom called the medical offices in France the next day. She spoke to Dr. DuBois, the surgeon whose name Dr. Long had written on the business card in his office. The same surgeon who years earlier had trained with Dr. York in craniofacial surgery. Mom spoke to the man and, after much back-and-forth, scheduled a consultation and the surgery. Financially, my family couldn't afford for my dad not to work, so he stayed in California, while Mom, Zan, and I made arrangements to travel abroad.

At the next Girl Talk meeting later that week, I decided not to hide my upcoming operation from the girls. I didn't tell them I was having work done because I hated what I looked like or how risky the procedure was. But I did tell them how the midface surgery I'd had at their age changed what I'd looked like and how I hoped this operation would help me look and feel like myself again—whatever that meant. I wasn't sure how much of my story was appropriate to share with them, so I told them about Crouzon syndrome and some of the surgeries Zan and I had had. I let them ask me questions about my face and my life. I hoped they'd see there was power in raw authenticity. That being our whole selves—showing up and letting people know you, flaws, complications, and all—is courageous.

———

Three weeks later, Mom, Zan, and I boarded a flight to Paris.

TWENTY-EIGHT

The moment the plane landed, I knew I'd made a mistake. There was a knot in my throat and a voice in the back of my mind screaming, *I do not want this*. As I exited the plane, strangers stared at my eyes, commenting on my appearance as I walked by. I didn't know enough French to tell what they were saying, but the body language for *disgust* translates easily.

The stares Zan and I received in Paris were more aggressive and intense than ever before. We were used to children staring and making comments, because they did not know any better. But as we walked through the Charles de Gaulle Airport, it seemed everyone—children and adults alike—took issue with our faces. Entire groups of people stopped to point at us. Some tilted their heads and squinted their eyes as though they were studying our appearance. Others seemed shocked and afraid, disgusted even. We could feel their eyes following our every move, and I wanted to crawl outside of myself.

"What is happening right now?" Zan lowered her head to the floor as we walked, trying to get the people around us to look away.

"I want to go home," I whispered to Zan as we stood at baggage claim. I waited until Mom was pulling a suitcase off the metal carousel to make sure she would not hear me.

"I do, too," Zan said, turning her body away from the people around us. "This was a mistake."

I'd felt it during the plane ride, but the surgery and our faces changing had all been an idea—a fantasy I wasn't sure would ever really happen. None of it felt real until the plane hit the tarmac.

I expected Mom to be upset or at least irritated by my desire to leave Paris the moment we arrived, but she wasn't. "Well, we're already here, so let's meet with the doctor and just see what he has to say." She flung her backpack onto the pile of luggage. "That way you both have all the information before you make a decision. Because once we get on a flight home, we cannot afford to come back again if you change your mind."

Zan and I nodded. Then Mom pushed the luggage cart toward the exit, as we followed closely behind.

—

Winter in Paris was colder than I'd expected. The chill of the wind bit through my sweatshirt as we walked from baggage claim through the sliding doors onto the pavement near the taxi queue. From the airport, we took a cab to a hotel on the outskirts of the city, near the Hôpital Necker on Rue de Sèvres. It was the oldest pediatric hospital in the world, and it was where, on Thursday, March 5, 2009, Zan and I were scheduled to have surgery at three o'clock in the afternoon. The date and time of the surgery played in my mind like a loop—a countdown. I was scared now. We were in a new country where we didn't even speak the language, hoping doctors we didn't know could help us—could make us beautiful. We'd had so many surgeries before, but never had we been willing to risk our lives—ourselves—in the name of beauty.

I leaned my head against the window of the taxi and stared at the streets busy with people as we drove through the city. The gloom of the gray sky matched my mood.

We stayed at the Hôtel Camelia on Boulevard Pasteur. The exterior walls were a soft beige, the color of limestone, and the name of the hotel sat above the windows in capital red letters. The building was tall and thin, sandwiched between restaurants and shops on a bustling street.

"Bonjour!" the concierge said when we entered the building.

"Bonjour," we said, distracted by the exceptionally tight lobby. We knew the hotel was small when we'd booked it, but there was hardly enough room for all three of us to stand with our luggage as we checked in. Mom took out the confirmation details she had printed before we left and placed them on the counter.

The concierge fiddled around on the computer for a moment, before collecting our room keys from the hook behind him.

"You will go right over there," he told us, pointing to a narrow stairway that curved as it went up. "Breakfast is held in the basement each morning from seven until nine."

We carried our bags from the entry upstairs. Our knees cracked from the steepness of each step. Once we reached the top floor, we looked down and sighed at the tight, coiled curve of the staircase. It looked like a snail shell.

Our room was far too small for the two beds it held. One was a full-size, which Mom and Zan shared. I slept in the bed next to it, an extra-long twin that was pushed against the wall. The bottom corners of the beds were so close together they nearly touched.

Mom said the room felt filthy as we dragged our luggage inside, and we all laughed together. The walls and the carpet were stained and worn, but I reminded myself that we were not in Paris on vacation. The flights from San Francisco to France had been expensive, and this little room with wall-to-wall beds was what we could afford.

"What's the bathroom like?" Mom asked, as she plopped down on the larger bed.

"I'm too afraid to look," Zan joked. We laughed again when she twisted the knob and the door swung outward. It only opened about halfway before running into the footboard.

I grabbed a clean pair of jeans and underwear and went into the bathroom to clean up.

"I can't believe how efficient this place is," I yelled from behind the closed door.

"What do you mean?" Zan asked.

I finished and flushed the toilet, before turning on the

shower. "Come here," I told Zan after opening the door again. When she poked her head in, I sat on the closed toilet seat and dramatically stretched out my legs. "It's so small in here, I can shower, pee, and brush my teeth at the sink all at the same time." Zan and I roared with laughter. "It's brilliant!" I told Mom to come look.

She laughed, then pretended to cry.

"I think we're in hell," I joked.

"Nah. I think this might be worse," Mom added, playing along.

"Well, at least it's sort of fun." I smiled and closed the door again, then stepped into the shower. The ice-cold water shocked me to my core. "I take that back!" I shouted. "This is not fun!"

"What's the matter?" I heard Zan yell.

"It's freezing!"

It was after seven o'clock by the time I finished my shower and got myself dressed. Paris was nine hours ahead of San Francisco, so to our bodies it felt like it was ten o'clock in the morning.

"Back to bed?" Mom pulled back the comforter of the full-size bed and climbed beneath the covers.

When we woke up from our nap hours later, our room was black like the sky outside. The red numbers on the clock next to the bed said it was nearing two in the morning. Mom stretched her arms above her head and yawned. I knew when I saw Zan's shadow sit up in bed that she was awake, too.

"What's the plan for dinner?" I asked.

Mom laughed mid-yawn.

"I don't think many people will be out to stare at us right now." I lifted the covers off my legs and stood up.

"Well, I guess it doesn't matter," Zan added. "Because there's no food here, anyway."

"Wait, what?" I flicked the switch on the wall, and the dim yellow light on the ceiling flickered on. I sat down on the edge of my bed and looked at Mom and Zan. "Are you joking?"

"Nope. Mom went downstairs like half an hour ago to find out what restaurants are around here, and the guy at the desk said there's nothing open right now."

Mom nodded. "He said a cab to the only restaurant he knew would be open would cost like a hundred dollars."

"There aren't any, like, drugstores nearby?" I asked.

This triggered Mom's memory, and she waved her hands around excitedly. "Oh, wait! I do have dinner!"

Zan and I exchanged confused glances as Mom rolled to the other side of the bed and grabbed the carry-on bag she'd brought with her on the flight. She unzipped the pockets, pulled out a handful of assorted snacks, and spread them across the bottom of the bed. There were M&Ms, pretzels, and Biscoff cookies.

"Dinner is served," she said, smiling proudly.

"Oh my God," Zan laughed. "I'll take some M&Ms."

"Where did you get these?" I asked.

"They were left over from the plane! Both of you were sleeping, so I saved all your snacks!"

I grabbed one package of pretzels and sat cross-legged at the bottom of the bed. We spent our first night in Paris laughing and eating airplane food.

———

The next morning, our moods were far less cheerful. We all woke up at six thirty with the pain of hunger roaring in our stomachs. We threw on clothes and at seven o'clock on the nose, we made our way down the stairs and into the basement. When we entered the breakfast room, I saw my reflection in the mirror along the back wall. I quickly looked away. Breakfast was orange juice and stale croissants.

"It's better than nothing." Mom was always upbeat and optimistic, even when it was hard to be.

We took our orange juice and croissants to one of the tables and sat down. After breakfast, we returned to our room. We still had two days before meeting with the surgeon, but none of us had any desire to leave the hotel. We did not want to explore Paris. Zan and I did not want to be seen.

Mom spent the rest of the day reading and napping. While Zan watched episodes of *The Bachelor* on her laptop, I tried to watch an episode of *Gilmore Girls* on mine. I had downloaded every season of the show before we left San Francisco, but I could not focus on it. I was distracted by memories of everything we'd been through and nervous about meeting with the doctor.

There was something about being in Paris that made me think of the journalist who had written about us when we were kids. I wondered if after writing the article—after comparing our faces to Picasso—she ever thought about us again. *Was she still in Paris?* I wondered. *Did she ever regret her comparison?*

My mind shifted to Picasso himself. Sitting beneath a blanket in the twin-size bed with my laptop in front of me, I thought about what it had been like for Picasso in Paris. To be surrounded by so much beauty—the culture, the architecture, the people. The same extreme beauty that made me feel so out of place that I did not want to leave our hotel room. I imagined him walking around Montmartre with Françoise Gilot, like I'd read about in her memoir years before, and sipping coffee at Café de Flore. *So much of Picasso's artwork exists somewhere in this city*, I thought. I opened a new tab on my laptop and searched for how to find it.

There was an entire museum filled with it on Rue de Thorigny in the Marais. For a moment I was excited at the possibility of seeing these works in person, of coming face-to-face with the paintings my face supposedly resembled.

As I scrolled through images of Picasso's artwork on my computer, I felt a lump in my throat. It was the same lump that appeared when I'd found the article for the first time. Everything I learned about him fueled my shame, but I was so tired of being angry. I was tired of being angry about my ugliness, I was tired of being angry about the way people treated me, and I was tired of hating Picasso. More than that, I was tired of living in a world that valued a man like him over the lives of the people he hurt.

I closed my laptop and lay down in my bed. The idea of seeing Picasso's artwork in person felt like confronting the man himself. I was already in Paris to confront my ugliness. I didn't have it in me to face him, too. *Maybe I'll see a Picasso in person one day*, I said to myself, *but not today*.

———

Zan and Mom woke me up hours later. "Do you want food?" Zan asked me.

I rolled over to face my sister. The sky was dark again, but I was jet-lagged and disoriented. "What time is it?"

"Like six o'clock." Zan stood over my bed as she buttoned her coat.

I groaned and put my hands over my face. "In the morning?" I was so tired, my body felt like it had been drugged.

"No, it's night. Mom found a pizza place that's really close. We're going to go check it out. Come on."

"That's okay. You guys go ahead." I was surprised that after how we'd been treated in the airport, after how many people stared at us, Zan was willing to venture out onto the streets of Paris. I was hungry, but not yet hungry enough to risk more public humiliation.

Mom poked her head in from the bathroom. "You sure, Bella?"

I nodded and fell back to sleep.

I was awake when they returned an hour later with food for me. "It was so good, sis." Zan was happier than she'd been all week. I opened the box to find that the pizza was still hot. The crust was thick and covered in mozzarella and scoops of ricotta cheese. The flavors were rich and delicious. I'd forgotten how good it felt to eat real food.

The next night, Mom got restaurant recommendations from a different concierge. After three days of experiencing Paris only from the window of our room, I mustered enough courage to leave the hotel with them in search of dinner. Outside, the traffic signals and lights from the shops illuminated the sidewalk. There was a certain freedom in my lungs as we walked the several blocks through busy streets and open markets, past bustling cafés. People going in all directions rushed by us, and the energy was electric. Strangers on the street stared the way they always stared, but their glances did not linger.

Across the street sat a small restaurant with a red awning and outdoor seating. As I stepped onto the road to cross the street to the restaurant, Mom grabbed me by the shoulders and violently yanked me back onto the sidewalk. In the place where I'd stood just seconds earlier was a man splayed out on the concrete, his bike a nearby mess of twisted metal, his legs crossed over each other like a pretzel. The cab driver who'd struck him sat in his car with his hands on the wheel and his mouth gaping open. I stared at the scene, my heart beating rapidly, my body shaking uncontrollably. On the edge of the curb, with my mom's arms still wrapped around me, I thanked her for grabbing me.

Slowly the man with the crumpled bike rolled over on his side, before standing up. My heart was still racing, my focus still on that brief moment between life and death. That instant, that millisecond when everything changes, when life is taken.

———

Dr. DuBois's office was on Rue de la Pompe in the sixteenth arrondissement of Paris, a Right Bank district on the western side of the city. Of the twenty districts in Paris, it was the third wealthiest and included famous museums, elite schools, and part of the Arc de Triomphe. The entire area was extravagant and picturesque. We took a cab to the office from our hotel on Boulevard Pasteur. It was the first Sunday in March, and the streets were empty as we drove by them. Some of the intersections where five or six streets suddenly came together reminded me of San Francisco. How good it would feel to see my dad and my brother and my sisters, to hold my cat and sleep in my own bed, I thought. I ached for home.

When we arrived at the medical office that afternoon, we found that the entrance to the building was blocked by black iron doors that were locked from the inside. We knocked and rang the bell, but nobody came. When Mom called the phone number Dr. DuBois had given her, it rang and rang and rang. We were outside for fifteen minutes before we saw a tall, thin man with dark brown hair sprinting toward us.

"I'm so sorry. I'm so sorry. Please come in," Dr. DuBois said as he opened the door. He had been on vacation with his family until early that morning, and we were just grateful he was willing to meet with us.

Once inside, we climbed a spiral, dimly lit staircase to reach the surgeon's office. Inside, the rooms were dark and empty, but I marveled at the elaborate architecture and intricate designs on the ceiling. The sound of my feet against the marble floor echoed through the halls. When we sat down in front of the surgeon's desk, we made brief introductions before jumping right to the reason for our visit.

"So, you want your eyes straight and closer together?" Dr. DuBois squinted at me and then at Zan, before walking over and putting my face in his hands. He massaged my cheeks in a circular motion and gently raised the outer corners of my eyes. He repeated this several times before moving on to Zan. It was uncomfortable but did not hurt. Dr. DuBois was silent for a moment, before clearing his throat. He stood back and put his fingers to his nose and mouth as if he was praying, but he did not speak.

"I'm sorry, I cannot help you," he finally said. "I do not think it will work."

My mind went numb and I stared at the office window behind the man's head.

"There is so much scar tissue." He said he could feel it with his hands when he pinched our cheeks. "Charles—Dr. York can do surgery to help break it down."

"That was the same issue Dr. York ran into, but he said there was nothing else that can be done."

"He can do it," Dr. DuBois assured us. "It's just little fat injections from the belly into the cheeks. The fat will help break up some of the tissue and fill in this area." He placed the tips of his fingers along each of his cheekbones to show where he was referring to.

"Can we do it here?" Mom asked. "Dr. York was adamant there was nothing else he could do for them, and I don't want to turn around and go home only to be out of options again."

"I can call him?" Dr. DuBois reached for the phone on his desk.

Mom's eyes lit up when he gripped the handset, and she nodded. "Yes please. That would be great."

Dr. DuBois dialed a number and sat with the phone to his ear while it rang.

"Charles," he said into the receiver. "It's Philippe DuBois." Mom, Zan, and I listened as they exchanged pleasantries. "Listen, I have the Henley twins and their mother in my office right now." Dr. DuBois explained the situation and what he thought would work. "So you'll do it?" he said finally.

My eyes widened with anticipation and hope. A moment later, Dr. DuBois hung up the phone and looked at us seated in front of him. "Dr. York says he will do it."

"Can we get that in writing?" Mom teased. "I'm just kidding. We love Charles. He's practically family at this point."

Dr. DuBois nodded, and it was clear he understood the emotional investment that occurs with long-term patients. "I understand," he said. "You want to look a certain way. Especially after so many surgeries. But Dr. York is very skilled and is familiar with the girls' case. I trust he will do the best job."

"We appreciate the time you've spent with us today. You have been an immense help," Mom told him. We took turns shaking Dr. DuBois's hand. When we left his office, we walked back through the dim building, across the marble floor, down the staircase, and out the door where we'd come in.

By that time it was nearing dusk and starting to rain, but we began walking the three miles back to the hotel anyway. Admiring the ornate and spectacular buildings as we walked the streets in the cold, crisp air felt like a meditation of sorts.

"Will Dr. York be upset that we came here?" I looked at Mom as she walked next to me.

"I hope we didn't hurt his feelings," Zan added.

"You let me worry about that." Mom pulled a map from her purse to make sure we were heading in the right direction.

After a block, I stopped walking and looked at Mom again. "Momma, I'm so sad." Standing there on a sidewalk in Paris, I finally began to cry.

"I know, baby." She hugged me. "I know." Zan draped her arms over us and Mom and I pulled her in. The entire trip was a complicated mix of devastation and relief.

We caught a flight out of Paris the following morning.

TWENTY-NINE

When I think of the ways Zan and I were limited by how we were viewed, I think of *The Weeping Woman*, a colorful and distorted 1937 painting of Dora Maar, the talented surrealist photographer who was mostly known for being one of Picasso's lovers for nearly a decade. Picasso viewed painting as the more respectable medium, and during their time together—from 1936 to 1945—he encouraged Dora to pursue painting instead. This was how his abuse started. Soon it became physical and emotional, too. Sometimes he'd leave her unconscious on the floor after he beat her.

In painting Dora as *The Weeping Woman*, Picasso portrayed her as having sad, dark eyes, with the outer corner of each eyelid tilting downward like Zan's and mine. Though she was stunning in real life, on the canvas she was deformed and crying—weeping. The painting was meant to symbolize the bombing of Guernica during the Spanish Civil War. The shapes that made up Dora's disfigured face were meant to evoke pain. The asymmetry in her features was meant to convey the violence and suffering that occurs during war, but what did that say about Dora as the woman behind the painting? I wondered. How did she feel about her face being used to symbolize human suffering?

Picasso's use of disfigurement was how he made art from Dora's tears and her suffering. But it also demonstrated his hatred of women. "For years I've painted her in tortured forms, not through sadism, and not with pleasure, either; just obeying a vision that forced itself on me. It was the deep reality, not the superficial one . . . Dora, for me, was always a weeping woman." Picasso's claim that a disfigured image of Dora forced itself on him overshadowed who she was as a person and as an artist. "Women are suffering machines,"[9] he claimed. In her book on the artist, *Picasso: Creator and Destroyer*, Arianna Huffington wrote about how the majority of the work Picasso created from the late 1930s through 1940 "consisted of deformed women, their faces and bodies flayed with fury. His hatred of a specific woman [Dora] seemed to have become a deep and universal hatred of all women."[10]

Though Picasso didn't care about Dora as anything beyond a subject in his paintings, she refused to accept Picasso's truth as her own. "All his portraits of me are lies. They're all Picassos, not one is Dora Maar,[11]" she once told writer James Lord during an interview. James went on to remind Dora that she would always

---

9   *The Weeping Woman*, painting by Pablo Picasso (1937), www
.pablopicasso.org/the-weeping-woman.jsp.

10   Huffington, *Picasso: Creator and Destroyer*, p. 254.

11   James Lord, *Picasso and Dora: A Personal Memoir*, 1993, p. 123.

have a legacy due to Picasso's portraits of her being hung in museums all over the world. "Do you think I care?" Dora asked him. "Does Madame Cézanne care? Does Saskia Rembrandt care? Remember that I, too, am an artist."[12]

I like to imagine her holding his stare and demanding that he see her—really see *her*—instead of the woman Picasso painted her as.

———

By the time we returned home from Paris, Zan and I had been accepted to nearly every school we'd applied to. On March 5, 2009, the day my surgery was originally scheduled for, I received an email congratulating me on my acceptance to the University of Vermont.

"I got in!" I screamed, laughing, as I read the message out loud to Zan. "I got into UVM!"

Zan and I jumped and screamed together in excitement. We had always dreamed of college but never actually imagined life beyond our surgeries. We were too used to being told we were not good enough. For the first time in so long, I had hope that things would get better.

My parents were thrilled and proud. Every weekend, they took Zan and me to tour the schools we'd been accepted to in California. We looked at San José State and Sonoma State, but neither of them spoke to me the way I'd hoped they would.

---

12   James Lord, *Picasso and Dora: A Personal Memoir*, 1993, p. 123.

Once I narrowed down my list of schools to the University of Oregon and the University of Vermont, I decided I would base my decision on the vibe I got from each of the campuses. What mattered to me most was how I was treated when I got there. Both schools were beautiful and had good education programs, but I wanted more than that. I wanted to feel a sense of belonging, like I was a part of the university and the university was a part of me. I wanted to *want* to wake up in the morning and attend classes on subjects I was interested in. I wanted to read books and study literature and history and philosophy. I wanted friends who felt like a second family and people to talk and laugh and exchange ideas with. I wanted to sit in historic classroom buildings and wonder about all the people who had sat there before me and what they'd accomplished once they left. I wanted to be like everyone else and exist in public without being stared at or pointed to. I wanted to be happy.

Marissa and Alexis offered to take me to tour each campus. In early April 2009, Alexis and I drove eight hours up to Oregon. When we arrived, we wandered around the campus until we found the admissions office and got a campus map. But even after unfolding it, I was not sure what to look for, so we wandered around some more. The campus was beautiful, with brick buildings and rich greenery. I liked the school, but I didn't feel the spark I'd expected to. There was no voice in my head screaming, *This is the one.* That night we stayed at a motel on the outskirts of Eugene and drove home the next morning.

Two weeks later, I met Marissa in New York and together we flew to Vermont, where we stayed at a Holiday Inn halfway between the airport and campus. After checking into the hotel, we took a shuttle to the university. When the driver turned down South Prospect Street and pulled over next to one of the administrative buildings, I stepped out of the van and stood frozen with awe. The campus was unlike anything I had ever seen before. The buildings were old and beautiful, and the air outside felt clean and light. There were no billboards in sight, but the mountains were visible from every angle. Marissa and I thanked the driver and crossed the street to the admissions office. We spent the afternoon on a tour of the campus and ate lunch in the university's Davis Center. All day, groups of students walked past us, talking and laughing, on their way to class. They didn't stare at me when they passed. They didn't even realize I was there. *This is it*, I thought. *This is what I want.*

Marissa could tell by the way I was quiet and to myself that I was contemplating my desire to attend. "It's going to be okay, Bella," she told me. "It will be an adjustment no matter where you go, but you can do this."

I nodded and smiled nervously.

Our second day in Vermont was the last day to make a decision before the enrollment deadline. I hardly slept that night, and instead lay awake in bed thinking about what life would

be like in Vermont. Zan had already confirmed her enrollment to University of the Pacific, where like me, she planned
to go into the education program and become a teacher. She'd
wanted to stay close to home and to our family. She liked the
idea of attending a smaller school with small class sizes, where
she wouldn't be just another face in a lecture hall. I wanted the
opposite. I wanted to be anonymous.

Going to school in Vermont meant living three thousand
miles away from each other. What would it be like without Zan
and my family? Would they forgive me for leaving? Would it all
be one giant mistake? I didn't know what would happen if I left,
but I did know things could not continue as they were.

I finally fell asleep just after four that morning. When my
alarm went off at eight thirty, I sat up and looked over to find
Marissa already dressed and ready for the day. I felt the sheet I'd
wrapped around my waist in the night and was relieved to find
it wasn't covered in urine. *It's a sign*, I thought.

"Good morning, sleepyhead." Marissa turned to face me.

"I'm going to do it," I said. "I'm ready to commit." My heart
had decided on attending before my head caught up.

"Yeah?" Marissa was a level of excited I should have been.
"So, Vermont it is then?"

"Vermont it is." I almost couldn't believe I was saying it,
but as hard as it would be to leave home, I knew it was what
I needed. Zan and I needed to figure out who we were on our
own and without our medical history defining us.

That afternoon, Marissa paid the $495 for me to confirm my enrollment. After, we walked to the bookstore, where she bought us matching gray sweatshirts with UNIVERSITY OF VERMONT CATAMOUNTS in white letters across the front.

My bed-wetting stopped for good after that.

———

When I returned to California, I told the Girl Talk girls that I would be moving to Vermont for college. They hugged me excitedly and said they'd miss our weekly chats. We spent our final meetings holding after-school bake sales to raise money for a local animal rescue.

At the end of May, though I had technically finished my senior-year coursework months earlier, I was invited to the high school's senior awards night. The ceremony was held at a Pentecostal church down the road from the school. Mr. Davis came and sat in the audience with my family.

"Watch me get an award for perfect attendance," I joked.

About a quarter of the way through the ceremony, a man in a suit and tie stood at the front of the room and introduced himself as a corporate representative from Comcast. He talked about the Comcast Leaders and Achievers Scholarship Program, which awarded high school seniors for academic achievement and community service. When I heard the man call my name and announce I had won a scholarship, it felt like an out-of-body experience. I walked awkwardly to the front of the room and shook the man's hand, before returning to my seat. The rest of the ceremony was a daze, as I was still riding the high of my scholarship win.

Mrs. Keene closed out the festivities by thanking everyone for attending. Then she gave a speech about leadership and community service and announced she had a final scholarship award to pass out.

"This student has been through a lot over the past four years," she said. "And I'm grateful I had the opportunity to mentor them during their time at Redwood Creek High School." Everyone in the audience looked around, trying to figure out who she was talking about. I was as shocked as everyone else when Mrs. Keene asked me to return to the front of the room. She did not mention any specific award or scholarship, but when I got to the podium, she handed me a certificate and motioned for me to stay.

"I have not had this happen before," Mrs. Keene said with a slight laugh into the microphone, "but I think you're going to want to just stay put up here for a moment." She told the audience that the scholarship certificate she had handed me was not the only award I would be receiving that night. Mrs. Keene reached out and gently squeezed my hand, before carefully removing a small stack of papers from behind the podium. The scholarship organizations I'd submitted my applications to earlier that year had notified each of the winners' high schools. I found out when one by one, Mrs. Keene read a list of thirteen scholarships I was being awarded. Then she placed an achievement medal around my neck. My parents cried. Mr. Davis cried. It took everything in me not to cry, too. For the first time, I was being recognized for something I'd done, not for what I looked like.

———

I grew up feeling like Dora, the weeping woman—my face a disguise masking who I really was. But like Dora the artist, I refused to be a subject in someone else's painting. In November 2019, nearly eighty years after Dora first began showing her artwork, her legacy as an artist—not Picasso's lover—was celebrated in an exhibition at Tate Modern in London. When I think of how it felt to stand in front of my teachers, my classmates, and my family and receive the scholarships I'd worked so hard for, I think of Dora finally getting the recognition she deserved. Because like Dora, Zan and I had to learn that we were more than a subject, more than a muse, more than our faces. We were artists, and we too had the right to decide who we were.

THIRTY

I moved to Vermont in June 2009. Mom and Zan flew with me to Burlington to help me get settled. I'd been accepted to participate in the Summer Enrichment Scholars Program, a summer program for underrepresented first-year students at the University of Vermont. For the month of July, I was to live in a dorm room on the second floor of Hamilton Hall with eighteen other incoming freshmen. I would spend my mornings taking classes in anthropology and psychology, and my afternoons working in the disability office on campus.

I hadn't actually considered what it would be like to live on my own. I had never been away from home, from my parents, or from Zan for an extended period of time. When I was away, I'd always had at least one family member with me.

After spending three days with me in Vermont, Zan and Mom dropped me off at my dorm room for the summer. It was pouring rain and they were running late to the airport, so we had the cab pull over in front of the building and unload my belongings onto the pavement. They hugged me tight before jumping back in the car. As I watched them drive away, I prayed they'd miss their flight and be forced to turn around—to stay with me a while longer.

By the time I got my stuff up the stairs and into my room, my hair and clothes were soaked from the rain. The sun came out just as I finished drying off and unpacking. I sat on the edge of the twin-size bed and looked out the window at the green lawn in the center of a circle of dormitories. With nobody around, it was eerily quiet. For the first time in my life, I was truly alone.

We didn't have to check in with the others in the program until later that evening, so I ventured outside. I walked back down South Prospect Street, where Marissa and I had first visited months before. From the corner of South Prospect and Main, I could see the blue of Lake Champlain at the bottom of the hill. When I reached downtown, I stopped at the Ben & Jerry's for an ice cream cone, before walking the rest of the way to the lake. I sat on the dock and stared out at the water for an hour or so before heading back.

The welcome barbecue was held in front of the Blundell House, a small gray-and-white building that looked more like a portable classroom than an office. On the grass next to it were rows of white plastic tables and folding chairs. Students and staff were gathered outside, talking and laughing. Everyone seemed so comfortable, like they all knew each other. When I reached the grass, I smiled awkwardly and looked around for someone else who seemed out of place like me. I found an empty chair at an empty table and sat down. I focused my attention on the smoke from the grill wafting into the air, but all I could think about was how much I wished Zan was with me. I'd spent so much time alone with her, just the two of us, I wasn't sure how to be without her.

A few moments passed before someone sat down at my table. She had shoulder-length black hair that swooped over to hide one side of her face. "I'm Pema," she said. "Who are you?"

I laughed nervously at her blunt delivery. "I'm Ariel," I said, and shook her hand. I stuck by her the rest of the night but barely said a word.

When I got back to my room after the barbecue, I called Mom's cell phone and begged her to let me come home. "Please," I sobbed. "I'll enroll in a different school. I miss you so much."

"I know it's hard, Bella."

I held my breath, trying to muffle my cries as Mom spoke.

"It's going to take some time to adjust, but you're going to be so glad you did it. We are so proud of you. We love you so much."

"I love you, too." My words were choppy and hard to get out.

I called home crying every day for the next four days. On the fifth day, when Mom didn't answer her phone, my dad called me back instead.

"Ariel, you have to stop calling Mom," he told me.

A surge of embarrassment rushed through my bones. My incessant calling had upset her.

"She doesn't know I'm calling right now, but she's in the bathroom crying because she doesn't know what to do."

My dad realized the harshness of his tone was not translating, so he softened his voice. "I know this is hard. We miss you and we want you here, but this is something you wanted to do, and you have to see it through."

"Okay." I was hurt and ashamed for having reached out to them, for having displayed such vulnerability, only to be told I needed to get over it.

"Don't call Mom," my father continued. "If you have a problem, call me instead."

"I said okay."

"I'm not trying to be mean," Dad told me. "I love you."

I told him I loved him, too, and got off the phone as quickly as possible.

My dad told me later that our phone call that afternoon was one of the hardest ones he had ever made. He said he got into his car so many times to come get me. "I mapped out the distance," he said. "I told Mom I could be to you in three days and have you home within a week." At one point, he even got into the car and made it a couple of hours before he forced himself to turn around. "It was something you needed to do," he said. "I had to honor that." My father's tough love held me accountable. It forced me to hold myself accountable, too. He knew it was going to take work for me to create the life I wanted, and it was up to me to make that happen.

That weekend, the students in the summer program were split up into three volunteer teams. Six of us were sent to pull weeds at the Intervale, a community farm along the Winooski River, and six were sent to plant flowers at the Shelburne Museum. The rest of us were sent to spend the day at the Boys & Girls Club in the Old North End of Burlington.

I knew walking into a building filled with children and teenagers was a bad idea, but like I did before every operation, I shut my mind off and forced myself to act as though everything was fine. From the moment I walked in, the kids stared at me the way one stares at the road in front of them when they're driving. They pointed at my face and pulled the outer corners of their eyelids down and laughed. I spent the afternoon wandering from one room to another, wishing for a way to make the hands on the clock go faster so I could leave.

At a debrief that evening, our group leader asked us to pull our chairs into a circle so we could all face each other. "Does anyone want to share a bit about your experience and what you learned today?" she asked us.

Pema raised her hand. "All the kids kept staring at Ariel. They didn't want to play with her. They kept calling her ugly."

"Oh my God," I muttered. I was humiliated.

"How did that make you feel?" the leader asked Pema.

I didn't stick around to hear the answer. Without a word, I stood up and left the circle. I pushed the doors open and listened to them slam shut behind me as I walked down the steps onto the sidewalk and made my way back downtown toward the water. Tears blurred my vision while I walked, but I dialed Marissa's number into my cell phone as quickly as I could manage.

"Hi, Bella!" Marissa answered.

"It's never going to change," I bawled into the phone.

"Oh, honey. What happened?"

I stood on the corner of Main Street with tears and snot flowing down my face as I recounted my day of volunteer work and Pema's comments. "I'm just so tired of this," I said.

As I stood on the street corner talking to Marissa, a white university van pulled up next to me. Pema was in the passenger seat and our group leader was behind the wheel. "You want a ride?" they asked me. I said no and kept walking. When I got back to the dorms, Pema was waiting for me outside my door.

"Can we talk?" she asked me.

"I have nothing to say," I told her as I placed my key into the handle and unlocked my door.

"Are you okay?" She looked worried.

"Not really, no."

"Please, can we talk?" she begged again.

I opened the door, flicked the light switch, and motioned for her to come in. "Fine. Five minutes."

"I feel like I upset you."

"I mean, I basically got called ugly all day and then you all tried to have a conversation about it like I wasn't even there. So, yeah. I'm a little upset."

"Ariel, I'm sorry," Pema said. "I didn't realize."

"How did you not realize . . ." I could feel myself on the verge of tears and so I stopped myself.

"English is not my first language," Pema explained. "And so sometimes the words . . . they come out a little bit different than I mean them."

I stayed silent and listened as she spoke.

"I was upset for you," she said. "I did not like how they treated you today. They were so mean. I wanted to understand why they said those things."

This had not occurred to me. "I'm used to this," I told her. "I just ignore it. Bringing it up in front of everyone just made me feel worse."

"I'm really sorry," Pema said, as she wiped a tear from her cheek.

"It's okay." Now I was crying, too.

After our conversation, Pema and I grew close. For the rest of the summer, we sat together in class and stayed up late doing homework every night. When she didn't understand the way something was worded, I explained it. When I was having a bad day, she listened to me vent. We helped each other.

Pema only stayed in Vermont for one year before returning home to New York. She was more excited about the social aspect of college than the academics, and the school gave her one semester to decide which one she wanted to prioritize. She was gone the following year. My closeness with Pema had made it hard to make other friends. She understood me in such a way that meant I no longer had to explain myself or my experiences. Her nonjudgmental attitude was rare among my peers, and so I clung to it, expecting it to always be there. After her departure, I made an effort to lean into my other friendships.

During my sophomore year, I roomed with another friend, Corinne, who I'd met in the education program freshman year. We had most of our classes together, and though we both had enrolled at UVM thinking we wanted to become teachers, we were opposites in every other way. She was graceful and elegant. She listened to classical music and joined the competitive ball-room dancing team. I listened to country music, indie music, and Top 40, and scheduled my academic courses around my favorite television shows. She was also an entire fourteen inches taller than me. When I stood next to her, I looked like her kid sister.

After Pema left, Corinne became one of my only friends in Vermont. I think she noticed, because she was quick to include me in anything she did. She had nightly dinners where she and her friends talked about *Doctor Who* and other television shows and movies that excited them. At times it felt like they were talking in code. I had never heard of most of what they talked about, and even when I didn't understand what they were saying, I enjoyed learning about their interests. Mostly, I liked that I never once heard them discuss their appearance or anyone else's. Before long, Corinne's friend group was my friend group, too. Evie, Nathan, Gretchen, Molly, and Danielle made me feel like I had a place in Vermont, like I belonged there. Soon there were trips to the downtown farmers' market for maple pumpkin muffins and concerts at Higher Ground to see Walk the Moon and Matt and Kim. There were sunrise hikes, weeknight dance parties, and evenings spent on Church Street and Lake Champlain. Yet the more my new friends included me, the more I realized I would never fit in easily the way other people seemed to.

In October 2010, they invited me to travel with them to Washington, DC, for the weekend to attend the Rally to Restore Sanity and/or Fear.

"What is it?" I asked.

"You know Jon Stewart and Stephen Colbert?" they asked me. I didn't.

"Have you seen *The Daily Show*?"

I hadn't. They tried to explain that the rally was an event promoting educated discussion in our country, where extreme views dominated the political landscape. I had no idea what they meant, but I agreed to attend anyway.

The week before we were set to leave, when Corinne and I got back to our dorm room after dinner, I brought up the rally again. "So wait, it's being held at the National Mall?" I asked her. "How is everyone going to fit?"

Corinne stopped what she was doing and stared at me intently. "What do you mean?"

"I mean, it sounds like there will be a lot of people. How are we all going to fit inside a mall? How will we see what's going on? None of this makes sense to me."

I had never seen her laugh so hard.

———

At the root of all my struggles was my desire to belong. I couldn't change who I was, but I could take control of who I was becoming. On December 29, 2010, while home in California for winter break, I had the surgery to break up the scar tissue around my eyes. Dr. York took a small amount of fat from Zan's and my bellies and injected it into the area around our cheekbones, just as Dr. DuBois had described when we met him in Paris. We'd go into the operating room in the morning and be home by early afternoon.

It had been three years since my last surgery, and I'd forgotten how to silence the pain I felt. When I returned home from the hospital, I went straight to my bedroom. My dad could hear me crying from the other room. When he opened the door, I was lying on my back in the center of the bed, staring upward at the ceiling as tears spilled down the sides of my eyelids and into my mess of tangled hair. The room was dark, save for the slivers of light peeking in through the cracks of the blinds. He walked over, stood next to me, and took my hand in his. "It's going to be okay," he said, rubbing the top of my hand with his thumb. "I'm going to go get your pain medicine right now. Do you need anything else while I'm out?"

"No, thank you," I said between tears.

A few minutes after Dad left, Aaron arrived with his girl-friend, Vanessa. When they, too, heard my cries, Aaron opened my bedroom door.

"Belle." My brother's tone was sweet and comforting. Vanessa stood just inside the doorway while Aaron made his way to the side of the bed, as Dad had done minutes before. "Are you okay?"

"I hurt so bad." I arched my neck backward into the pillow, sending tears rushing down my forehead and into my hairline. The roots of my scalp were wet with sweat and tears, and snot dripped from my nose.

Aaron placed his hand on mine. "Do you need anything?"

I shook my head no. "I'm just so tired of this."

My brother sat down on the edge of the bed next to me. "Tired of surgery?"

"I'm so tired of hurting. It hurts so bad. I always hurt so bad." I was crying harder now.

"I know, Belle. I know. It's going to be okay. In a few days you're going to feel better, and it will be like none of this ever happened."

I wiped my face with my left forearm and closed my eyes. "I don't want to do this anymore." I turned to look at my brother. "It's not worth it. I don't want to do any of this anymore."

"It's okay, Belle. You don't have to." Aaron sat and listened until Dad returned with my medicine. Then he got me a glass of water and watched me swallow the pills, which kept me asleep for the next several hours. When I woke up the next morning, my belly still ached from where they had sucked the fat from my stomach and my face throbbed from where it had been injected.

It was the last surgery Zan and I ever had on our faces.

THIRTY-ONE

Two weeks after the operation, I returned to Vermont with cheeks so swollen, I looked like a chipmunk. It was the middle of January and snow blanketed everything in sight. My belly still felt painfully hollow. When I moved, it felt as though my organs were going to suddenly free-fall and spill out onto the floor beneath me. For months, I used the roll of twelve-inch-wide gauze the hospital sent me home with to keep my torso tightly wrapped beneath my clothes. It was uncomfortable, but I liked the way it hid the soft rolls of my stomach. I still struggled with accepting my appearance and was recovering from what had, at that point, become full-fledged bulimia, but the decision to be done with surgery was my first step toward healing.

When I returned to college, I found a therapist in Vermont who specialized in eating disorders and began an outpatient treatment program. As much as I'd appreciated my childhood therapist, it felt good to meet with someone who didn't know every painful detail about the appearance-altering surgeries that defined my adolescence. As soon as people found out about the surgeries I'd had, all we discussed was the trauma around my medical past. I could finally place my eating disorder at the forefront and get the help I needed while I worked through the trauma at the core of my illness: my appearance. In the months following my last surgery, my recovery became my main priority. I began attending weekly Zumba and yoga classes and seeing a nutritionist.

That January, I switched my major from education to English and political science. Teaching was noble and something I aspired to, but I wanted more content-specific courses. I wanted to read and write and study everything I had missed in high school. I was drawn to political courses, because I'd missed so much school and I wanted to better understand how our government worked and how societal values influenced the world around me. Once I changed my focus of study, the majority of my classes were held in Old Mill—a beautiful brick building that overlooked the university green.

My first introductory course for political science was on early political thought. The classroom was split down the middle by a ramp and steps that gradually increased the height of the seats as it neared the back of the classroom. It reminded me of a movie theater.

My professor stood behind the media center at the front of the room as he lectured about Plato, Aristotle, and what early governments looked like. My class was held first thing in the morning and I was too tired to focus on political theory, so I opened my laptop and browsed the internet instead. Every few minutes, I would stop scrolling and look intently at the whiteboard and projector screen behind my professor and pretend to take notes about what he was saying.

One morning in class that spring, I spent the lecture hour doing my own research for an upcoming paper. In reading Plato and Aristotle, I learned more about the early treatment of people with disfigured faces and bodies. Plato, I found, was obsessed with physical health and strength. Aristotle, I discovered, believed in the golden ratio. In *Poetics*, he said that for a living creature to be beautiful, they had to "present a certain order in its arrangement of parts."[13] In *Metaphysics*, he added, "the chief forms of beauty are order and symmetry and definiteness, which the mathematical sciences demonstrate in a special degree."[14] He also believed parents should be forbidden from raising children with disfigurements. He even tried to make this a law. If I had been born in ancient Greece, I realized, Zan and I would have been murdered. How could my professor talk about early societies without ever mentioning that some people were never even allowed to live in them? I continued down the rabbit hole, unsure of what I was originally looking for. All I knew was people like me were seen as weak and inferior—a punishment for those around them. The way society viewed Zan and me, the way we were treated and ridiculed, was the

---

13   Aristotle, *Poetics,* volume 2, p. 2322.
14   Aristotle, *Metaphysics*, volume 2, p. 1705.

result of hundreds of years of dehumanization. I felt validated and heartbroken all at once.

To distract myself, I opened a new tab on my laptop and scrolled through news and entertainment sites. I searched for Picasso, only to find that his 1932 painting *Nude, Green Leaves and Bust* had recently sold for a record-breaking $106.5 million. I clicked the link and stared at an image of the painting—an abstract depiction of Marie-Thérèse Walter in the nude. I smiled when I read the news of the sale, because even with years of discrimination and oppression targeting people like me, it confirmed something I had spent years questioning: There was both beauty and value in faces that were different—in faces like Zan's and mine.

In fall 2011, I enrolled in an introductory creative writing course taught by Chester Brimley. In class, we covered everything from short stories to memoir and read books like *Fun Home* by Alison Bechdel and *A Million Little Pieces* by James Frey. In November, he told us our next assignment was to write a ten-page mini memoir.

For the next week, I sat in my dorm room and stared at a blank computer screen. There was so much I wanted to write about and so much I wanted to say, but I had no idea where to start. How to pack twenty years of life into ten pages? Every time I wrote a sentence, I cried.

The morning our memoirs were due, students shuffled into

class and began removing layers of sweaters and coats. It was early December and our last class before everyone went their separate ways for winter break. Outside, the snow had yet to fall, but the sky was gray and hazy, and the trees were bare. I sat nervously as Professor Brimley pulled students' essays up on the projector screen in front of the room. He told us that normally he would've asked us to print one copy of our paper for each student in the class, but why waste paper when he could just use a projector? One by one, he read each essay aloud as we followed along. When he finished reading, he asked students to offer feedback on what did and did not work well in the piece and why. Then he gave his own feedback before moving on to the next story. I was one of the last students to go. I stared down at my desk while I listened to him read my ten-page glimpse into what life after seventh grade had looked like for Zan and me. I liked the way my words sounded when they came from someone else's mouth. It was like I had released them, like they no longer held the same power they once did. I did not think my paper was any kind of literary masterpiece, but it was mine and I was proud of it. When Professor Brimley finished reading through my submission, the room fell silent. My words were still projected onto the board in the front of the room.

I spent the next month curled up on the couch in our cool, dark living room. The shades stayed drawn, and the doors remained locked. My eyes remained glued to the silent television. Day after day. I can't even tell you what I watched. Or what I ate. I can't tell you much of anything about that time, because it's still raw. It's still real. And I can still taste the blood and smell the IV drip. I can still hear the cries and I can still recite the prayers. I can still retrace the scars and live it again and again and again.

"Wow," he said. I peeled my eyes away from the wall to see my professor still staring at the computer screen in front of him.

"I normally try to reserve my comments for last, but this might just be the finest memoir I've ever received from an undergraduate student," Professor Brimley said. He lifted his eyes from the screen and looked at me. "Well done, Ariel. Really. Well done."

—

After class, I celebrated the end of the semester by going downtown and treating myself to a hot chocolate from Muddy Waters, a cozy coffee shop on Main Street with brick walls and exposed wooden beams. I liked it there because patrons often wrote notes on the backs of their receipts and folded them into the cracks of the walls. Sometimes I'd stop in for a drink just so I could see what people left behind. That afternoon, after I read all the notes I could find, I walked to the bookshelf near the door. I crouched down and, with my index finger, traced the titles as I read through them. I froze when I saw that on the bottom shelf was a copy of *Life with Picasso*. I quickly brought it back to a table with me. Finding it again was like being reacquainted with an old friend.

For the next few hours, I sat in a U-shaped booth with shiny red upholstery and a black table in the center. I sipped my drink and skimmed the book until I reached a page I did not recognize. From there, I finished it. In rereading *Life with Picasso*, entire sections stood out to me that I had not remembered noticing before. Like how Françoise lived in Picasso's shadow, and after ten years and two children together, she finally left him. When this happened, Picasso told her that she would be nothing without him. That the only success she would ever find as an artist would be in her association with him. When this did not dissuade her from leaving, he refused to ever see their children again. He severed all ties with her and made sure everyone he knew did as well. "But in doing so," Françoise wrote, "he forced me to discover myself and thus to survive."

Despite Picasso's threats, Françoise remade herself away from his power, influence, and abuse, just as I was trying to do with my disfigured face. I no longer wanted to be defined by my appearance or haunted by the article that compared my features to an artist I hated. *Their faces resembled the work of Picasso.* I thought of cubism and Françoise Gilot and what it meant to be limited by how others viewed our identity. Because for me, Picasso and his art symbolized my disfigured face and the way society treated me because of it. I found comfort knowing that after Françoise left Picasso behind, her life went on. She remarried, continued painting, and wrote her memoir, which she even dedicated to him. In telling her story and dedicating it to the man whose abuse she experienced, Françoise reclaimed her power. And maybe, I thought, by flipping the script, so could I.

It was cubism, after all, that showed perspective mattered. In that moment, I rephrased the line that haunted me. *Their faces resembled the work of Picasso? No*, I scoffed to myself. *Picasso's artwork was inspired by faces like theirs.* If anything, Picasso drew inspiration from faces like Zan's and mine, from our stigma and mistreatment. Disfigured faces like ours had existed for far longer than Picasso or his art. We were not made in his image, nor did our beauty lie in it. Still, I could not help but wonder how different my life—our lives—would have been had that one line, that one comparison, that one article not been written. How different my sister and I would have been, had we been written about from a different perspective, from a place of equality instead of ignorance. But we weren't. I wasn't.

After writing a piece of my story for class and listening to Professor Brimley read it out loud, the power in the process transformed me. It made me understand Françoise in a way I had not before. By writing, I could come face-to-face with the truth—my truth. I could piece my experiences together and take them apart, until I understood them. I could claim ownership over the person I was and come to terms with both the things that happened to me and the mistakes I had made. Like

Françoise, I could find healing in rewriting the narrative and telling my story on my own terms. I told myself Picasso would have been lucky to have been able to see the true beauty in unique faces like mine. How much better his artwork would have been had he understood a woman as more than her beauty, and disfigurement as more than a symbol of pain and fear and suffering.

My face did not resemble the work of Picasso. I *am* a face for Picasso.

AUTHOR'S NOTE

While I wrote this book as honestly and as accurately as I could, trauma changes us and alters our brains. It makes us question things we thought we knew. So to present you with the most honest version of my story, I interviewed family and friends. I read over one thousand pages of my medical records and consulted my childhood journal. Zan even let me read *her* journal. In researching my life, I saw myself and my story through more than just my own perspective. I try to address any memory-related inconsistencies throughout the story because part of my journey to healing has involved coming to terms with the truth, even when it's hard or it hurts or it doesn't portray me in the most positive light. Even when my version of truth does not align with someone else's.

In telling my story, I knew I wanted to write about my family's love and dedication for my twin sister and me, and our love and appreciation for them. And I did. But I also tried to include the complicated, messy parts, too, because healing isn't linear. Sometimes it's one step forward and three steps back. But my parents' actions were always motivated by love and informed by the knowledge they had at the time. As were our surgeons'. Would they handle everything the same way now as they did when I was a child? No. And neither would I. But none of us are the same people now as we were back then.

This book takes place in the 1990s and early 2000s, when there wasn't as much information about Crouzon syndrome and the impact of beauty-focused treatment on mental health. I still remember typing the names of my upcoming surgeries into Google to try to get an idea about what the recovery process would look like, but it would rarely yield helpful results. I was privileged to have access to top medical care from world-class surgeons. They saved my life, and for that I am grateful.

While finishing the first draft of the book, I returned to therapy to deal with my PTSD and the anger that fuels it. My therapist compared my anger—my trauma—to a cup of coffee. She said having anger build up inside you is like walking around with a cup of hot coffee that's filled to the brim. If you bump into someone, the coffee will splash on you and them, and hurt both of you. But if you dump some of that coffee out, bumping into someone may cause the coffee to swish around in the cup a bit, but it won't hurt you or the people around you the way it used to.

What I didn't realize going into the writing process was that I wasn't the only one in my family who was traumatized by the surgeries Zan and I had. My family and I were all walking around with full coffee cups, trying to take care of each other while struggling to take care of ourselves. Writing this book was my way of dealing with the trauma that fueled my childhood and young adulthood. It was my way of dumping the coffee from my mug so that I had room to experience everything life still has to offer. It was my way of letting go and moving on. Of choosing to continue loving a world even when it didn't always love me back.

ACKNOWLEDGMENTS

This book has been burning within me since I was a child. Writing it was one of the hardest things I have ever done. There were times I didn't think I would be able to do it, and I could fill a novel thanking everyone who has helped me make my dream of writing this book a reality.

This book is for my family.

Thank you to my amazing twin sister, Zan. I know this story is as much yours as it is mine, and so I thank you for your blessing in writing it. It's been a long, hard road, but I'm thankful I got to travel it with you.

To Mom and Dad. From the first time I told you I wanted to be a writer, you celebrated my words. This book exists because you encouraged me to dream big and keep going, even when I felt like giving up. Thank you for always telling me to stand up and speak my truth no matter how hard it is or what anyone else says. Your strength, kindness, and resilience inspire me, and I'm so proud to be your daughter. *Thank you* will never come close to enough.

To my siblings and their spouses: Alexis and Dave, Marissa

and David, and Aaron and Vanessa. Thank you for being the best siblings I could ever ask for. Thank you for the many nights, phone calls, and text messages spent reminiscing. Thank you for laughing and crying with me as we talked through the many experiences that made us all who we are. And of course to my beautiful nieces and nephews—I love you all so much.

To Natalie Newell and Vanessa Lola, my wonderful friends turned family. Thank you for being the highlight of my childhood.

For Dawn "Dawn-Dawn" Kennedy, for always being there anytime I need you.

To Leann, Shanna, Grampy, and of course Gerry. I can still hear your "yippee!" all the way from heaven.

I have so much love and appreciation for my incredible agent, Rachel Letofsky, and the entire team at Cooke-McDermid. Thank you for everything you do. And to Eric Smith for making the introduction. Thank you so much to everyone at FSG/Macmillan as well—Joy Peskin, Elizabeth Lee, Kelsey Marrujo, Teresa Ferraiolo, Lelia Mander, Celeste Cass, and Valerie Shea—and especially my amazing editor, Grace Kendall, who asked all the right questions and helped me tell my story in a way I am so proud of. This book would not exist without you.

A big thanks to Paul Ngo for the cover photo, artist Shira Barzilay for the cover art, and to the designer, Aurora Parlagreco, for the vision behind it. And to Veronica Cabrera for making my hair look camera-ready.

To my University of Vermont family: Jonathan DeAngelis, Claire Hopkins, Mackenzie Wise, Beryl Frishtick, Ashleigh DiLaurenzio, Annie Lerch, Briana Rainville, Sarah Muller, and Leann Olson. Thank you for your friendship and support all these years. I started really trying to write this book in college, and you always cheered me on. For that I am so grateful. A special thanks to Beryl Frishtick and Jonathan DeAngelis, who happily read countless drafts and sat on the phone with me for hours talking through each section. And to Claire Hopkins, who let me talk about my book as much as I wanted without getting annoyed.

Not having the best experiences with teachers growing up has made me extra grateful for the remarkable educators I did get to learn from. I have nothing but respect and gratitude for Henry Bailey, Diane Faber, Jessica Lawrence, Mathew McLean, Shirley Dawkins, and Jeff Torquemada. To my writing professors at University of Vermont: Greg Bottoms, whose course introduced me to my love for narrative essays, and Philip Baruth, who believed in me more than I believed in myself.

To my colleagues and friends at University of the Pacific, both past and present: Melanie Hash, Eileen Camfield, Rhonda Bryant, Sophia Vu, Miranda Heaney, Elizabeth Purnell, Eddie Cardenas, Betsy Hooper, Luly Sbeta, and my 2019 Masters of Education in Student Affairs cohort and professors. To my team in the Office of Services for Students with Disabilities: Danny

Nuss, Morgan Northcutt, Antoinette Peoples, Emily Marino, and Henry Nguyen. Shout-out.

To my friends in the disability, disfigurement, craniofacial and/or physical difference communities who inspire me every day: Brooke Spurlock, Mikaela Moody, Morgan Lakusta, Melissa Blake, Alice Wong, MariaLuisa Mendiola, Nathalia Freitas, Jenny Kattlove, Tom Head, John Altmann, Ashley Eakin, Crystal Marshall, Lara Ameen, Carly Findlay, Jenny Woolsey, Emma Johnson, Alaina Leary, and Rasheera Dopson. To Selma Blair, whose advocacy has shown the beauty and power of vulnerability and authenticity.

To Lilly Dancyger, for publishing the essay that started it all.

To Karie Fugett, Teagan Sturmer, and Kelsey Green, my writing buddies, who held me accountable and gave such helpful feedback. To Naseem Jamnia and Britni De La Cretaz, who provided feedback on early sections of this book. To Joanell Serra, who let me use her home as a writing retreat. To Andrea and Allison at Writing Class Radio, Erin Khar, and Ana McNaughton, who lent a hand when I needed it. To Reema Zaman and Gayle Brandeis, for your kindness and support. Thank you also to Lola and the entire Garcia family. To the Binders.

To the people who shared their stories and memories with me: Jennifer Reichhold, Kathleen Jones, Becca Garetz, Danae Hall, Caitlin Hernandez, Leah Foltz, Austin Price, Rachel

Miller, Hillary Harvey, Jenna Famular, Lucia Rubin-Cadrain, Durieka Campbell, Monica Albertoni, Zoe Holmes-Higgins, and Caitlin Rahn. Thank you also to Roxana Duran, David Watkins, Bridget Cohen, Amy Kaplan, Julie Geddes, Callie Little, and Sharon Andrews.

To Angel Herrera, whose Zumba class got me through college. To the Let's Make Art community and Sarah Cray, whose watercolor projects got me back into art and painting. This was my lifeline while working on my first draft, and I'm grateful such a positive and supportive art community exists. To Taylor Swift, whose music has been my happy place for so many years—especially while writing.

To all the friends who have been most understanding when I canceled plans or didn't reach out, because I was all-consumed by writing this book. Thank you. To everyone who has ever taken the time to read something I've written, it means more to me than I will ever know how to convey.

To my incredible doctors and nurses. I owe the entire craniofacial department at Children's Hospital Oakland my life. To Dr. Martin Chin, Dr. Bryant Toth, Dr. Maureen Herd, Dr. Montgomery Kong, Dr. Daniel Birnbaum, Dr. Richard Kerbavaz, Dr. Bernard J. Drury, Dr. John McQuitty, Dr. Otis Paul, Dr. Donald Linck, Ginny Curtin, Peg Langham, and so many others. From the bottom of my heart, thank you.

To Françoise Gilot, Jacqueline Roque, Dora Maar, Marie-Thérèse Walter, Olga Khokhlova, and Fernande Olivier: the

ACKNOWLEDGMENTS

incredible women and artists behind Picasso's success. Françoise Gilot, I spent much of this book talking about *Life with Picasso*, and I mean it when I say your story changed my life. Your strength and courage made me believe in a better future. Your words helped me heal.

Lastly, to my fellow Cranio Warriors, this book is for you. May you always see the beauty in being exactly who you are.

SOURCES

Aristotle. *The Complete Works of Aristotle*. Edited by Jonathan Barnes. 2 vols. Princeton, NJ: Princeton University Press, 1984.

Chin, M., and B. A. Toth. "Le Fort III Advancement with Gradual Distraction Using Internal Devices." *Plastic and Reconstructive Surgery* 100, no. 4 (September 1997): 819–832. https://doi.org/10.1097/00006534-199709001-00001.

Davis, Caitlin. "How One Surgeon Changed the Lives of Patients with Crouzon Syndrome Worldwide." *Quintessence Publishing*, June 23, 2017. www.quintpub.net/news/2017/06/how-one-surgeon-changed-the-lives-of-patients-with-crouzon-syndrome-worldwide/#.X6dx4y2z06g.

Gilot, Françoise, and Carlton Lake. *Life with Picasso*. New York: McGraw-Hill, 1964.

Huffington, Arianna S. *Picasso: Creator and Destroyer*. New York: Simon & Schuster, 1988.

Marlowe, Lara. "Sex on the Canvas: Picasso's Most Erotic Year Laid Bare." *The Irish Times*, February 17, 2018. www.irishtimes.com/culture/art-and-design/visual-art/sex-on-the-canvas-picasso-s-most-erotic-year-laid-bare-1.3392315.

Richardson, John. *A Life of Picasso: The Cubist Rebel, 1907–1916*. New York: Alfred A. Knopf, 1996.

RECOMMENDED READING

Brown, Keah. *The Pretty One*. New York: Atria, 2019.

Eco, Umberto, ed. *History of Beauty*. Translated by Alastair McEwen. New York: Rizzoli International Publications, 2004.

Eco, Umberto, ed. *On Ugliness*. Translated by Alastair McEwen. New York: Rizzoli International Publications, 2011.

Findlay, Carly. *Say Hello*. Sydney, NSW: HarperCollins Publishers Australia, 2019.

Grealy, Lucy. *Autobiography of a Face*. Boston: Houghton Mifflin, 1994.

Head, Tom. *Crouzon Syndrome: A User's Manual*. 2020.

Leduc, Amanda. *Disfigured: On Fairy Tales, Disability, and Making Space*. Coach House Books, 2020.

Patchett, Ann. *Truth & Beauty*. New York: Harper Perennial, 2005.

Strings, Sabrina. *Fearing the Black Body: The Racial Origins of Fat Phobia*. New York: New York University Press, 2019.

Wong, Alice, ed. *Disability Visibility*. New York: Vintage, 2020.

Woolsey, Jenny. *Ride High Pineapple*. Pearls of Wisdom Press, 2016.